T0355204

Chaitanya

Chaitanya

A Life and Legacy

Amiya P. Sen

OXFORD
UNIVERSITY PRESS

OXFORD
UNIVERSITY PRESS

Oxford University Press is a department of the University of Oxford.
It furthers the University's objective of excellence in research, scholarship,
and education by publishing worldwide. Oxford is a registered trademark of
Oxford University Press in the UK and in certain other countries.

Published in India by
Oxford University Press
2/11 Ground Floor, Ansari Road, Daryaganj, New Delhi 110 002, India

First Edition published in 2019

ISBN-13 (print edition): 978-0-19-949383-8
ISBN-10 (print edition): 0-19-949383-9

ISBN-13 (eBook): 978-0-19-909777-7
ISBN-10 (eBook): 0-19-909777-1

Typeset in Adobe Jenson Pro 10.7/13.3
by The Graphics Solution, New Delhi 110 092
Printed in India by Nutech Print Services India

For my mother, Himani Sen, *kirtan* singer par excellence, who taught me to savour good food just as much as soulful music.

Contents

Preface

This work will please neither the pious Vaishnava nor the probing scholar. In the first case, it might be set aside for a palpable lack of faith; in the second, for not employing a rigorously scholastic apparatus. I have deliberately refrained from using copious notes and citations, which, I now realize, would have added more volume than weight. This work is essentially a story that a historian has narrated to himself, a story that sustains itself largely through an intellectual interest in a life that was quite extraordinary in its public appeal if not also in personal achievements.

All through my writing career I have tried to alternate between serious academic writing, with its burden of methodological rigour and political correctness, and the not so serious yet reflexive works which, thankfully, do not necessarily have to carry that burden. The first is aspirational: writing with an eye on my own intellectual growth; the second I produce for the sheer joy of writing. It is reassuring to know that given all my professional limitations, I have so far been capable of producing both with some regularity.

I have approached this work with some caution and deference. My first worry has been about working on a historical period with which I have never been sufficiently familiar, either in terms of relevant sources or even a general grounding in the subject. I cannot claim to have effectively overcome such limitations at any stage of writing this book and yet, what inspired me, kept my interest alive, and helped overcome most of my inhibitions was the very intensity and grandeur of the tradition that I had chosen to study. The delicateness of feeling and imagination in Vaishnava songs and poetry or the stirrings of deep faith and passion that I have detected in both common people and better known practitioners have moved me considerably. At some level, this study of Chaitanya and the Vaishnava tradition has also been an intensely personal journey that meandered through memory, affect, and nostalgia, rediscovering and reaffirming certain cultural roots that had languished and withered over time through sheer neglect and disinterestedness.

My interest in Bengal Vaishnavism was first aroused in the early 1990s upon reading a book that had been officially banned by the government of West Bengal following considerable public pressure. In the early 1990s though, abruptly withdrawing books from circulation was not as common or as hastily performed as has been the practice in recent times. All the same, but for the fact that I was at the time located in Oxford, I might never have had the opportunity to lay my hands on a book that had dared to put in print only inferences drawn from relevant sources. I remain grateful to the late Professor Tapan Raychaudhuri who, at the time, had very graciously gifted me a copy of the book. Having re-read the book more recently, I could muster only empathy for the hapless author for it would seem as though contemporary authors and publishers have very adroitly and effectively mastered the art of circumventing such publishing disasters. Whereas the book that faced public censure had only hinted at certain scandalous 'misdeeds' allegedly committed by Chaitanya's close companion Nityananda, a work published as recently as 2013 and which casts doubt on the ancestry of Chaitanya himself, has escaped public attention altogether, simply by locating this within the realm of fiction!

Some scholars and colleagues, I fear, would object to my claims of a discernible movement of Vaishnava 'revival' occurring in colonial Bengal. For one, they might consider the term 'revival' itself being loaded and problematic. On my part though, I would prefer to set aside this controversy for now and instead draw greater attention to the fact that even in a provincial culture deeply permeated by Sakti worship and Tantra, there really has not come about a comparable movement among Saktas. In terms of the influence that it has cast over the literary and cultural world of the Hindu Bengali, Vaishnava devotional culture—both in pre-modern and modern Bengal—appears to be truly ubiquitous. However, having said that, I would prefer that this culture be taken for what it truly was: many-layered, complexly structured, and polygynous. In substance, I have argued that contrary to commonplace beliefs, Gaudiya Vaishnavism or the religion associated with the life and work of Chaitanya and his close followers is not quintessential Vaishnavism in Bengal but merely the dominant one.

This work does not claim to be a history of Bengal Vaishnavism, far less of Bengali Vaishnavism. I would strongly contest the view that the expressions 'Bengal Vaishnavism' and 'Bengali Vaishnavism' could be used interchangeably. In my understanding, the former represents only one of the several Vaishnava sub-schools located within the larger collective we may reasonably identify as 'Bengali Vaishnavism'. Midway through writing my manuscript, it also dawned upon me that I was fast veering towards writing a general history of Vaishnavism in Bengal, which was far from my intentions. I do hope that I have suitably corrected myself. My concern consistently has been with Chaitanya as a biographical and religious subject on whom no critical account has been produced in a long time, at least not in the English language. Given also the fact that this work was intended to be a biography, I have refrained from engaging in any depth or detail with the intricate theology, ritual works, or the literary productions of Gaudiya Vaishnavas, the bulk of which, in any case, appeared well after the passing away of Chaitanya. This work does not also go into the theoretical aspects of *bhakti*, which many scholars have earlier attempted quite admirably. On the whole, I write from the perspective of a historian and not as a scholar of religious studies.

I have consciously steered away from 'insider' accounts as, for instance, by Oudh Bihari Lal Kapoor or, more recently, by Steven J. Rosen, which tend to obfuscate the distinction possible between a biography and hagiography. To date, the English language work that comes the closest to being an authoritative and critically framed biographical account of Chaitanya is by A.K. Majumdar. However, a lot has been written on the subject since, much of it in Bengali. On the occasion of the 500th birth anniversary celebrations of Chaitanya in 1986, valuable literature was added to Chaitanya studies, much of which still remains useful and unsurpassed in merit or originality. Regrettably, however, such 'vernacular' perspectives, if I may call these so, have still not entered the world of English language scholarship. Even at the cost of some immodesty I would have to argue that one of the strengths of this work lies in its purposive attempt to get English language scholarship into a meaningful conversation with the Bengali.

In writing this biography, I have gainfully employed older and valuable studies of the Chaitanya movement. But for its ideological predisposition, which seeks to place Vaishnavism and Christianity on a comparative scale, Melville T. Kennedy's account still remains very insightful and informative. For me, the works of Sushil Kumar De and Ramakanta Chakravarti, otherwise aptly regarded as classics in their respective fields, represent two studies in contrast. The first, relying far more on Sanskrit language sources than the Bengali, is essentially an intensive study of Goswami literature, rhetoric, rituals, and theology. Its historical chronology stretches only as far as the late sixteenth or the early 17th century and neglects almost everything thereafter. In a work of about 700 pages, De devotes less than 40 to the 'Life and Personality of Chaitanya'. Chakravarti's narrative, by comparison, is so sprawling, inclusive, and unwieldy that the focus on Chaitanya within the work becomes quite diffused. One area within Chaitanya studies that still awaits its scholar is the history of Gaudiya Vaishnavism in Vrindavan, especially in relation to other Vaishnava *sampradayas* settled in the region. One work that appeared to be promising but which I could not sufficiently use is Prabhudayal Mittal's *Chaitanya Mat Aur Vraj Sahitya* (1962).

This project has been pursued over two successive stages: first at the South Asia Institute, University of Heidelberg, Germany, where I held the Heinrich Zimmer Chair between 2014 and 2017; and, thereafter, as Sivdasani Fellow at the Oxford Centre for Hindu Studies (OCHS), University of Oxford, United Kingdom, during Hilary Term, 2018. I take this occasion to especially thank the librarians and staff associated with both these institutions. Collectively, they opened up a whole new world before me, introducing me to the virtually unfathomable domain of Vaishnava Studies. My professional location in Delhi often denied me the opportunity to consult libraries and repositories in Kolkata for any extended lengths of time. Thankfully, the digital revolution has now made matters considerably easier. The newly opened Bhaktivedanta Research Centre at Kolkata has a fast-expanding collection of rare books and primary source material, some of which has been of use to me. However, I would be greatly remiss if I spoke only of my luck with source material. I have been luckier with the help and companionship that my friends have always extended to me at various stages of my intellectual journey, typically by way of indulging in successive rounds of smoky Lapsong Souchong tea sipped at our favourite Oxford pub. Some of them such as Lucian Wong, Ferdinando Sardella, Rembert Lutjeharms, Santanu Dey, and Måns Broo are first-rate scholars of Vaishnavism and have often rescued me from the bewildering impasse into which I occasionally descended while working on this book. At an international conference held recently in Kolkata, I had the pleasure of also meeting Ravi Gupta and Kenneth Valpey, whose works I have long admired. I remain grateful to Shaunaka Rishi Das, director of the OCHS, for his engaging kindness and hospitality. Shaunaka, if I may add, is one of those Vaishnavas who has a contagious smile and a great sense of humour. I am grateful to Professor Gavin Flood, also of the OCHS, who very kindly attended my seminar presentations at Oxford and made me rethink some of my settled opinions. This is an apt occasion to also thank Nandana Nagaraj, secretary at the OCHS, who helped a technologically regressive man such as me in numerous ways. Nandana is also trained as and is a practising advaitin and I very much enjoyed the occasional exchange of notes we had over lunch. It is only apt that I also use this occasion to affectionately recall my association with friends from Heidelberg: professors Axel Michaels, Hans Harder, Gita Dharampal-Frick, Rahul Mukherjee, William Sax, and Subrata Mitra. To Dr Martin Gieselmann and his wife, Manu, I remain grateful for the help and hospitality they ungrudgingly extended during my entire stay at Heidelberg.

It is quite fortuitous that Varuni Bhatia's *Unforgetting Chaitanya* has appeared in print before my own work will. Her nuanced and well-crafted work has allowed me to anchor deeper into the Chaitanya tradition in Bengal. I do also hope that she will graciously overlook my occasional disagreements with her line of argument.

My friends from Delhi and Kolkata, Malabika Majumdar, Tapati Sengupta, and Nandan Dasgupta, have stood by me in difficult and distressing times and I take this opportunity to convey to them how greatly I value their camaraderie and support.

Needless to say any errors of fact or argument occurring in this book are entirely mine.

Amiya P. Sen
New Delhi

Glossary

achintya	inconceivable
Advaita	the philosophy of non-dualism
advaitin	a practitioner of the philosophical school of Advaita Vedanta; a non-dualist
adhikaar	ritual right
adhikari	literally, one who holds an entitlement but also an office conferred by Goswamis on people expected to regulate the social conduct of initiated followers, Boshtoms, and Bairagis
adhyay	chapter
ahetuki bhakti	devotion free of any personal rewards or expectations
akhra	ghetto
alankara	rhetoric
ananda	pure bliss
angina	courtyard

antaranga sevak	intimate follower
aruna	glowing red
avadhuta	a radical ascetic, usually associated with Saivism
avatari	the source of all avatars
Bairagi	literally, one who renounces; typically used for Vaishnava singing mendicants
bairagya	detachment
bajra	a type of coarse grain
baniks	literally, merchants
bhadralok	genteel people
bhagavat pathaka	a ritual narrator or interpreter of the *Bhagavat Purana*
bhakta	devotee
bhakti	devotion
bhedabheda	a philosophical school juxtaposing unity and difference, usually identified with the philosophers Nimbarka and Bhaskara
bhoga	the path of sensual indulgence
bibek	withdrawal
Boshtom	a male Vaishnava mendicant, usually from the lower castes
brahmachari	celibate
caturmasya	the four months comprising the rainy season
chandal	a caste ostracized by upper-caste Hindus; associated with scavenging and activities considered ritually 'unclean'
Dabir Khas	an office corresponding to that of personal secretary
dasa	slave, servitor
dasakshari	literally, that with 10 syllables
dasyabhava	the mood of the servant; one of the several moods that Vaishnavas are encouraged to adopt in their religious life
daya	compassion
deha	the body
deshi	indigeneous
devadurlabha	qualities rarely found even among gods

dhikr	a state of God-remembrance and intense ecstasy in Sufi Islam
digvijayi	literally, world conqueror; also a title conferred on outstanding scholars
dikshaguru	the teacher who specifically tutors a pupil in some special religious or philosophical doctrine and also initiates him/her into a religious order
dvaitadvaita	a school of thought which juxtaposes philosophical dualism with non-dualism and is comparable to the position held in *bhedabheda*
dwija	twice-born
gambhira	a cramped room in the Jagannath temple premises where Chaitanya spent his last days
Gaurnagaravada	an eroticized form of revering Chaitanya, practised mostly in district Nadia
Gaurpramayavada	a religious view or theory which projects Gaur (Chaitanya) as the Supreme Principle and object of worship
goala	milkman
gopa	cowherd
gopi	cowherdess, pastoral women from the Mathura–Vrindavan region
gotra	clan, a term also used in Hindu ethnography to indicate exogamy
gramya katha	crude or uncultured words
grihastha/grihi	householder
grihini	housewife
gunjamala	a garland made of wild berries
Hinduani	Hindu spirit
hladini shakti	the energizing power or principle that animated the Godhead
jati	ordinarily translated as caste
Jatra	rural theatre
Jnan Yoga	the path of gnosis
jnani	the male who pursues the path of gnosis
kadcha	notes
Kali yuga	This is one of the four *yugas* or epochs into which Hindu-Brahmanical reckoning of time is

	divided; considered extremely degenerative and perverse, representing a world turned upside down
kama	lust
kamini	sensuous woman
kanchan	wealth
kapat	fake
kamandalu	ascetic's water pot
karmakar	blacksmith
kartal	cymbals made of metals, usually brass or bell-metal
kathak	an expert narrator or interpreter of important Hindu texts
kaupin	the hermit's/ascetic's loincloth
kavya	poetics
Kazi-dalan	humbling of the Kazi
khetrapal	guardian angel
khol	a drum made of treated clay used in *kirtan* singing
kirtan	Hindu devotional songs identifiable with both Vaishnavas and Saktas
Krishna-Yatras	rural theatrical performances based on the life of Krishna
Krishnaparamyavada	a religious view or theory that projects Krishna as the Supreme Principle and object of worship
kulin	of exalted pedigree
laukik satkriya vidhi	daily rites of passage
lila	divine sport
madhura	sweet, blissful, erotic
madira	wine
mahabhava	the supreme state of pining and devotion revealed by Radha for her lover, Krishna
Mahabhavaprakasha	the manifestation of the Supreme State of Bliss
mahajans	spiritual leaders; also used for gifted Vaishnava poets
mahant	the spiritual and administrative head of a monastery or congregation

mahotsava	Vaishnava feasts held to mark special occasions
malakar	garland maker
malsa bhoga	community feasting
mama	maternal uncle
Mangal Kavyas	poetic literature composed in medieval Bengal on various folk deities such as Chandi, Dharma, Shitala, and so on
manjari sadhana	a form of Vaishnava worship in which the practitioner assumes the mood of a *manjari* or a female servant of the *gopis*
manoharan	conquest of the mind
markat bairagya	literally, the renunciation of the monkey, denoting a renunciation that was faked and specious in intent
mathas	monasteries
Muffasil	areas contiguous to towns but not as densely populated; a kind of hinterland
mukhya	main
mukti	salvation
namsakariya	verses written in obeisance to a venerated Vaishnava figure
nayika	heroine
nedas, nedis	male and female followers of late, degenerate Buddhism
ojha	shaman or priest
pada	verse
padabali	Vaishnava devotional verse
panda	local priests and ritual specialists attached to Hindu shrines and pilgrim spots
paragana	an administrative unit used in medieval India
parakiya	a psycho-religious theory which claims that for the male practitioner, higher forms of love leading to spiritual experiences is best realized in the company of a woman other than one's wife
paramaguru	guru's guru
parastree	a woman other than one's wife

parinamavada	a metaphysical theory which believes the world to be an actual transformation of God/Absolute/Brahman, typically identified with dualist philosophers such as Madhva
path	ritual reading
pathaka	professional reader and interpreter of religious texts
patita	literally, the fallen; outcaste
phagu	coloured powder
pir	a Muslim saint or holy figure
prasada	the leftovers of offerings made to gods and taken to be highly potent when consumed by devotees
prem	love
raganuga sadhana	the path of inwardly generated passion
rasa	a mood or manifestation and part of classical Hindu aesthetic theory; also, aesthetics
sadhaka	male spiritual practitioner
sadhana	spiritual praxis
sadhya	object of worship
saguna	that with tangible properties or qualities
sahaja	natural
sahebi	Western
Sakar Malik	an office corresponding to that of chief minister
sakhi	female companion
sakhya bhava	the friendly mood; relating to God as a friend or companion; a mood especially practised by Vaishnavas in their religious life
salgram sila	an iconic representation of Lord Vishnu or Narayana
sampradaya	sect
sankhari	conch shell maker
sankirtan	Vaishnava collective devotional singing
santans	literally, children
sanyas	asceticism
sanyasi	ascetic
sarvamukti	spiritual redemption for all irrespective of gender or caste

shakha	branch
shakti	literally, power, but metaphysically taken to represent Feminine Power
shastrarth	scholarly disputation
shikshaguru	the secular teacher
shringara	the erotic mood, one of the nine principal *rasas* or moods in Hindu dramatic theory
shruti	literally, that which is heard; also representing the Hindu-Brahmanical canon consisting of core Vedic literature
shrutidhar	a man with an extraordinary memory
Shudras	the fourth and the lowest placed among the four Vedic *varnas*
siddhanta	theology
smarta	a practitioner of *smriti* or orthodox Hindu rites and conventions
smriti	Hindu legal texts
sripat	a Vaishnava Holy seat or centre that also developed into organizational centres
su-daridra	a man with a paltry income
sudarshan chakra	Lord Vishnu's discus
sutibra narapati	the most valiant ruler of men
suvarnabanik	goldsmith, trader in gold or gold ornaments
swakiya	a psycho-religious theory which is socially more conformist and claims the opposite of parakiya
syahi	ink
tanti	weaver
tarja	cryptic message
tika	commentary
tol	Hindu seminary
tulsi	Holy basil
tyaga	the path of abstinence or renunciation
upadan	material cause
Vaikuntha	Krishna's heavenly or transcendental abode
vanprastha	the third of the four-stage Vedic theory by virtue of which the male householder abandons his domestic duties at a prescribed age,

	retreating to the outskirts of forests but without turning into an ascetic
varna	represents the Vedic four-fold social hierarchy, now dysfunctional
vastraharana	literally, the stealing of garments, an episode described in the *Bhagavat Purana* and commented upon in radically diverse ways by later day commentators
vilas	literally, luxury or indulgence, but actually representing a hagiographic work related to a saint or a holy figure
viraha	the intense pain of separation, especially between lovers
vivartavada	a metaphysical theory which takes the world to be merely an appearance or illusion brought about by God/Absolute/Brahman; typically identified with Advaita philosophers such as Sankara
vyakaran	Sanskrit grammar
vyakhya	exposition
vyavastha	religious fiat
yati	ascetic
yavana	originally a term used for Ionian Greeks but later used pejoratively for Muslims
yugal sadhana	ritual spiritual praxis conducted jointly by a man and woman
yugala	combined, joined
yuga	epoch, cosmic age
yugavatar	an avatar befitting an age

1 Introduction

In evaluating the life and work of Krishna Chaitanya (1486–1533) and its historical legacy, ones is confronted with a set of three related questions. First, there is the issue of whether or not Chaitanya could be rightfully acknowledged as the founder or originator of the Vaishnava religion and culture in Bengal; second, whether Chaitanya Vaishnavism is justly called Gaudiya Vaishnavism; and third, whether historically the term 'Gaudiya Vaishnavism', also known as 'Bengal Vaishnavism', could be used interchangeably with 'Bengali Vaishnavism'. The first question has an important bearing on the questions that follow. Upon assuming that Vaishnavism in Bengal did indeed originate with Chaitanya, the third question loses much of its significance. We are then (wrongly) led to believe that the Vaishnavism launched by him and his associates was quintessential Vaishnavism in Bengal rather than the dominant form among many overlapping streams of Vaishnava religious and cultural consciousness. In this work I have argued quite to the contrary.

The query underlying the second question is how a specific geo-political region in Bengal—Gaud in north Bengal—and once the political seat of the Bengal Sultans is taken to denote the entire province of Bengal, even in extra-political terms. In the pre-modern era, different sub-regions within the province of Bengal were known by different names which also vitally determined matters such as social and ethnic identity, especially among upper-bracket castes. Thus, the terms 'Rarh' and 'Banga', representing south-west and east Bengal respectively, were also often affixed to Brahmin or Kayastha communities originating in these areas. Hence the terms 'Rarhi Brahmin' and 'Bangaj Kayastha' came into being. It is not certain just when the term 'Gaudiya' came to represent a provincial identity. And yet, we do encounter this in the early modern era. Rammohun Roy (1774–1833) wrote a book on Bengali grammar known as *Gaudiya Vyakaran* (1833). The relevant questions to ask here are whether the use of the term 'Gaudiya' affixed to Vaishnavism in Bengal is a pre-Chaitanya or a post-Chaitanya phenomenon and second, just what social or cultural compulsions determined this choice.

In as much as it implied the worship of Vishnu or one of his several Puranic manifestations, there is little reason to doubt that Vaishnavism or Vaishnava culture in Bengal antedates Chaitanya. Into this was integrated the mythology and a devotional culture surrounding Radha and Krishna that was considerably old and pan-Indian in scale. In medieval Bengali culture, influenced as it was by that of neighbouring Odisha and Mithila, there was a thriving religious cult which had been passionately celebrating these figures through song and dance. A popular saying in Bengal is '*Kanu chhada geet nai*', without Krishna there could be no songs. Hagiographies on Chaitanya refer to his passing through a site called Kanair Natshala, close to Ramkeli in north Bengal, which traditionally hosted Krishna-*yatra*s and, possibly, even puppet shows based on Krishna lore. The *Subhashita Ratnakosha*, an anthology of verses from early medieval Bengal, describes communities of singers making daily rounds of the villages at dawn, singing about the glory of the Lord. Chaitanya himself is known to have been a great admirer of the poets Jayadev and Vidyapati who wrote in Sanskrit and Maithili respectively and whose literary production spanned the 12th to 14th centuries.

In Bengal, the ruling dynasty of Senas switched their loyalties from Sadashiva to Vishnu and patronized poets who specialized in Krishna *lila*. There was also something idiosyncratic about the way local poets or bards perceived the love-play of Radha and Krishna. In some Bengali traditions, the relationship between Radha and Krishna was doubly illicit and scandalous since Radha also happened to be Krishna's aunt. Rustic and erotic in its literary usage and flavour, the *SriKrishnakirtan* (Devotional Songs in Praise of Krishna) of the medieval Bengali poet Badu Chandidas (c. 13th to 14th century) depicts Krishna as a lecherous trickster, using every ruse to persuade Radha to grant him sexual favours, and Radha too, at the end of exhausting love-play, deserts Krishna and leaves him for dead! Since Chaitanya is known to have savoured the poetry of Chandidas, the *SriKrishnakirtan* was in all probability known to him. However, as Chandidas also appears to be a generic name and not that of a specific individual, there could have been other Chandidases before his time with whose poetry Chaitanya might have been familiar. At the time of Chaitanya's birth, there were already small communities of Vaishnavas scattered along the Ganga in places such as Nabadwip, Kulingram, and Srikhanda.

In 1473, Maladhar Basu of Kulingram translated the *Bhagavata* and one of his descendants, Ramananda Basu, later became a close companion of Chaitanya. Nabadwip, by itself, could boast of the presence of pious Vaishnavas such as Advaita Acharya, Sribas, and Gangadas Pandit, most of whom were migrants from the district of Sylhet and subsequently joined Chaitanya's movement. One of the early hagiographical sources on Chaitanya, the *Chaitanya Bhagavata* by Vrindavan Das, reports how the veteran Advaita—older to Chaitanya by many years and troubled by the visible decline in moral and religious life within his community— was preparing to invoke the warrior hero Krishna, who might suitably punish the wicked and restore dharma. The widespread belief in the avatarhood of Chaitanya was considerably reinforced by such legends. Madhavendra Puri, (c. 15th century) a key figure in the medieval Indian Bhakti movement and a guru-like figure to many important Vaishnavas of the period, is known to have visited Nabadwip sometime preceding Chaitanya's birth and been hosted by Jagannath Misra, Chaitanya's father.

In hindsight, therefore, it looks as though both Sushil Kumar De, one of the earliest researchers on Bengal Vaishnavism, and Ramakanta Chakravarti, a contemporary historian who continues to reflect and write prolifically on this subject, unwittingly erred on the side of imprecision when choosing a suitable title for their books. De's work, titled *Early History of the Vaishnava Faith and Movement in Bengal* (1942), would have us believe that it was the Chaitanya movement that represented the 'early' phase of Vaishnavism in Bengal, thereby implicitly ignoring the pre-Chaitanya phase. Ramakanta Chakravarti too, as it would appear, has been arbitrary in his selection of dates. His *Vaishnavism in Bengal* (1985) spans the period of 1486–1900. The first of these dates, as we know, coincides with the birth of Chaitanya, which once again ignores or obliterates the pre-Chaitanya period in terms of Vaishnava culture and history in Bengal. His closing date, one has to say, is even more arbitrary since the year 1900 does not mark an important event, episode or the close of a distinctive period in the history of Bengal Vaishnavism.

The conflation of the expression 'Bengal Vaishnavism' with 'Bengali Vaishnavism' has seen even greater persistence than one would expect. In 1939, the well-known Sanskrit scholar and Indologist, Pramathanath Tarkabhushan (1865–1944) argued that Vaishnavism in Bengal had to be treated synonymously with Gaudiya Vaishnavism. Though contested quite promptly by Sushil Kumar De, who rightly found Vaishnavism in Bengal to be multiple and polygynous in character, Tarkabhushan's thesis continues to have channels of expression to this day. The author (Santanu Dey) of an otherwise excellent dissertation on neo-Vaishnava movements in colonial Bengal, produced as late as 2014, has the following to say:

> On my part, I use the terms Bengali Vaishnavism and Gaudiya Vaishnavism in a more or less exchangeable manner throughout this work.

A close scrutiny of our sources, however, dispels such arguments. It is, indeed, somewhat surprising that modern-day scholars should so carelessly overlook differences or disagreements going back to the 1870s. In his *Annals of Rural Bengal* (1868), colonial ethnographer W.W. Hunter (1840–1900) observed how many people in Bengal who worshipped both Vishnu and Chaitanya did not count themselves among Vaishnavas. Here Hunter was possibly referring to the tradition of *panchopasana* or *panchayatana* (which accepted an eclectic mix of five chosen deities) prevalent in Bengal and elsewhere. Other scholars have rightly drawn our attention to the problems of defining 'Bengal Vaishnavism' itself. The

American missionary Melville T. Kennedy, author of an important study on the Chaitanya movement published in 1925, aptly reminds us of the underlying difficulties:

> There is no clearly defined cult binding on the whole sect, organizing its life as a homogenous unit. On the contrary, there is a vagueness about it all, an utter absence of anything approaching sectarian organization, an ignorance and lack of leadership and an indefinitiveness of ideas and practice that almost warrants the conclusion that the use of the term sect is altogether a misnomer.

Here, it would be important to acknowledge that Kennedy's critique was inspired neither by an evangelist zeal nor by a gross unfamiliarity with the subject. Though never entirely objective in his observations, Kennedy proved to be quite extraordinarily sympathetic when commenting upon certain aspects of Gaudiya Vaishnavism that attracted ire and cynicism from his fellow workers. For one, he disagreed with views—originating from both Indian observers and Western—that took lower-class practitioners of Chaitanya's religion to be incorrigibly affected by gross immorality. And even otherwise, his observations on the social stratification and religious life among Vaishnavas in contemporary Bengal can be taken to be quite apt and astute. For instance, Kennedy was one of the earliest authors to admit that Chaitanya was more a religious reformer than social. I imagine that at the time he argued thus, Kennedy would have been quite unpopular with several Indian commentators and authors who firmly believed otherwise.

The social world of Gaudiya Vaishnavism was indeed vastly differentiated. To begin with, differentiation arose over the varied social origins of Vaishnavas in Bengal, ranging from the Brahmin or upper-caste Goswamis with ecclesiastical powers, to the nondescript and socially much-despised Jat Vaishnavas, who—in the opinion of pioneering scholar of Bengal Vaishnavism Joseph T. O'Connell—represented a *jati* without a corresponding *varna* status. Outside these categories, but loosely forming a part of the Vaishnava collective were Boshtoms and Bairagis, aptly described as mendicants who lived by begging. Neither of these categories found favour with either colonial ethnographers or upper-caste members belonging to mainstream Vaishnavism. They were generally taken to be renegades with disreputable pasts, indolent by habit, disrespectful of social conventions, and quite infamous for leading a freewheeling life in ghettos called *akhras* in the company of concubines, euphemistically called *sevadasis* (female helpers). Some observers even suspected them of foeticide since they were rarely, if ever, found to have children. It is equally possible that some of these were erstwhile Buddhist or Vaishnava Sahajiyas or even Tantriks, Bauls, and Fakirs who had mastered sexual techniques in strictly controlled laboratory-like conditions. But there was differentiation within mainstream Vaishnavism too. Kumud Nath Mallik, the author of a standard descriptive account of district Nadia in West Bengal and a biography of Chaitanya, noticed four different kinds of Vaishnavas in the region: first, worshippers of Vishnu who neglected to worship Chaitanya; second, those who worshipped Krishna through the medium of Chaitanya; third, those who worshipped only Chaitanya; and fourth, the community that called itself Vaishnavas but followed a very different set of rites and customs compared to those ordinarily practised by Vaishnavas. Mallik's observation was that of these, the first was the least common and the fourth the most popular. Author and a member of the Indian Civil Service, Romesh Chunder Dutt (1848–1939) noticed that in his time, there was a clear cleavage between the 'respectable' and the not so respectable Vaishnavas. All 'respectable' Vaishnavas, Dutt observed, had adopted the Hindu way of life and recognized the caste system, and that it was only in the villages and among the lower classes that the religion of Chaitanya was found to prevail 'in all its integrity'.

Recent anthropological research has revealed the prevalence of other Vaishnava traditions in Bengal besides the Gaudiya. June McDaniel, who has carried out extensive researches into the religious life and culture of rural Bengal, speaks of 'folk Vaishnavism'. This, unlike the form identified with Chaitanya and his followers, was not monotheistic in practice. In this tradition, Krishna appears to play multiple roles: folk hero, a fertility god, or protector of villages. More importantly, this tradition relied more on the efficacy of miracle work than some densely formulated philosophical doctrines. It was also brazenly utilitarian in its approach and character. Idols not known to deliver the desired results are known to have been unceremoniously thrown into rivers or else relegated to unknown, unpopular, or remotely located shrines.

In delineating the complexities embedded in the term 'Vaishnavism', it would be apt to also recall that what goes by the name of Gaudiya or

Bengal Vaishnavism was not entirely the creation of Bengali Vaishnavas themselves. In hindsight, one could justly separate Chaitanya as the source of inspiration behind a religious movement and as an institution builder. There is little reason to doubt the charismatic and enduring influence that he cast over successive generations, mainly through his magnetism and personal example. And yet, the construction of the system now identified as Gaudiya Vaishnavism, which includes a bewildering corpus of writings on theology, philosophy, and rituals, is more justly attributed to the Vrindavan Goswamis. It is interesting to note that the majority of the Vrindavan Goswamis were of southern provenance and never went back to Bengal once they had settled in Vrindavan on the instructions of Chaitanya. The Goswamis secured the patronage of both the contemporary Mughal state and local Hindu potentates ruling the arid regions bordering Vrindavan. It was also through them that Gaudiya Vaishnavism acquired two important features which, notwithstanding its chequered history, have survived to this day. First, there is the impressive array of temple architecture that can legitimately boast of being counted among the finest in north India (although some of the original temples were ravaged and replaced) and second, the institutionalization of both devotional singing and a library movement that was the key to sustaining the world of Vaishnava scholarship. More important, the Goswamis also thought and wrote in cosmopolitan Sanskrit and not, as it were, in the colloquial or the vernacular. Their object of adulation and reverence was more Krishna than Chaitanya, which seems quite consistent with their larger project of revitalizing a far older transregional Krishna worship and refurbishing Vrindavan not as an extension of a local Vaishnavism centred in Nabadwip, but as a pilgrimage centre of pan-Indian importance.

However, the conflation of 'Bengal' Vaishnavism with the 'Bengali' has other unresolved dimensions too. For one, we may identify some figures from modern Bengal who actively supported the cause of Vaishnavism without formally adhering to it in a sectarian sense. Three figures that readily come to mind here are Bejoykrishna Goswami (1841–1899), belonging to the Advaita lineage of Santipur, his disciple Bipinchandra Pal (1858–1932), and famed novelist and thinker Bankimchandra Chattopadhyay (1838–1894). Bejoykrishna, for some time a member of the Brahmo Samaj, deserted it eventually to be initiated by a Nanakpanthi guru at Gaya Hills. His monastic name, as revealed through sources, was Achyutananda Saraswati. Given the fact that traditionally one could seek multiple *shikshagurus* (teachers) but not *dikshagurus* (ritual initiators into a religious order), Bejoykrishna's identity as an orthodox Vaishnava, mcuh less Gaudiya Vaishnava, comes under some doubt. That apart, Bejoykrishna remained quite eclectic in his habits and religious routines: he adorned himself with *rudraksha* beads associated with Saivite ascetics, had a Muslim follower by the name of Shaukat Ali who, quite uniquely, was admitted in the presence of the *salagram sila*, an iconic representation of Vishnu, and could count several tonga-drivers of Mathura among his disciples. None of this, as far as I know, was true of other Gaudiya Goswamis. Pal was initiated by Bejoykrishna, but presumably not as a Vaishnava monastic, since the latter never took a monastic name. Also, there is surprisingly little in Pal's writings, otherwise quite copious, on Chaitanya himself. Rather, he appears to lean towards either an abstract Universalism suffused with Hegelian idealism or else a larger defence of Hinduism as against non-Hindu religions.

The more startling exception, however, is Bankimchandra. Due to the fact that he modelled his Krishna on the lines of the historical Jesus, it is commonly presumed that he had little or no personal faith in the deity. In truth, however, Bankimchandra belonged to a Vaishnava household which had instituted the daily worship of Krishna as the family icon. Reportedly, he also had deep faith in and respect for this particular icon and would turn to it for relief in times of acute personal distress. Unlike many men of his class, he fully believed in the concept of avatars and was greatly enthused by the literary and aesthetic beauty of Vaishnava songs and poetry, some of which he suitably incorporated in his novels. And yet, Bankim also stops short of admitting several ideas and concepts fundamentally important to the Gaudiya Vaishnava way of life. First, Krishna was for him an avatar, albeit the most exemplary, but this was still different from the Gaudiya view which took him to be the *avatari*, or the source of all avatars. Second, Krishna was as much the ideal man as an emanation of the Divine; in fact, Bankim's argument in his magnum opus, *Krishnacharitra* (2nd revised edition, 1892), was that the Lord's divinity was most tellingly related to his ability to fully function as a man. It might as well be said here that Bankim's persistence with the 'fully human exploits of the Divine' seems to run counter to the *Bhagvad*

Gita (Song of the Lord, 2nd century BCE) itself (*adhyay* IX, verse 11) where Krishna warns us against misconstruing his divine descent as a purely human manifestation. Arguably, this warning failed to alert him, since in his commentary on the *Gita*, Bankim never got beyond the fourth *adhyay*. He also had no scruples about food and drink and did not think that the choice of food consumed had any association with the quality of a man's religious life. In an essay that he wrote in the 1880s, a Vaishnava mendicant is seen feasting on mutton curry and hoping to be invited next to a dish of fowl curry cooked by a Muslim.

Interestingly enough, this is not as bizarre or fanciful as it prima facie appears. We have the testimony of Bipinchandra Pal to show this. Pal tells us that he once found a pious Vaishnava from Nabadwip relish cooked wild boar. Given that the boar (*varaha*) was one of the avataric manifestations of Vishnu, this does seem quite bizarre, but also suggests multiple layers of Vaishnava faith and practices.

Bankim's historicism led him to substitute the eroticized, pastoral figure from the Vraj country with a historical warrior hero from the *Mahabharata*, which, in turn, seriously qualified the *Bhagavat Purana* as a source book for the life of Krishna. The dramatic episodes surrounding the life of Krishna, as narrated in the *Bhagavat*, were interpreted by Bankim metaphorically rather than literally—including the infamous *vastraharana* episode which depicts a juvenile Krishna indecorously stealing the clothes of women bathing in a tank, leaving them helpless and acutely embarrassed. Contrary also to Gaudiya theology, Radha was for him the ideal worshipper—*aradhita* or the human soul venerating the Divine—and not Krishna's partner in perennial love-play. In Gaudiya theology, Radha was *hladini shakti*, the energizing power or principle that animated the Godhead; in Bankim's view, by contrast, the mood that Radha revealed towards Krishna was affection mixed with compassion (*daya*). Above all, Bankim had little regard for either Chaitanya or the emotive *bhakti* that came to be associated with him. In his novel, *Anandamath* (1882), he plainly calls it 'false' and virtually scoffs at the Vaishnava for whom merely striking a note on the *khol* (a drum used in Vaishnava singing) was enough to throw him into fits of ecstasy. Later in this work, we shall have occasion to see how Bankim contributed to reinforce his argument—appearing quite regularly in the literature of late 19th-century Bengal—about an over-eroticized, effeminate, and emotionally charged Gaudiya faith and culture, regrettably contributing to the very enfeeblement of the race. This casts some doubt on the thesis, somewhat unqualifiedly accepted today, about Chaitanya and his religion being integral to the politically sensitized *bhadralok* discourse that was desperately trying to shake off the ignominy of colonized subjectivity.

In the context of a biographical–historical study of religious subjects, such as the present one, it is of utmost importance to determine just what helped a saint or religious teacher achieve extraordinary popularity across a wide cross section of people. There has been a tendency in contemporary scholarship to explain such phenomena largely in terms of a given historical or political context. A very persuasive line of argument has been adopted by modern scholars in the case of the Bengali saint and mystic Ramakrishna Paramahamsa (1836–1886), who in his time enjoyed as great a measure of popularity as Chaitanya. They project him as a panacea for the great duress enforced upon a subject people by a culturally alienating way of life, racial discrimination, and the depressing poverty perpetrated by colonialist methods of surplus extraction. In this view, Ramakrishna virtually becomes a captive either of *bhadralok* social and political anxieties and imagination, or else of middle-class existential problems that appear to get more exacting with time. In other words, the power or popularity of the saint is seen to be derived from his pandering to the tastes or hidden desires of a class who think that the saint speaks what they are most anxious to hear. They also believe that it is in his presence that they are encouraged to make culturally romantic escapades into an idealized world—a world of mythical time and unspoilt native innocence. The problem with such formulations, however, is that it overlooks how Ramakrishna's own categories of thought or preferences could have been meaningfully different.

It is undeniably true that a good number of Ramakrishna's followers were unemployed young men or hapless clerks subjected to a demeaning life of petty colonial employment, abject subordination, and racist humiliation inflicted by the white employer. And yet, Ramakrishna's own understanding revolved around not so much the issue of class or caste as the line separating the man of the world (*sansari*) from those who had not fallen captive to worldliness. In degenerative *Kali yuga*, Ramakrishna believed that all men, irrespective of their class or rank, were susceptible to the lures of wealth (*kanchan*) and sensuous women (*kamini*). *Bhadralok* exasperation or anxieties born of colonized subjectivity do not appear to have affected him. As a Protestant missionary J.N. Farquhar once put it quite aptly and eloquently, Ramakrishna's whole life was driven by the singular belief that God-realization was the *summum bonum*, the essential substance, of human life and that nothing else really mattered. Personally, I would like to say much the same for Chaitanya. Both Chaitanya and Ramakrishna operated from within a world framed by an upper-caste Brahmanical culture and given the underlying continuities that lie within this world, notwithstanding obvious discontinuities, a certain collapsing of historical contexts looks quite possible.

Predictably, recent explanatory models employed in the case of Chaitanya and his religion are not dissimilar to those used for Ramakrishna. In recent and very influential books on the Chaitanya movement in colonial Bengal, devotional cultures are seen to be deeply intertwined with questions of nationalist identity and the devotional community itself becomes a working model for national integration. That Chaitanya was indeed a cultural icon for the colonized Bengali is indisputable. Bengal, having lost its political independence early, found no icon comparable to what Sivaji came to represent for colonial Maharashtra. Not even Pratapaditya of Jessore who briefly fought the Mughals and, for a while, attained popularity in Swadeshi Bengal could attain this position. The Bengali cultural investment in Chaitanya, therefore, comes closest to R.G. Bhandarkar's (1837–1925) projection of the medieval Maratha saint-poets as seers and prophets, who first aroused the people against all forms of injustice and oppression and then lay the very foundations of the nascent Maratha Empire. For modern Bengal, as it occurs to me, the linkages drawn between the formation of a devotional community and the larger, aspirational nationalist identity is not very clear and existed more in the realm of *bhadralok* imagination than in pragmatic politics. Writing in the 1940s, literary historian J.C. Ghosh, in what turns out to be provocatively critical work, argued that by embedding themselves in the national tradition, Vaishnavism and Bhakti had virtually 'drugged the national consciousness', and that through a combination of emotional abandonment and mystical rupture, these had simply provided to people the most insidious escape routes from the harsh realities of life.

In any case, neither nationalist rhetoric nor injured cultural pride are tropes that will sufficiently explain the success of the Chaitanya movement in pre-colonial Bengal, and here, we might more reasonably examine if this movement somehow created new social spaces for people with a range of aspirations.

The historian Tanika Sarkar interprets the Gaudiya movement as a successful attempt at community building, whereby hierarchically and disparately placed social groups are integrated into a devotional community supported by congregational worship and emotional bonding. She sees medieval Bengal as having consciously adopted certain strategies of uniting the Hindu community, of which three are readily identifiable. First, there were *smriti* regulations that demanded conformity to prescribed ways of social and ritual life; second, the production of a new literary genre, collectively labelled 'Mangal Kavyas', which adopted the inclusive strategy of co-opting popular deities into the Brahmanical religious fold; and third, the method adopted quite effectively by Chaitanya and his associates, using resources drawn almost entirely from a Sanskritic–Brahmanical cultural world and yet questioning the social and ritual supremacy of the Brahmin. Prima facie, the third can be said to anticipate the methods or strategies employed for much of the *bhadralok* reformism in 19th-century Bengal. It cannot be simply fortuitous that Hindu reformism in Bengal of this period was almost exclusively dominated by the Brahmin and only occasionally by the non-Brahmin upper-caste reformer. Arguably, this method had the twin advantages of making change socially more acceptable but also fortifying regulatory functions and powers of the Brahmin as sanctioned by tradition. By Sarkar's own admission, its disadvantage lay in the failure to attract certain classes such as artisans, tribal chiefs, or more generally, lower castes. In hindsight, however, this theory does not accurately fit in with historical reality.

Bimanbihari Majumdar's (1889–1969) researches on the biographical sources on Chaitanya's life and work reveal the movement to be dominated by Brahmins and upper castes. However, this can also be quite misleading since, presumably, Majumdar went by identifiable names appearing in the numerous biographical and quasi-biographical works, spanning from the 16th to the 18th centuries. Surprisingly, he could also discern the jati standing of the people, so identified since the biographies appear to have made no special effort to conceal this. This is surprising given the repeated warning uttered in contemporary Vaishnava literature and by Chaitanya himself that for the Krishna devotee, jati was not something to be reckoned with. It could well be the case, therefore, that biographers and hagiographers actually drew some delight in conveying how the movement proved attractive even to the 'respectable' classes. All the same this does not take away from the fact that Vaishnava space expanded both vertically and horizontally in Chaitanya's time and immediately thereafter. William Ward, writing in the early 19th century, estimated the Vaishnava population of Bengal as roughly about a third of the total Hindu population. Even after allowing for a degree of misguided inaccuracy in such estimates, the fact remains that we are, indeed, looking at a substantial Vaishnava presence in Bengal, later also borne out by decennial census reports. The Vaishnava population standing outside Majumdar's enumeration of what might be reasonably deemed as only the Gaudiya Vaishnava figures would have comprised very largely communities of peasants (such as the Mahisyas and Kaivartas), pastoralists (such as Gops and Goalas), artisans (such as Kansaris and Karmakars), and traders (such as Suvarnavaniks, Gandhabaniks, and Sankhabaniks). In Mallabhum, Midnapore, and adjoining areas, Gaudiya Vaishnavism also managed to recruit some tribal chiefs, as can be gauged from the proselytizing activities of Shyamananda and his chief disciple, Rasika Murari.

A further question that arises from Sarkar's thesis is the following: Just what was it that led Chaitanya and his associates to attempt an integrated community? Was it the fear of forced conversion to Islam or a combative resistance against an allegedly oppressive state? Incidentally, both these have been cited as possible reasons in historical literature. Some scholars have taken the Chaitanya movement to be a delayed reaction to the Muslim conquest, citing Bejoy Gupta's *Manasa Mangal* (1484–5) which alleges brutal atrocities carried out particularly on Brahmins and Hindu holy men in the reign of Sultan Jalaluddin Fateh Shah. Others have gone on to suggest how Gaudiya emotionalism itself was induced by the 'anarchic conditions' produced by the Muslim conquest. The demographic balance between Hindus and Muslims was an issue that apparently agitated several *bhadralok* interlocutors by the late 19th century. The Brahmo poet–singer Trailokyanath Sanyal (1868–1915), who wrote a tract on Chaitanya in the 1880s, anticipated in some ways U. N. Mukherji's theory of the Hindus as a 'dying race'. After him, the modern Bengali author Girijasankar Raychaudhuri (1885–1965) observed that but for Chaitanya's mission, the Hindus of Bengal would have been outnumbered by Muslims. Writing in the 1930s, Satish Chandra Dey, another modern biographer of Chaitanya, was sorely disappointed over the fact that the state of Vijaynagar did not come to the rescue of Odisha when attacked by Sultan Hossain Shah (who reigned between 1493 and 1519) of Bengal. More recently, scholars have expressed strong disagreement over theories proposing Islamic influences on Chaitanya and his movement. Bangladeshi scholar Enamul Haque was perhaps the first to propose this in a well-known article of 1968. But on the whole, scholars of Vaishnavism appear to have taken greater exception to the remarks of K.A. Nizami in 1961, to the effect that 'there was hardly any saint of the *bhakti* school who had not passed some of his time at a khanaquah'. 'It is now almost a political creed to assert dogmatically,' A.K. Majumdar countered, 'that medieval (Hindu) saints were influenced by Islam.' The historian R.C. Majumdar was irked at the praise that Hindu poets and scribes had for contemporary Muslim rulers; for instance Chaitanya's biographer Jayananda, who conferred upon Sultan Fateh Shah the epithet of '*Gaudachandra*' (the moon shining over the kingdom of Gauda) or Vrindavan Das himself, who described Hossain Shah as '*sutibra narapati*' (the most valiant ruler of men). 'Three hundred years of political servitude and religious oppression,' alleged Majumdar, 'had caused such spinelessness among Hindus.'[1]

---

[1] In her reminiscences, political revolutionary Bina Das reports an interesting instance of Vaishnava 'meekness'. Following the violent riots of 1946 at Noakhali, the residents of village Noakhala, Police Station Ramganj, majority of whom were Vaishnavas, organized a *sankirtan* party just so that people would feel reassured about peace and normalcy returning to the region. A companion of Bina Das by the name of Mridula Dutta, who had watched the proceedings with some interest, later told Das how the same people who sounded so energetic were hitherto the very embodiment of deference and docility. Bina

Fortunately, Joseph T. O'Connell's researches on the way Gaudiyas perceived Muslims help look at the problem more objectively. O'Connell demonstrates how it was rare for Gaudiyas to produce an exposé on just what it meant to be a Hindu. One of the rare instances when this did occur is related to Chaitanya's confrontation with the Kazi of Nadia, as reported in some hagiographies. The episode concludes with Chaitanya telling the Kazi how all Hindus (implicitly including the Vaishnavas) refrained from eating beef. O'Connell also claims that typical Gaudiya citations of the word 'Hindu' occur only in 'confrontational contexts'. A perusal of our sources will generally support this view but there are occasional exceptions. Quite uniquely, in the *Chaitanya Bhagavata* of Vrindavan Das, a Kazi is seen reminding Haridas, in all probability a Sufi follower of Chaitanya, that the Muslims considered their food to be polluted in the presence of a Hindu.

Other than Chaitanya accosting the Kazi of Nabadwip, there are other similar instances reported in hagiographies. The Kazi of Ariadaha (in modern North 24 Parganas) was dumbstruck at the fact that local Vaishnavas had taken out *kirtan* processions in defiance of his orders. The Vaishnava Gauridas Pandit of Kalna quarrelled with the local Kazi and was then forced to spend some time in hiding. Jayananda's *Chaitanya Mangal* speaks of one Balaramdas assaulting a '*yavana*'. On the other hand, Chaitanya himself was known to behave quite cordially with Muslims. Further down this work, we shall have occasion to learn of the great respect that he showed to Haridas Thakur, personally carrying his dead body to the coast of Puri for burial. The *Chaitanya Bhagavata* notes his unexceptionable behaviour even towards non-Hindus: '*Yavaneo Prabhu dekhi kore boro preet, sarvabhute kripaluta Prabhur charit*' (Chaitanya treats even the yavana with warmth and friendliness; it was in his very nature to show compassion to all). Given the great regard in which Chaitanya held Haridas, this may not be tendentious exaggeration. *Chaitanya Charitamritam* (Nectar-like Life of Chaitanya, c.16th

---

Das admits that this had led her to wonder if Vaishnava meekness was not behind the violence and suffering perpetrated upon Hindus of the region (Bina Das cited in Sanyal, Hiteshranjan. *Bangla Kiraner Itihas*. Calcutta: Centre for Studies in Social Sciences and K.P. Bagchi, 1989, p. 244.)

century) by Krishnadas Kaviraj also narrates how on his way back to Puri from Vrindavan, Chaitanya had an extended dialogue with a Muslim *pir* on the theology of Islam, an event that ended in the conversion of some Pathan wayfarers to Vaishnavism. Generally speaking, in all instances of Chaitanya's meetings with Muslims, it is the 'superiority' of Hinduism and the Hindu way of life that is ultimately upheld. The point worth pondering over is just how in a Smarta-Brahmin dominated Nabadwip, Chaitanya could have gathered even a passing familiarity with Islam.

I have disputed the credentials of Chaitanya as a reformer, in the social field as well as the religious. The problem here is both semantic and with the intentionality of 'reform'. In my understanding, 'reform' is a relatively modern term, with no corresponding words in either pre-modern Indian vernacular or in Sanskrit. More important, it carried an ideological baggage that developed only in colonial India and among those who receive western education. Though emotionally committed to Krishna *bhakti*, Chaitanya reveals a remarkable catholicity towards gods outside the Vaishnava fold, including purely local shrines and deities. He had no qualms about paying homage to deities associated with the Sakta-Tantra cult, as borne out by his life both in Nabadwip and the subsequent tours of peninsular India and the north. Contrary to what 19th-century Hindu reformers—modelling their values or strategies on Anglican Protestantism—would have liked to believe, Chaitanya was not opposed to idolatry, nor did he categorically reject the institution of the guru. His daily routine at Puri, where he spent the second half of his life, included a visit to the shrine of Jagannath; and, in some ways, his devotional ecstasy and mysticism was inspired by his *paramaguru* (guru of gurus) Madhavendra Puri. In its barest details, Chaitanya's religion was simple and unencumbered by any particular religious regimen, pedantic learning, or ornate ritual practices. For him, sincere God-remembrance in itself potentially carried the power of removing any ritual defilement, moral shortcomings, or the stigma of sinfulness. A story is told about Subuddhi Ray, who was once in the employment of Sultan Hossain Shah and whom the Sultan turned into an outcaste by forcing him to consume un-Hindu food. When Ray asked the local pandits how he may expiate for his sins, they recommended that he consume a quantity of burning fat. On seeking the advice of Chaitanya himself, he was told that he might more effectively overcome his condition simply by retreating to Vrindavan and spending the rest of his life there in God-remembrance. Subuddhi Ray did as advised by Chaitanya, eking out a modest but honest living in Vraj by selling firewood. Many others, possibly driven by similar anxieties, or even dissimilar ones, have followed suit since that time.

In truth, however, Chaitanya's approach to *smarta* ritualism was ambivalent. Contrary also to what has been often asserted by some modern biographers, he did not actively campaign against caste nor did he entertain any reformist visions of an egalitarian society. While insisting that the Vaishnava devotee was outside the reckoning of caste and creed, Chaitanya himself would accept food only when cooked by a Brahmin, with only one known exception. That he refused to be drawn into a social rebellion of any kind can be deemed from his support of both Haridas Thakur and Sanatan Goswami, two of his closest followers, in their decision not to enter the Jagannath temple at Puri for fear of ritually polluting its premises. Haridas, as has been noted above, was a Muslim and Sanatan considered himself to be disqualified, having served a Muslim employer (Hossain Shah) for a long time. The hagiographies report that Chaitanya took this to be an exemplary instance of the true devotee respecting the *maryada* (sanctity) attached to an institution. Not surprisingly, one of Chaitanya's biographers, Jayananda, goes on to suggest that the advent of Chaitanya was necessary for the restoration of the Brahmanical order in a depressingly degenerate age of Kali.

Chaitanya did not scrupulously follow the rules of *sanyas* either, even though he remained quite sensitive towards any public criticism on this account. Even after he had accepted sanyas, Chaitanya would not refuse invitations to sumptuous meals, ordinarily forbidden to a Hindu *sanyasi*. In one instance, food was served to him in a dish made of gold. In his early life, he also had a voracious appetite, even provoking rude comments from eye witnesses. Above all, Chaitanya consistently entertained a Brahmanical fear of the temptations of the female body and would come down very harshly on a follower who had violated the rules of *male* continence. In one such tragic instance, a devotee by the name of Choto Haridas (Haridas Jr.) was banished permanently from the community for daring to beg for some rice from a woman. Despite repeated intercessions from his close followers, Chaitanya refused to re-admit Haridas into the community, eventually forcing the man to take his own life.

However, it must be granted equally that his respect for social conventions could be qualified, at least in theory, by his equally strong commitment to the formation of a devotional collective. Within this religious formation, rules of social and ritual commensality did not really matter. Chaitanya is known to have insisted several times that even the ritually defiled *chandal* was fit to be a saint or guru if he was sincere in his devotion to Krishna. Conversely, even the Brahmin did not qualify for this position if he was not. Vaishnava *sankirtan* processions, which became something of a public spectacle, did not respect caste hierarchies and, in modern/colonial Bengal, attracted both Brahmos and Christian groups such as the Salvation Army. Thus, a degree of both conformism and non-conformism appears to have marked the life of Chaitanya. We might also add that it was at best a spiritual democracy that Chaitanya tried to create, not the social. In this instance, an egalitarian, non-discriminating religious identity was somehow foisted upon a vastly differentiated social order, albeit quite precariously.

I have taken Chaitanya to be a good organizer, even though he left behind no organization. Nor did he consciously wish to create one. It would appear as though the devotional collective grew around him quite freely and spontaneously, aided, of course, by his charismatic presence and the active dedication of his devotees and followers. A close scrutiny of our sources reveals that Chaitanya had a certain vision and recognized that its effective realization required a certain degree of planning and foresight. Well before he visited Vrindavan in 1515, Chaitanya had sent two of his followers on a reconnaissance mission. He followed this up with instructions to both Goswamis Rup and Sanatan to permanently settle down at Vrindavan so that they might implant upon an old Hindu pilgrim site the nucleus of a new and growing religious movement. Apparently, his plans or visions for Vrindavan and native Nabadwip were perceptibly different. The former he understood in the light of both a devotional hub and the scholastic centre of pan-Indian importance; for the latter, he focused on proselytization and an active devotional culture.

This emerges more clearly from his instructions to his most trusted companion, the maverick *avadhuta*, Nityananda. Quite early in his life at Puri, Chaitanya forbade Nityananda to be a part of the contingent that visited him during the annual Rath Yatra festival, instructing him to concentrate on evangelical work among ethnic Bengalis instead. A modern work named *Pashanda Dalan* (The Overcoming of the Heretic, 1862) by one Ramlal Mukhopadhyay takes Nityananda and not Chaitanya to be the chief protagonist of Vaishnava *bhakti* in Bengal. Nityananda, though also of Brahmin birth, was widely despised for his open violation of social conventions. For one, he would openly take to drinking; at times he would adorn himself in expensive silks and gold ornaments unbecoming of a sanyasi. But above all, he attracted the displeasure of the Brahmin community by turning from an ascetic into a householder, marrying not once but twice, and raising a family. It is believed that he agreed to marry on the instructions of Chaitanya himself. If true, this would also suggest Chaitanya's intentions of projecting Vaishnavism as essentially a religion of householders. From another perspective, it is indeed quite extraordinary that Chaitanya should allow himself to be flanked by Nityananda and Advaita, two close companions who exhibited very contrary habits and qualities. The first was instinctively bohemian in his habits and the second pious but conservative. Perhaps, in some way, they also reflect the two faces of Chaitanya himself.

Extant hagiographies on Chaitanya speak of his leadership qualities: his attention to small details and matters of protocol; his ability to enter into personalized conversations with devotees and followers, and so on. Sisir Kumar Ghosh (1840–1911), active in the field of Indian political journalism and the author of biographies of Chaitanya in both English and Bengali, once made an insightful point about his biographical subject. His point essentially was that Chaitanya could surprise people by combining in himself two very contrary qualities of dispassionate withdrawal and active involvement. People were indeed touched by his piety, humility, and gentleness, but they were doubly impressed by the activism and spiritedness he revealed on some issues. An interesting and persuasive argument, now advanced by some contemporary scholars based on available evidence, is that Chaitanya consciously encouraged his deification by residents of Nabadwip, however immodest that might have looked, only so that he may instil in them qualities of courage and fortitude. This, he felt, was necessary for a people looking up to a leader who might lead them in their fight against both the social tyranny of orthodox Brahmanism and injustices perpetrated by the local ruling class.

Such qualities, apparently, best came to light when Chaitanya led an unarmed population into defying an arbitrary order imposed by the

state. He is also known to have paid great attention to matters of protocol and conducted proceedings in a manner that apparently kept all
his followers happy. Thus, he would praise the cooking of his devotees
and make his companions feel at ease, but also ensure that in a formal
gathering of the Vaishnavas, each person would be seated in a manner
and at a place befitting his personal status. Apparently, such qualities led
Vrindavan Das to repeatedly assert how Chaitanya truly knew how to
win over devotees ('bhakta badaite Gaursundara jaane'). Chaitanya had
no use for scholarship but respected the scholar and even as a sanyasi
who had deserted his friends and family, consistently revealed a great
concern for the well-being of his aged mother. One can only wonder if
he spared some thought for his young, forlorn wife, Vishnupriya, but
in this instance we might justifiably add that the pathos and pangs of
separation that the young wife may have felt has been amply celebrated
in Bengali literature.

One is tempted to argue that in the 19th century, Chaitanya was
more a subject of tendentious public discourse than an object of deep-
seated reverence, at least in the colonial metropolis of Calcutta. There
were, however, notable exceptions such as Kedarnath Dutta Bhaktivinod
(1838–1914), who firmly rejected the joining of Vaishnava piety with
a political life. In fact, his open avowal of loyalty to the Crown and the
colonial government in India might have even exasperated and embarrassed the likes of Bankimchandra and Sisir Ghosh, who were otherwise
his close friends and contemporaries. We do not also know enough
about the life that prominent Goswami lineages led, whether in Calcutta
or outside.

In Calcutta itself, an expanding Vaishnava space was mostly used up
by the creation of modern assemblies and associations. These assemblies
and associations increasingly concerned themselves with weeding out
'deviant' forms of Vaishnavism than with the strengthening of Vaishnava
piety. We do occasionally hear of institutions specifically dedicated to
Chaitanya; for instance, the Kolutallah Chaitanya Sabha (1861) and its
organ, SriChaitanyabhaktikaumudi Patrika or the Gauranga Samaj and
Sri Chaitanya Patrika (both from 1899). The Gaudiya community in
Vrindavan itself ran two periodicals—Chaitanyamatabodhini Patrika
(1892) and the Gaudeswar Vaishnava (1899)—committed to the propagation of the idea. On the other hand, more broad-based institutions

such as the Hari Sabhas (associations or congregations for the worship of Vishnu/Krishna) proliferated more rapidly. By 1898, there were as many as 29 Hari Sabhas in Calcutta and its adjoining areas alone. Going by Kennedy's account, there were but few public temples in Calcutta exclusively dedicated to Chaitanya, an observation which runs counter to the fact that most of the opulent families in early colonial Calcutta were Vaishnavas by persuasion. Were they specifically Gaudiya Vaishnavas and, in that time, was it possible to be one without formally identifying with the Chaitanya cult? By comparison, Radha–Krishna temples abounded in Calcutta and there were a good number of *akhras* hosting itinerant Boshtoms and Babajis. In the Marwari districts of north and central Calcutta, there were *akhras* which exclusively catered to visitors from Mathura and Vrindavan and other up-country sites, indicating some religious traffic between these regions, presumably only seasonal.

That Chaitanya himself should fall into neglect is also evident from close studies of extant Vaishnava fairs and festivals. Contemporary surveys carried out in chosen districts of West Bengal reveal that the number of fairs or festivals dedicated to local *mahants* and saints exceeds that dedicated to Chaitanya. Perhaps there is a vicious pragmatism here that had taken root over time. It has been noticed for instance that among rural agricultural communities, annual celebrations for mahants or saints are carried out on a larger scale if coinciding with a good harvest.

While Calcutta does not appear to have paid any special homage to Chaitanya, we have evidence of at least one instance when his birthday was celebrated with much fanfare. This occurred on 27 March 1899 with multiple sankirtan parties congregating at College Square and Beadon Square in north Calcutta. This seems to have been preceded by three successive meetings organized at the Classic Theatre, the Oriental Seminary, and the City College, all located in north Calcutta on the 5th, 14th, and 28th days of Falgun, *Bangiya San* (Bengali year) 1306, corresponding roughly to the period between February and March 1899. Invited to speak at one of these gatherings, Dr Mahendra Lal Sarkar (1833–1904), founder of the Indian Association for the Cultivation of Science (1876) reportedly argued how Chaitanya was the 'sole refuge of the Bengalis'. An interesting aside to this is the incident reported in the contemporary Bengali press of how he angrily reacted to Sister Nivedita's (1867–1911) public lecture on the goddess Kali (held at Albert Hall,

Calcutta, on 13 February 1899). Sarkar found this to be an irresponsible act of upholding antiquated beliefs and gross superstition.

In his history of Bengali literature published in 1872, Mahendranath Chattopadhyay suggested that the flowering of Bengali language and literature first began in the days of Chaitanya. To this we might add two more notable developments: first, the remarkable ways in which Vaishnava literature recast non-Vaishnava literary concepts, categories, and expressions; second, the wide recognition that Chaitanya and his cult received from a variety of religious sects and sub-sects located in Bengal. In his classic study of Bengali Sakta devotional literature, Sashibhushan Dasgupta has drawn attention to the 'Vaishnavization' of Uma, the daughter of the mountains and Siva's consort, and how other Sakta imageries and expressions too were palpably influenced by Vaishnavism. In late middle Bengali literature, Krishna rescues Radha from a scandalous disgrace by turning into the Sakta goddess Kali just when it seems that her secret trysts with him would be discovered by suspicious relatives and neighbours. It is no less interesting that a host of Sakta-Saiva works from post-Chaitanya Bengal should acknowledge the extraordinary presence of Chaitanya in contemporary Bengali literature and culture. These typically include Mangal Kavya compositions such as Mukundaram's *Chandi Mangal*, Khemananda's *Manasa Mangal*, and Rameswar's *Sivayan*.

There is, however, also an unsavoury side to this penetrating and wide-ranging influence. Melville T. Kennedy, influenced as he was with his own study of Bengal Vaishnavism, once made the rather unjustifiable remark that Saktaism demonstrated neither a spiritual nor an aesthetic influence over Bengal. It seems to have escaped him that the Gaudiya Vaishnava concept of Radha as the animating power of Krishna comes from Sakta-Tantra or that the source of the major Vaishnava smriti work, the *Haribhaktivilas* (compendium of Gaudiya Vaishnava rituals and rites, c.16th century), lies in Tantra. It would also be quite appropriate to take on board the substance of Sakta objections to Vaishnava devotional expressions, in particular, the *kirtan*. These were particularly active in Chaitanya's early days in Nabadwip and caused some unpleasantness between the two communities. The Sakta hostility arose from the fact that unlike the Vaishnavas, they did not pay equal heed to the collective religious praxis as they did to the personal. In effect, their spiritual communion was largely based on a highly personalized relationship with the divine, quite susceptible to an isolation of the self and esoterism. It is but natural that they disliked a method of worship that was not only public in character but also supported by persistently loud music and ecstatic dancing. In Nabadwip, Sakta objections were reinforced by the strong presence of Smartas and the Nyayyikas, the practitioners of Hindu personal law and the philosophical school of Nyaya respectively, both steeped in orthodox Brahmanism. Among those who categorically rejected the avatar status of Chaitanya were Brojonath Vidyaratna and Bhuvanmohan Vidyaratna, both scholars from Nabadwip.

There has been a certain school of opinion in modern Bengal which claims, perhaps not entirely unconvincingly, that the Vaishnava population of medieval Bengal was substantially recruited from the rapidly declining world of Buddhism. Arguably, there are resonances of the Buddhist *sangh* in the Vaishnava devotional collective or, for that matter, of the Mahayana ideal of *sarvamukti*. What might have also helped such recruitment is the anti-Brahmin, if not also anti-Brahmanical, stance of Chaitanya and his early followers. Sometime in the 17th century, Nityananda's son, Birbhadra, is known to have recruited a few thousand *nedas* and *nedis*, in all probability, Buddhist monks and nuns.

It would be sheer condescension to claim, as has been often done, that Chaitanya brought a religious life to the masses. I am more inclined to believe that his popularity sprang in good measure from the ability to foist upon quotidian religious beliefs and practices, certain ideas or ideals drawn from high Sanskritic culture that proved quite attractive. Goswami theology preferred *bhakti* or a sustained devotional life to *mukti* or salvation. It relied on purely mental processes to transform the material body into the divine and labelled it as *raganuga sadhana* or the path of inwardly generated passion. This does not quite seem to be the case with common men and women. For them, the body itself had to be the site of moral or spiritual virtues or the lack of these. It is thus that the recurring cycle of human births and deaths was just as abhorrent to practitioners of quotidian and sharply deviant religions as it was to high Brahmanism. For the former, paradoxically, the body was the site of spiritual experimentation, but also an encumbrance that had to be ultimately conquered and overcome. Sexo-yogic exercises relied on the instrumentality of the body and bodily actions without necessarily falling prey to sheer bodily pleasure. In essence, this too was a form of *sadhana* or spiritual praxis, albeit following radically different methods and routines.

For the lower-class recruit, the attraction for *mukti* became more compelling, perhaps, when stripped of references to one's social standing and commonplace ritual observances. From this perspective, Chaitanya's call for *ahetuki bhakti*, devotion free of any personal rewards or expectations, may not have appealed to the masses as much as it appealed to those located in upper-class culture. For the masses, a devotional life could not be altogether unrelated to expectations of rewards in this life or the next. The colonial ethnographer, William Ward tells us that in Calcutta 'all women of ill fame' took to the religion of Chaitanya so that they might at least be granted decent funeral rites. On one level, this looks like sheer opportunism, empty of all faith or ideological moorings. However, it has also been recorded that such public women, when asked to perform Vaishnava devotional singing, preferred to take a ritual bath and a change of dress before they commenced their singing. In their opinion, this was necessary for transiting from everyday worldly life to the realm of the holy. It would be no exaggeration to say that Chaitanya and his religion brought to such classes of people, a more immanent sense of the Divine and the celebration of that which was uncompromisingly holy.

While the contemporaries of Chaitanya perceived him and related to him in various ways—as an avatar, saint, mystic, friend, the ideal devotee, or the undisputed leader of his community—closer to our time, his images have been inscribed only on specific registers and filtered through certain lenses. For one, *bhadralok* sensibility with regard to his life and teachings has been consistently characterized by a puritanism which refuses to acknowledge important differentiations in cultural contexts or modes of communication. As late as 1995, in their edition of the *Chaitanya Charitamritam* by Krishnadas Kaviraj, Tarapada Mukherjee and Sukumar Sen quite purposively misinterpreted the purport of a Sanskrit verse from the medieval anthology of Indian verses, *Kavyaprakasha*, which Chaitanya is believed to have recited before his followers at least thrice. This verse poetically narrates the feelings of a woman who wistfully recollects her pre-marital lovemaking with the lover who later became her husband. She then goes on to confess how, though related by matrimony to the same man, she still entertained an irrepressible urge to return to the pleasures of her unmarried love life. In substance, the verse could be taken for an adverse comment on the predictability and placidness of love within marriage as against the unpredictable and, for that reason, more intense experiences of love occurring outside wedlock. In translating this verse into Bengali, Mukherjee and Sen rendered the Sanskrit '*Kaumaryaharan*' (the loss of virginity) into '*manoharan*' (conquest of the mind). But an even worse instance occurs in Ramakanta Chakravarti's *Bonge Vaishnava Dharma* (Vaishnava Religion in Bengal) where our author rules that such a 'crude erotically charged verse' could not possibly have been uttered by Chaitanya. Sadly, he does not leave us with any clue on just why this should be so. Implicitly, Chakravarti also suggests that it was Krishnadas who quite inexcusably imputes his own ideas or intentions on to Chaitanya. In the pages to follow we shall have occasion to locate many such instances. This one, I dare say, was not one of them.

Also worth pondering over is the changing character of Chaitanya Vaishnavism over time. As I recall, on my only visit to Vrindavan, undertaken several years ago, my local guide would proudly point to the raised platforms, often laid out in the open, under which Goswami luminaries lay buried and which visitors and devotees perennially criss-crossed on foot. This appeared to be a practical and sincere execution of Chaitanya's advice to his followers to be as humble and unassuming as the lowly grass which everyone habitually and quite unmindfully trampled under their feet. On my more recent tour of Mayapur, I have been forced to notice what a few might even call megalomaniac dreams of empire building. A friend observed that the dome to the new shrine that is now being built at Mayapur may turn out to be more imposing than that of St. Peter's in Rome! Across the river, in old Nabadwip, some residents now complain of there being two Chaitanyas, one that was *deshi* (indigenous) and the other, *sahebi* (Western). They also feared that one would very soon completely marginalize the other.

2   Sources on the Life of Chaitanya

The production of biographical literature, more precisely of hagiographies, was a distinctive feature of middle Bengali literature and entirely the contribution of Vaishnava poets and authors. Hitherto, no social or religious figure of pre-modern Bengal had ever been treated as a biographical subject. However, between the 16th and 18th centuries, no less than 11[1] biographical works were produced on the life of the medieval saint and mystic Chaitanya, all of which are now available in print. This list excludes works which speak of Chaitanya

---

[1] These are as follows: *Chaitanya Charitamritam* by Murari Gupta, *Chaitanyacharitamrit Mahakavya, Chaitanyachandrodaya Nataka* and the *Gauraganoddesdipika* by Kavi Karnapur (Paramananda Sen), *Chaitanya Bhagavata* by Vrindavan Das, *Chaitanya Mangal* by Lochandas, *Chaitanya Mangal* by Jayananda Misra, *Gauranga Vijaya* by Chudamani Das, *Chaitanya Chandramrita* by Prabodhananda Saraswati, *Swarup Damodarer Kadcha* by Swarup Damodar, and *Chaitanya Charitamrita* by Krishnadas Kaviraj. This list is not arranged chronologically.

only peripherally and whose authenticity is still in some doubt. I shall presently return to the question of 'authenticity'.

Of the 11 biographies, five were originally written in Sanskrit and were subsequently translated into Bengali and other Indian vernacular languages. To these may be added about a dozen works in Odiya that appeared between the mid-16th and 19th century. Among major Odiya works pertaining to the religious life of Chaitanya, one could include *Sunya Samhita* (Discourses on the Philosophy of the Void, c.16th century) by Achyutananda, *Chaitanya Bhagavata* (Verses in Adoration of Chaitanya, c.16th century) by Iswar Das, *Gauranga Bhagavata* (Verses in Adoration of Chaitanya, n.d.) by Bhagavan Das, *Madhuchandrika* (Sweet Moonlight) by Haridas, and *Premataranagini* (The Flowing Currents of Love, c.17th century) by Sadananda Kavisurya. Two important Odiya manuscripts that may or may not have been printed yet are *Chaitanya Vilas* (Verses in Praise of Chaitanya, c.17th century) by Madhava Das and *Chaitanyalilamrita* (Verses on the Divine Play of Chaitanya, c.16th century) by one Madhava Pattanaik. Given the fact that Chaitanya spent about half his life in Puri, the importance of such works as a source of information on our subject cannot be doubted. Finally, there are works to which references have been made at various places but manuscripts for which have not been located yet, far less printed. We know of at least five such works: *Srikrishnalilamrita* (Verses on the Divine Play of Srikrishna, c.16th century) by Iswar Puri, *Mahabhavaprakasha* by Kanai Khuntia, *Chaitanya Mangal* (Auspicious Verses on the Life of Chaitanya, c.16th century) by Gopal Das, *Gauranga Vijaya* (Verses Proclaiming the Glory of Chaitanya, c.16th century) by Paramananda Puri, and *Chaitanya Sahasranama* (A Thousand Verses on the Life of Chaitanya, c.17th century) by Vasudev Sarvabhaum. Some of the names listed above are those of individuals closely related to the monastic life of Chaitanya and their testimony, had they been available, would have proved invaluable as source-material. The *Chaitanya Charitamrita* by Krishnadas Kaviraj also speaks of a Sanskrit biography composed by a Bengali devotee of Chaitanya but which failed to pass the scrutiny of his intimate followers and is now irretrievably lost. Another Sanskrit composition called *Chaitanya Charita* by one Gopinath Kanthavarana is available only in excerpts, cited in a modern work, *Banger Jaitiya Itihas* (The National History of Bengal, 1927) by Nagendranath

Gupta. Among useful biographical works that are still available only in manuscript form, we could mention the *Gauralilamrita* (Verses on the Divine Play of Chaitanya, c.17th century) by one Bangshidas (Calcutta University Manuscript [Mss] Collection, mss. no. 3996).

New biographies and readings of Chaitanya's life continued to be produced well into the colonial era, when, no doubt, they originated in a very different set of cultural or ideological needs or compulsions. In an environment deeply permeated by a buoyant provincialism, relating the life and message of Chaitanya to the pressing question of defining a Hindu-Bengali identity was certainly important. However, Chaitanya also increasingly came to be seen as a figure of pan-Indian importance, which then facilitated the purposive blending of a provincial cultural identity with a larger Hindu nationalist rhetoric. The 19th century in particular, with its growing awareness of the self and of history, paid greater attention to individuality, human mediation, and cultural distinctiveness. And, quite evidently, the growing intellectual acceptance of such new concerns encouraged the production of serious and sophisticated biographical literature. Apart from those on Chaitanya himself, copious hagiographical accounts were also produced in respect of his major devotees and followers, of which the famed Vrindavan Goswamis are an apt example (see Appendix C).

However, notwithstanding a growing attention to accuracy and detail, there persisted in the public mind considerable misinformation about certain key events in the life of Chaitanya. Early 19th-century works remained patently guilty of carrying such misinformation. A work called *Pashanda Dalan* (1862) by Ramlal Mukhopadhyay relocates the famous episode concerning the chastisement of two rouges of Nabadwip, Jagai and Madhai, in the town of Katwa. Yet another collection of essays called *Prabandha Ratna* (Jewel-Like Essays, 1884) takes Rup and Sanatan Goswamis to be courtiers of Akbar, whereas, in truth, they were in the employment of the Bengal sultan, Hussain Shah. Even in post-independent India, Nirad C. Chaudhury wrongly called Vrindavan Das the first biographer of Chaitanya. Given the prodigious research on Vaishnava history and literature that was undertaken all through the 19th century, such claims prima facie appear inexplicable. Further down this chapter I also briefly introduce what was certainly a biography (*Govindadaser Kadcha*) but the authorship of which still remains under a cloud. In this particular case, determining the identity of the author was crucial since on this rested both the historical age of the work and its credibility. But for the *SriKrishnakirtana* by Badu Chandidas, believed to have been composed sometime between the 13th and 14th centuries, no other work has produced such persistent controversy in modern Bengal among scholars and laymen alike. The controversy around the *Kadcha*, which erupted in the closing years of the 19th century and resumed about 30 years later, was, in some ways, unique. First, unlike that related to the *SriKrishnakirtan*, this was a controversy that commenced upon the publication of the text, not before it. Second, rather than affect the Vaishnava community alone, it created acute differences of opinion even within the world of lay scholarship. Perhaps the intensity of the controversy was also somewhat related to the fact that it was, on some level, deeply personalised. Most critics take the *Kadcha* to be a modern work falsely claiming to have been composed in Chaitanya's time. More often than not, this led to the rejection of the work itself which appears to be somewhat uncharitable and unjust. Even assuming that this was but a modern 'fabrication', one still needs to explain why it surfaced at a particular time and context. Also, it is one thing to allege text torturing and tendentious interpolation and quite another to claim that the work never existed in pre-modern history, even in a rudimentary form. Most hagiographies on Chaitanya are lamentably inaccurate, inconsistent, and careless with historical and biographical details and the *Kadcha* is no exception.

The problem of 'authenticity' is a complex one and arose in perceptibly different causes or contexts. For one, the allegedly 'inauthentic' emerged in the light of differing readings of Chaitanya and of his message over time. By the mid-17th century, when Gaudiya Vaishnavism had developed a visible orthodoxy in matters of self-definition, the issue of authenticity naturally assumed great importance. By this time, Vrindavan had developed into a productive centre for formulating distinctive ideas related to aesthetics, literature, liturgy, religion, and philosophy. It clearly sought to define or regulate the way Gaudiya Vaishnavism perceived itself even without an established mechanism of control and in the face of palpably deviant ideas in vogue elsewhere. Quite naturally, ideas or practices originating in Vrindavan were not always unqualifiedly accepted and it is reasonable to assume that at least until the early 17th century, there remained considerable differences of opinion between Vrindavan and Bengal in matters of doctrine and even more so on conducting the everyday life of the Vaishnava. In the absence of a central organization, difference and dissidence within Gaudiya Vaishnavism were quick to surface. Here, it is important to remember that especially in Bengal, many who claimed to be followers of Chaitanya were drawn more towards the idea of creating a new social and ritual space for themselves than by pure religious ideology, which, in any case, was riddled with inner contestations. The problem of authenticity was further compounded with several quotidian and dissident religious groups, based mostly in Bengal, appropriating elements of belief and practice identified with mainstream Vaishnavism and claiming these as their own. The Vaishnava Sahajiyas, for example, who residually carried elements of Tantra and esoteric Buddhism, made inroads into Vaishnava orthodoxy by attributing works propagating their own theology and ways of life to well-known Vaishnava writers and theologians of Vrindavan. This was the kind of appropriation that most hurt the orthodox, whether in Bengal or elsewhere.

In an interesting act of inversion, the Sahajiyas claimed that rather than represent the 'true' spirit of Chaitanya's religion, Goswami theology was but a surreptitious entry into the world of Vaishnava life and devotion and worse, a mischievous misrepresentation of the fundamental teachings of that saint. That apart, different geo-cultural settings, established traditions, and tactical requirements served to perpetuate different modes of thinking and palpably different practices at these two places. Reportedly, non-Bengali Vaishnavas of Vrindavan, even when belonging to the Gaudiya camp, took exception to the way the Bengali Raghunath Das Goswami indiscriminately ate the leftovers of people belonging to various castes. In part, conflicting perceptions of Chaitanya's life and message also originated in the fact that different groups of followers came to be acquainted with him at different stages of his life. Most devotees or followers based in Bengal were drawn to the pre-monastic Chaitanya whereas the Goswamis and their associates based in Vrindavan knew him only as an ascetic. Understandably enough, Goswami theology could not fully come to terms with either *Gaurparamyavada*, which projected Chaitanya as both the *sadhya* and *sadhana*, that is, the object of worship as also the means of worship or *Gaurnagaravada*. This inspired highly erotic poetry describing the young, pre-monastic Chaitanya in amorous dalliance with the women of Nadia. The first the Goswamis promptly rejected since they stood by *Krishnaparamyavada*, which regarded Krishna as the Supreme Deity and Chaitanya only an emanation; the second they found to breed both moral impropriety and threateningly 'specious' theology. For the Vrindavan Goswamis, the privileging of Krishna over Chaitanya as the object of deification was increasingly meant to prioritise a pan-Indian religious system over that which was cultic and provincial. The followers of Chaitanya in Nadia, on the contrary, saw him as an iconic figure who had visibly transformed local social and religious life.

All the same, it would be simplistic to argue that differences in doctrine and praxis between Vrindavan and Bengal arose in differing cultural locations alone. A careful examination of biographies will reveal that in the post-Chaitanya period, the Vaishnava community in Bengal itself was affected by recurring disputes and differences. In his *Chaitanya Bhagavata*, the biographer Vrindavan Das was quite contemptuous of *Gauranagarvada*, the school led by the poet Narahari Sarkar of Srikhanda in Burdwan. Personal predispositions, too, coloured the way episodes and events associated with Chaitanya were represented by his biographers. Vrindavan Das, born to the widow Narayani in circumstances that appear plainly scandalous (explained in detail later), introduced a great degree of violence into the well-known episode of Chaitanya and his followers accosting the Kazi of Nadia for prohibiting *sankirtana* processions (community singing) in the town. In this narrative, Chaitanya's followers are seen setting fire to the Kazi's place and ruining his garden, resulting in the Muslims' collectively deserting their settlements in panic. Arguably, some of this appears to reflect the anger and affront that Vrindavan Das suffered on account of his widowed mother being made to appear before the local Kazi to clear her 'sullied' character. In *Chaitanya Charitamrita* by Krishnadas Kaviraj that followed *Chaitanya Bhagavata*, the violence is considerably toned down. As an author based in Vrindavan, Krishnadas' interests were more didactic in nature and he found greater contentment with making the Kazi accept the 'superiority' of Krishna *bhakti* over his 'newly founded' faith (Islam). Clearly, differences in narratives often followed from differing subjectivities and subjectivities themselves were derived from varying social and individual contexts.

A related and recurring problem is that of interpolation. In 1929, at a meeting held at the Albert Hall, Calcutta, the scholar-theologian, Sundarananda Vidyavinod argued that but for *Chaitanya Bhagavata, Chaitanya Charitamrita*, and *Chaitanya Chandrodaya Nataka* of Kavi Karnapura, all other biographical works pertaining to Chaitanya had been subjected to tendentious interpolation. The problem of interpolation was indeed a recurring one in pre-print culture. Printing helped to standardize texts and in an emerging print culture, it was common practice for scholars and editors to carefully collate extant manuscripts. Manuscripts, though, were often at the mercy of patrons, theologians, and copyists who manipulatively modified the text in keeping with their own understanding or preferences. In the context of Bengali Vaishnava literature, this is comparable to strategies employed by *kirtan* singers who, when performing in public recitals, were known to deliberately alter words originally occurring in songs or poems, the exact import of which they were unable to determine. There was considerable carelessness with the authorship of verses too. Historian Bimanbihari Majumdar testifies to the fact that he heard famed *kirtan* singers of his time singing the verses of Jnandas under the colophon of Govindadas and attributing the verses of Murari Gupta, Chaitanya's first biographer, to Bangshibadan Thakur, a close follower of the saint. Interpolations in biographical literature also occurred in cases where an existing work was, for some reason, left incomplete. This is clearly the case with the narrative of *Chaitanya Bhagavata*, which appears to end rather abruptly. In 1924, Ambikacharan Brahmachari, a Vaishnava theologian attached to the Vaishnava *Sripat* (Vaishnava religious centre) at Denur, West Bengal, claimed to have found three missing chapters to this work, which, upon scholarly scrutiny, have been found to be spurious. In the case of the *Srikrishnachaitanya Charitamritam* (The Life of SriKrishnachaitanya, c.16th century), a Sanskrit biography of Chaitanya authored by Murari Gupta, the printed text does not match older manuscripts in which only the life of Chaitanya at Nadia is narrated. Evidently, events related to Chaitanya's subsequent life at Puri were added at a later stage to make the work look more pious and comprehensive.

And yet, printing by itself did not always lend credibility to a work. We have already cited the case of Murari Gupta. Another short biographical work commonly known as *Swarup Damodarer Kadcha* (Notes of Swarup Damodar, n.d.) was printed at the popular Battala Press in

19th-century Calcutta but was almost universally dismissed as a work of doubtful authenticity.[2] We do know, however, that such a work existed since respectful reference has been made to it by later hagiographies, chiefly, the *Chaitanya Charitamrita*.

In general, post-17th century works need to be treated with greater caution. Being removed in time from their main subject by nearly a century, they seldom had access to first-hand information. On the other hand, the continued production of such late biographies reflects an acknowledgement of a dynamically expanding Gaudiya movement in terms of both geographical space and ideology. Also palpable was the pressing cultural urge to publish important Vaishnava texts that would better define the community of practising Vaishnavas and facilitate Vaishnava self-definition. By the late 19th century, publishing houses committed to the printing of Vaishnava works had emerged even in places at some distance from Calcutta, as for instance the Radharaman Press at Behrampore (Murshidabad). That apart, the printing and public circulation of biographies of well-known post-Chaitanya Vaishnava leaders was now an important way of not only commemorating such figures but also of proving and proclaiming a continuous cultural momentum. From this perspective, the *Chaitanya Charitamrita* may not have been quite the 'final word' as Tony K. Stewart calls it. Thus, in the 17th and 18th centuries, older issues continued to be agitated, with new ones also being added.

As the Vaishnava literary and cultural world grew increasingly differentiated, biographies and hagiographies became instrumental in creating contesting sectarian loyalties. It is now reasonably well established that *Advaita Prakash*, a work attributed to one Ishan Nagar, reportedly in personal service of Chaitanya, and first brought to light in 1897 by the scholar from Sylhet Achyutacharan Chaudhuri, was in all probability the work of Chaudhuri himself. Though modern literary scholars such as Dineshchandra Sen (1866–1939) have similarly doubted the authenticity of Jadunandan Das's *Karnananda* and Nityananda Das's *Premvilas*

---

[2] I am aware of a subsequent edition published by Sunirmal Kumar from Midnapore in 1974. More recently, Nirmalendu Khasnabis has undertaken a study of this work in his *Swarup Damodar O Tahar Kadcha* (1991).

(both from the 18th century), they have had to otherwise depend on these very sources for historical information on the period. A recent study has argued that three extant texts, *Chaitanya Upanishad*, reportedly based on the *Atharva Veda*, *Nabadwipa Shatakam* (A Hundred Verses on the Glory of Nabadwip, c.16th century), attributed to Prabodhananda Saraswati, an ascetic follower of Chaitanya, and *Prema Vivarta* (The Diffraction of Love, c.17th century) by Jagadananda Das were actually authored by the well-known Vaishnava theologian of the colonial era Kedarnath Dutta Bhaktivinod. In his monumental study of biographical sources on the life of Chaitanya, *Chaitanya Chariter Upadan* (Materials for Compiling the Life of Chaitanya, 1959), Bimanbihari Majumdar has identified no less than 12 works from the post-Chaitanya period whose authenticity is under serious doubt.

In general, literature pertaining to the life of Chaitanya reveals little interest in historical sequence or chronology, as hagiographies are only apt to do, though one must also allow for exceptions. One important exception that comes to mind is Mahendranath Gupta's *Sri Sri Ramakrishna Kathamrita* (The Gospel of Sri Ramakrishna, first serialised in Bengali in 1897) with its precise dating and accurate descriptions of locale. In the preface to the work, Gupta even resorts to the use of the Indian Evidence Act, 1872, for classifying various kinds of evidence. One may justifiably argue that given their different historical contexts, hagiographies of Chaitanya and the *Kathamrita* are incomparable. And yet, modernity too is known to privilege faith over rational judgment. Majumdar's *Chaitanya Chariter Upadaan*, which otherwise follows the historical method, admits to have abandoned this midway. In his defence, Majumdar cited Tagore's poem *Bhasha O Chhanda* (Language and Metre, in *Kahini*, 1899) which claims that a character conceived in the poet's mind was always greater than that known to history. Here it is important to recall that Majumdar, notwithstanding his credentials as a historian, was also an initiated Vaishnava and composed religious poems under the colophon Nitai.

Quite evidently, hagiographies of Chaitanya do not attempt a rational or historical ordering of a life and its achievements; they remain more committed to the agenda of propagating a particular religious message. As the pioneering scholar of Bengal Vaishnavism, Joseph O'Connell once put it aptly that the biographers of Chaitanya were not professional historians but engaged devotees and for them, Chaitanya was not a historical subject but a man who was Divine Will manifested. There is considerable anachronism, too, in the way older hagiographers portray their subject. Thus, Krishnadas Kaviraj, the author of *Chaitanya Charitamrita*, attributes to Chaitanya ideas or doctrines that he himself developed over a century later. We shall have occasion to return to this question subsequently.

Just where did the hagiographers draw their material from? Evidently, accounts of Chaitanya's life and message originating in contemporaries and near contemporaries could be broadly divided into two categories: those derived from individuals who actually met Chaitanya in person and those who did not. In the first category, we may include several Vaishnava poets, contemporaries of Chaitanya and subsequently known as the *padabali* poets. Such poetry was directly inspired by the charismatic presence of the saint. It is here that one also finds the earliest physical descriptions of Chaitanya and of his early life in Nadia. However, whether as verse or in some other literary form, accounts belonging to the first category are not always more reliable. For one, contemporaneity did affect perspectives. The *padabali* poet Balaram Das tells us that Chaitanya insisted on redeeming and rescuing the destitute, the fallen, and *patita*. On close scrutiny, this appears to be a more pious perception than accurate historical reporting. There is little reason to doubt that the socially marginalised and persecuted found self-expression through the religious message of Chaitanya; and yet, it is just as plausible that Chaitanya was not a self-conscious social reformer with a perceptible social agenda who set out to carry out structural changes in his society. On the other hand, the best known accounts of Chaitanya, *Chaitanya Bhagavata* and *Chaitanya Charitamrita*, were both produced by men who had never met Chaitanya and whose fame as authors rests not just on the appealing quality of their piety or poetry but on the wealth and vividness of biographical detail. Of the hagiographers, only three are known to have met Chaitanya in person: Murari Gupta, Paramananda Sen (Kavi Karnapur), and Jayananda Misra. Of these, only the first had known Chaitanya for any length of time; Karnapur met him when he was barely seven and Jayananda, only as an infant. From this it is reasonable to conclude that at the time of composing their works, Karnapur and Jayananda had to rely on what in legal parlance could be called 'hearsay evidence', gathered either from their gurus or else fellow Vaishnavas. Murari Gupta is known to have relied on the testimony of Sribas Acharya, a leading devotee of Chaitanya from his Nabadwip days, Vrindavan Das on Nityananda (the prominent Vaishnava leader and evangelist, only second in importance to Chaitanya), Lochandas on the poet Narahari Sarkar, and Krishnadas Kaviraj on Goswami Raghunath Das (Chaitanya's companion in Puri for a long time). Whether directly or otherwise, Nityananda was the source of inspiration for several biographies; curiously, Chaitanya's other well-known follower, Advaita Acharya, is not known to have inspired any hagiographers.

There are, however, certain zones within biographical narratives wherein the sources of information are far from clear. In all, Chaitanya spent about six years of his life as a wandering ascetic, coinciding with some important developments in his religious life but for which, apparently, there are no reliable first-hand accounts. A case in point is the theological exchange that took place sometime in 1510 between Chaitanya and Ramananda Ray, Odiya governor of the Godavari district. The 'Ramananda Samvad', as reported in Krishnadas Kaviraj's *Chaitanya Charitamrita*, is the very foundation of the theory that speaks of an androgynous Chaitanya, combining in his person both Radha and Krishna. Allegedly, Krishnadas Kaviraj plagiarised the account from Kavi Karnapur, which then leaves us with the question: where did Karnapur derive this theory from? The issue is only further compounded if, in keeping with current thinking, we were to dismiss *Govindadaser Kadcha*—the only text that claims to cover his tour of south India—as an inauthentic and untrustworthy text. Given the circumstances, we are practically left with no choice but to fall back on the idea that on his return from his wanderings in north and south India, Chaitanya himself narrated his experiences in copious detail for his followers to prepare suitable notes. Prima facie this looks very unlikely.

It is only natural that a biographer would come to rely on preceding works of the same class. Krishnadas Kaviraj admits to have depended on Vrindavan Das, reportedly even to the extent of seeking his permission to begin his own work. However, this was not always the case. Thus, neither Vrindavan Das nor Jayananda mention the early work by Murari whereas Karnapur and Krishnadas do this quite selectively. The hagiographical work *Gauranga Vijaya* by Chudamani Das, possibly composed in the 1540s, mentions no comparable text that preceded it.

A distinction may justly be made between the 'major' and 'minor' hagiographies, and it is on the former class of works that our reconstruction of Chaitanya's life and message is primarily based. All hagiographical works on Chaitanya are marked by greater attention to poetry than history, but a few do this appreciably more than others. Some works, such as those of Lochandas and Jayananda were essentially meant to be publicly sung or else enacted in *jatras* and hence reveal a different narrative structure or linguistic preference when compared to texts that were meant for private reading. In the context of historically reconstructing the life and work of Chaitanya, these works generally assume a secondary position. Popularity and circulation of manuscripts is also a reliable measure of importance and here, *Chaitanya Bhagavata* and *Chaitanya Charitamrita* clearly overtake all others. More manuscript copies of the *Charitamrita* have been recovered than any other comparable work. By comparison, the works of Murari Gupta or Kavi Karnapur appear to have suffered primarily because they were composed in Sanskrit and accessible only to a select and committed readership.

However, works that could be classed as 'minor' are also known to yield useful and unique information. Thus, *Gauranga Vijaya*, of which only one manuscript copy could be found in all of Bengal and which remains a relatively unknown work, is the only text to offer a description of the house in Nadia in which Chaitanya's parents lived. From this work, we also gather that Jagannath Misra, Chaitanya's father, was also known as Purandar Misra. Similarly, Lochandas's *Chaitanya Mangal* informs us that Nityananda was popularly known as Kuber Pandit. However, alternate narratives appear most startlingly in Jayananda's *Chaitanya Mangal*. For one, this work shows Chaitanya's ancestors to have originated from Jajpur in Orissa and not Sylhet in east Bengal, as commonly believed. Reportedly, Jayananda gathered this from Madhava Pattanaik's *Chaitanyalilamrita*. By the 1920s, this sparked off a controversy between scholars based in Odisha and Bengal, with each group appropriating the Chaitanya cult for itself and indignantly contesting the claims of the other. Bengali scholars strongly disapproved of Jayananda's relying on an Odiya work that also allegedly claimed the poet Jayadev of *Gitagovinda*

(Songs on the Celestial Lord Krishna, c.12th century) fame to be a resident of Odisha. In Jayananda's work, quite uniquely, Chaitanya is also shown to have died of a septic wound he suffered in his foot, whereas all other texts suggest either his miraculously merging with Lord Jagannath or else washed away at sea. Most contemporary Vaishnavas considered Jayananda's reporting to be both incorrect and impious since, for them, a man who was taken to be an incarnation of God could not possibly have met with an ordinary death or died of common human ailments. Jayananda's work never attained the status or popularity of *Chaitanya Bhagavata* or *Chaitanya Charitamrita*. The only group to have put some value on the work are modern scholars who believed some of its descriptions to be quite realistic and unpretentious.

The following section briefly introduces select authors and texts that I consider vital to the reconstruction of the life and message of Chaitanya.

Murari Gupta: *SriKrishnachaitanyacharitamritam*

The manuscript of this work was first discovered in 1896, largely due to the initiative taken by political worker and pious Vaishnava author, Sisir Kumar Ghosh (1840–1911), and subsequently published by the newspaper *Amrita Bazar Patrika* in Calcutta. Murari was a Baidya by caste, a native medical practitioner, and one of the several migrants who had come from Sylhet to Nadia and had become intimate devotees and followers of Chaitanya. Older to Chaitanya in age, he was, for some time, a fellow student at the local *tol* (Hindu seminary) in Nadia. Though a Vaishnava, Murari's revered deity was Lord Rama and not Krishna. That he was given to the study of Hindu philosophy, particularly to the Vedanta school of thought, is apparent from the attention he gave to the *Yogavasistha Ramayana* (an anonymous quasi-Vedantic work based on a dialogue between Sage Vasistha and Lord Rama, c.8th–9th century). Murari's work, in fact, includes eight verses in praise of Lord Rama (*Ramashtaka*) but which, apparently, did not come in the way of either his reverence for Chaitanya or Chaitanya's own affection for his friend and companion. If anything, Chaitanya is known to have encouraged Murari to stay true and devoted to his personal faith. Together with Sivananda Sen, Kavi Karnapur's father, and poet Narahari Sarkar, Murari is identifiable with the group that adhered to the concept of *Gaurparamyavada* to which reference has been made above. In hindsight, this appears to have contributed to the neglect that he suffered from later Vaishnava authors and theologians. Those based in Vrindavan were reluctant to accept the idea of greater weightage being given to Chaitanya than to Krishna. But even within Nadia circles, ironically, Murari was under attack for not depicting Chaitanya as a Krishna devotee, even as a child. Whether in Vrindavan or in Bengal, authors did not find favour with the local religious community when presenting their personalised understanding of a subject.

The *SriKrishnachaitanyacharitamritam* (The Life of SriKrishna-chaitanya, c.16th century), also commonly known as *Murari Gupter Kadcha*, is a Sanskrit work of about 1,906 verses and most probably composed around 1535. Literary historians of Bengal, as for instance, the late Sukumar Sen, doubted if a work of such length could justly be called a *kadcha* (notes). This takes us back to the question of possible interpolation. All the same, Murari's is the most reliable, first-hand account in respect of Chaitanya's life and activities in Nabadwip, that is, prior to his departure for Puri as an ascetic. On the other hand, if the account of Chaitanya's life at Puri now included in the printed version is taken to be authentic, the work obviously could not have been completed in 1503 as claimed since Chaitanya accepted *sanyas* only in 1510.

Kavi Karnapur: *Chaitanyacharitamritam Mahakavya, Chaitanyacandrodaya Natakam,* and *Gauraganoddesdipika*

Kavi Karnapur (whose name literally means one who adorns the ear-jewel among poets) was reportedly the title conferred on Paramananda Sen by Chaitanya himself when seven-year-old Paramananda met the saint at Puri in the company of his father. Reportedly, the boy spontaneously composed verses befitting a gifted poet. Paramananda's father, Sivananda Sen, was himself a poet and a close follower of Chaitanya, who also organized and financed the recurring trip from Bengal to Puri (coinciding with the annual Rath festival) for Bengali devotees and followers. Karnapur authored several works but in this brief introduction we shall refer to only three.

Given his personal talent and valuable contribution to Vaishnava biography, literature, aesthetic theory, and rhetoric, Karnapur could justly claim a place among the famed Goswamis of Vrindavan, but this was a status which he was eventually denied by the Gaudiya Vaishnava community. His literary feats match those of the famed Rup and Jiva Goswamis. Rup produced two plays on Krishna *lila*, Karnapur two comparable works on Chaitanya lila. In the field of Vaishnava aesthetics, his *Alankarakaustava* (A Work on Rhetoric, c.16th century) matches Rup's *Ujjvalanilamani* (The Resplendent Blue Jewel, c.16th century). Rup produced the *RadhaKrishnaganoddesdipika* (An Inventory of the Intimate Followers of Radha and Krishna, c.16th–17th century), a work on the mythical characters associated with Krishna and Radha at Vrindavan, while Karnapur produced the *Gauraganoddesdipika* (The Shining Lamp on the Associates of Chaitanya, c.16th century), a comparable work associated with Chaitanya and his companions in Nabadwip. If Jiva excelled in campu literature (a literary form combining prose and poetry), so did Karnapur in his *Anandavrindavanacampu* (a dramatic work in both prose and verse proclaiming the glories of Vrindavan—the abode of bliss, c.16th century).

It has sometimes been suggested that Karnapur failed to win the status of a Goswami on account of his non-Brahmin birth and the possibility that he never settled in Vrindavan. On closer scrutiny, both these explanations appear flawed. Raghunath Das Goswami, one of the six Vrindavan Goswamis, was a Kayastha by birth and Raghunath Bhatt, who made no contribution to Vaishnava literature, was counted among the Goswamis. Ironically, Jiva, who never met Chaitanya, was revered as a Goswami while Karnapur was not, despite having met him. A visit to Vrindavan was not consistently a factor for determining the rank or status of Bengal-based Vaishnavas. Greatly revered Vaishnava figures such as Advaita Acharya or Narahari Sarkar never visited Vrindavan, and yet, they did not lose their importance or leadership qualities on that account. The most plausible reason for the exception lies in Karnapur identifying himself with *Gaurparamyavada*. For the Vrindavan Goswamis, the doctrinal value of Chaitanya worship was somewhat instrumental; for the most prominent of Chaitanya's followers in Bengal, this was substantive and critical. Short of overstating the case, it might be claimed that for Karnapur, Chaitanya was both the means and the end; for the Goswamis, he was but the means to a 'higher' end.

The *Chaitanyacharitamritam Mahakavya* (An Epic on the Life of Chaitanya, 1542) is a Sanskrit work, which, in the opinion of Sushil Kumar De, reveals a juvenile enthusiasm and rhetorical artificiality. If Karnapur was born sometime between 1524 and 1526, as commonly believed, we are indeed looking at the work of a young boy not over 18. Stylistically though, Karnapur adhered well to the conventions of classic Sanskrit poetics, which made free and evocative use of erotic imagery. There are vivid descriptions of the beauty of Laxmi's (the first wife of Chaitanya) breasts and of Krishna and the *gopis* engaging in *viparita sringara* (reverse coitus).

The *Chaitanyacandrodaya Natakam* (A Dramatic Work on the Life of Chaitanya—The Rising Moon, 1572) is believed to have been commissioned by the Odiya king Prataprudra, though this seems improbable since Prataprudra passed away in 1540, just seven years after Chaitanya did. This work proved to be unpopular with Vaishnavas, as also with modern scholars. Among other reasons, it was spurned by Vaishnavas for the way Karnapur, in defiance of Vaishnava conventions, critiqued the earlier work by Swarup Damodar, *Swarup Damodarer Kadcha*. In Bimanbihari Majumdar's view, only the son of a man of the stature of Sivananda Sen could have dared to do this without inviting the collective wrath of the community. Closer to our times, Indologist Rajendralal Mitra (1822–1891), who published the work in 1854 under the Asiatic Society of Bengal, was moved by puritanical thoughts. 'It (the *Natakam*) does not propose to itself,' Mitra wrote, 'the highest thoughts of social improvement ... (and is) more calculated to produce a hypertrophy of religious feeling. ... It is more suited to the temper of lazy monks than the requirement of honest citizens.'

Karnapur's *Gauraganoddesdipika* is important on two accounts: one, it appears to be the first work to have employed the term 'Goswami'; second, for suggesting that the followers of Chaitanya and Gaudiya Vaishnavism belonged to the Madhva Sampradaya, denoting followers of the medieval Vaishnava–Vedantin scholar from Karnataka. Modern research, however, has interpreted this affiliation to be motivated more by strategy and less by doctrine.

Vrindavan Das: *Chaitanya Bhagavata*

There is an apocryphal story to the effect that the name *Chaitanya Mangal*, which Vrindavan Das had originally given to his work, was changed to *Chaitanya Bhagavata* at the behest of the Vrindavan Goswamis. That the work was indeed known as *Chaitanya Mangal*, at least until the close of the 16th century, is borne out by Krishnadas Kaviraj's *Chaitanya Charitamrita*, which refers to it by that name. Possibly, Das's intention was to replicate the narrative intentions and style of the medieval *Mangal Kavyas*, popular ballads composed in praise of chosen deities; for Das, Chaitanya was Divinity itself.

Vrindavan Das's birth is shrouded in mystery and, in Sushil Kumar De's opinion, plainly scandalous. Reportedly, he was born to the widowed Narayani, a niece of Sribas who was a close companion of Chaitanya. This event drove a sharp wedge within the Vaishnava community in contemporary Nabadwip, and Narayani was summoned before the local Kazi to clear her name. The family subsequently settled her elsewhere, where she spent the rest of her life performing cleaning services at a temple, perhaps never altogether freed of social persecution. The 18th-century work *Premvilas* and, more recently, Vaishnava author and theologian Atul Krishna Goswami (1867–1946) suggest that Vrindavan Das was conceived before his father, Vaikuntha Chakravarti, passed away. However, legend has it that Narayani conceived upon eating a portion of a betel leaf (*paan*) that Chaitanya had chewed upon. Thus, not surprisingly, it was widely rumoured that the biological father was none other than Chaitanya himself. Vrindavan Das's own testimony took Narayani to be only four years old when she met Chaitanya, sometime in 1508. Assuming that a woman could not have conceived before she was 13 or 14 years of age, this puts the year of birth at 1518, long after Chaitanya had settled in Puri. On the other hand, there are reasons to doubt Vrindavan Das's testimony, for, going by some accounts, the news of Narayani conceiving was known to residents of Nabadwip even before Chaitanya left for Puri in 1510. Suspicions are also cast on Nityananda, who is known to have blessed Narayani with the birth of a son. This is an interpretation that was known even in the 1940s, since Satish Chandra Ray (1866–1931)—compiler of the well-known Vaishnava anthology *Padakalpataru* (An Anthology of Vaishnava Verses, 1915)—refers to it in the context of the researches of a contemporary 'historian-friend', now identifiable as Amulyachandra Sen. Sen's *Itihaser Sri Chaitanya* (The Historical Chaitanya, 1965) was banned by the West Bengal government, allegedly for offending public sentiments. Even a fig-ure as sympathetic to the Vaishnava movement as Dineshchandra Sen once wrote to say that 'even the warmest supporters of Nityananda do not recognize Vaikuntha Chakravarti as the father'. Some scholars have also pointed to the fact that in his *Gauraganoddesdipika*, Karnapur refers to Vrindavan Das as the 'Vyasa of the modern era', which indirectly supports the theory of his birth outside wedlock. Whether out of filial love or not, Vrindavan Das remained extremely loyal to the memory of Nityananda, even going to the extent of abusing and threatening those contemporaries who dared speak ill of him in a manner very unbecom-ing of a Vaishnava.

Very different dates have been assigned to the *Chaitanya Bhagavata*, ranging from 1535 to 1575. It seems reasonable, however, to settle on the period 1546–50. Internal evidence suggests that it was composed about 10 to 15 years after the death of Nityananda, by when Chaitanya's devotees and followers had already split into rival camps.

Vrindavan Das's chief agenda was to link Chaitanya's life and activi-ties to those of Krishna's. While Murari Gupta and Kavi Karnapur also perform this in some ways, they chose not to recast Chaitanya's life as thoroughly. In the *Chaitanya Bhagavata*, however, episodes in the life of Chaitanya are made to closely correspond to those in the mythical life of Krishna, often through the use of the miraculous. A disproportionately large space is devoted to Chaitanya's early life, especially between January 1509 and January 1510, which corresponds with his return from Gaya and subsequently accepting the life of an ascetic. On the other hand, the work overlooks certain important historical episodes connected with Chaitanya such as his tour of south India and of Mathura–Vrindavan and Benares. It is visibly lacking in details of Chaitanya's life at Puri, which is ample justification, one feels, for Krishnadas Kaviraj to have conceived of his *Charitamrita*.

A work marred by youthful impatience and impetuosity, the *Chaitanya Bhagavata* also exhibits the tendency to draw an exagger-ated picture of certain events. Vrindavan Das was fiercely loyal to the memory of Chaitanya. The pioneering historian of Bengali literature Ramgati Nyayratna (1831–1894) once remarked that if Vrindavan Das had had his way, he would have simply exterminated all those who failed to revere Chaitanya. And yet, as a source on the early life of the saint, the *Bhagavata* remains the single most valuable text. Its descriptions of contemporary Nadia, of its people, and of their daily lives are insightful and abundantly detailed. Barring the *Chaitanya Charitamrita*, more manuscript copies of this work have been unearthed in Bengal; and, in some way, Vrindavan Das's work remains a typically Bengali commentary on contemporary Vaishnava life. The *Charitamrita*, by comparison, was a significantly different text since it intended to bridge the two somewhat divergent worlds of Bengal and Vrindavan.

Krishnadas Kaviraj: *Chaitanya Charitamrita*

There is general agreement on Krishnadas's high reputation as a poet and scholar. Perhaps, the only person whose scholastic talent closely matched his was Kavi Karnapur. Krishnadas had ample knowledge of poetics, grammar, rhetoric, and scripture which he put to good use when writing the *Charitamrita*. It is not certain if he was by birth a Brahmin or a Baidya. Though the title 'Kaviraj' would otherwise suggest the latter, we also know that this was acquired not on account of his *jati* standing but because he was the author of the monumental *Govindalilamrita*, the largest single work in Bengali Vaishnava religious literature. In Bengal, the word 'kaviraj' is used for practitioners of ayurveda, usually belonging to the Baidya caste. However, the literary historian Sukumar Sen adds that Jhamatpur in district Burdwan, where Krishnadas was born, had no Baidya settlement.

Krishnadas belonged to a reasonably affluent family, as can be gauged from the fact that a priest was engaged for providing daily service to the family deity. Following a domestic squabble, Krishnadas left home. Legend has it that Nityananda appeared in his dream directing him to Vrindavan, where he reached either in 1554 or 1557, depending on whether or not the Goswamis were all alive then. This hypothesis is based on Krishnadas's admission that he received theological training from all the six Goswamis, which makes them his *shikshagurus*. However, he remains strangely silent on just who formally initiated him into the Gaudiya community, fulfilling the role of the *dikshaguru*. Krishnadas's dates are disputed. It is unlikely though that he was born in

1517, as commonly claimed, since that would have enabled him to meet Nityananda in person, not merely in his dreams. Also, going by Tony K. Stewart's claim that his magnum opus, the *Charitamrita*, was completed in 1615, Krishnadas would have had to be nearly a hundred years old at the time and there is also no reason to assume that he did not survive the *Charitamrita*.

The dates of the *Charitamrita* itself are no less disputed. In his *History of Bengali Language and Literature* (1911), Dineshchandra Sen suggests the date as 1581, but in *Chaitanya and His Age* (1923), he suggests 1615. Both J.N. Farquhar and Jadunath Sarkar agree on 1582. Prima facie, both 1581 and 1582 are problematic since the *Charitamrita* alludes to the Vaishnava classic *Gopala Champu* (a dramatic work in both prose and verse in honour of the infant Krishna, c.16th century), completed only in 1582. We also have it on Jatindra Mohan Bhattacharya's testimony that the oldest extant manuscript of the work, preserved with the Calcutta University Manuscript collection, dates back to 1020 Bangiya San (Bengali year), corresponding to 1613 CE. Two popular, albeit somewhat dubious, texts from the 18th century—Nityananda Das's *Premvilas* and Narahari Chakravarti's *Bhaktiratnakara* (An Ocean of Devotional Verses, c.17th century)—suggest that Krishnadas Kaviraj was grief-stricken and gave up his life upon hearing that the manuscript of the *Chaitanya Charitamrita* was lost following an act of robbery at Bonbishnupur in Bengal. The robbers mistook several valuable manuscripts, being transported from Vrindavan to Bengal, for precious treasure. In Stewart's view, the event took place sometime in 1599–1600. According to Stewart's own reckoning, the *Charitamrita* was not completed until 1615. Thus, it could not have been among the manuscripts so lost, whereupon the apocryphal story of Krishnadas's tragic death would also have to be regarded as unfounded in fact. However, the problem remains that if the work was completed before 1615, as could well be the case, it is not improbable that the *Charitamrita* was indeed en route to Bengal in 1599–1600. This by itself also does not also establish that its alleged loss led to the premature death of its author.

A plausible resolution to this problem is contingent on determining three related matters: the date by when the *Charitamrita* was completed, the date of the robbery, and the date of Krishnadas's death, natural or otherwise. Given the fact that few Vaishnava works agree with one another in terms of details, this could indeed prove to be a difficult task. Two other points of relevance must be considered alongside. It is highly unlikely that there was but only one manuscript copy of the work available in Vrindavan or that Krishnadas and the Goswamis risked sending it all the way to Bengal. Second, it is hard to impute a motive to either Nityananda Das or Premdas for suggesting that the senile Krishnadas had not died a natural death. Wantonly dramatizing the event could not have brought them extra acclaim.

Not surprisingly, the *Charitamrita* has attracted conflicting assessments and opinions. Of the religious classics produced in Bengal, this work attained a circulation surpassed only by the Bengali version of the *Ramayana* by Krittibas and of the *Mahabharata* by Kashiram Das. Once consigned to print, the wealthy of Calcutta commissioned local presses to produce special editions that used watermarked paper imported from Europe. The historian Jadunath Sarkar (1870–1958) was impressed enough to render a partial English translation of the work. And yet, it was also somewhat harshly criticized in certain quarters. The otherwise excellent history of Bengali literature in the English language by J.C. Ghosh (1948), found it 'laboured, ponderous and dull-devotional rather than historical'. Dineshchandra Sen, though otherwise consistently appreciative of Vaishnava literature and culture, felt that few had the ability to grasp its theological meaning. Earlier, there had also been some confusion about the exact identity of this work's author. Writing in 1851, Rev. Lal Behari Dey took it to be 'an abridgement of the larger work in Sanskrit by Vrindavan Das' when, in fact, Vrindavan Das's work was neither in Sanskrit nor more voluminous.

The *Charitamrita* does represent dense theology, even though its treatment of Chaitanya's spiritual life is otherwise both inspired and enlivening. Stewart found a manuscript copy of the work, said to belong to Krishnadas himself, being worshipped at a shrine located in Jhamatpur, his birthplace. Fully accepting the thesis originating from Chaitanya's personal companion at Puri, Swarup Damodar, and subsequently elaborated over an extended dialogue with Ramananda Ray, he projects Chaitanya not only as an androgynous figure but as actively preaching *madhura rasa*, an emotionally and erotically charged love for the Divine. This is in visible contrast with the picture presented by Vrindavan Das where Chaitanya is essentially understood as a *yugavatar* whose function was to punish the wicked and redeem humanity. On the whole, both the style and orientation of the *Charitamrita* are pedantic, leaning heavily on classicism. It consults no less than 75 Sanskrit texts, borrowing about 450 verses from the *Bhagavat Purana* alone. Whereas in the *Chaitanya Bhagavata*, the Divine could be invoked in the vernacular alone, in the *Charitamrita*, this turns bilingual in a queer amalgam of provincial Bengali and classical cosmopolitan Sanskrit. A feature that some Bengali readers in particular have also objected to is Krishnadas's recurring tendency to employ words or terms used in Hindi or Brajbhasha. This, however, is understandable in the light of his long residence in Vrindavan and perhaps also because like the Goswamis, his view of Vaishnavism as a religious and cultural order was more pan-Indian than centred on Bengal alone.

Biography sans Biographer? The *Kadcha* of Govindadas Karmakar

The *Kadcha* of Govindadas qualifies more as a biography than a hagiography. Prima facie, it is a down to earth account, narrated in plain vernacular without adhering to any established literary conventions or pandering to any sophisticated religious doctrine. Also, unlike other works it mostly does not employ miracles as a part of narrative strategy. On the contrary, Chaitanya, in this account, emerges as almost an ordinary mortal with commonplace qualities of head and heart. It was precisely this quality about the work that largely explains its unpopularity with the orthodox Vaishnava community.

Govindadaser Kadcha is reportedly the work of one Govindadas Karmakar, a man belonging to the community of *karmakars* (blacksmiths), who is believed to have served as Chaitanya's companion on his tour of peninsular India between 1510 and 1512. A work of about 2460 verses, it describes in some detail Chaitanya's travels between those years. As far as Chaitanya's tour of peninsular India is concerned, this narrative makes up for the significant lack of the *Chaitanya Bhagavata* and the rather sketchy account in the *Charitamrita*. For those who believe in its authenticity, the *Kadcha* also becomes the oldest work associated with the life and message of Chaitanya.

The manuscript of this work was 'discovered' by Jaygopal Das Goswami (1829–1916) of the Advaita lineage, serving as Head Pandit at a school in Santipur. Reportedly, Jaygopal found the manuscript with one Kalidas Nath, also of Santipur, which he then claimed to have sent over to Sisir Kumar Ghosh for inspection. Apparently, Sisir Kumar liked the work since an appreciative note appeared in his journal, *Vishnupriya Patrika* (a Vaishnava journal named after Chaitanya's second wife, started in 1890). Subsequently Ghosh is known to have sent it over to a friend, Sambhoo Chunder Mookerjee (1839–1894), sometime editor of the *Hindu Patriot*, and it was at this stage that the manuscript copy was misplaced. Reportedly, Jaygopal was able to procure another copy from a fellow resident of Santipur, Harinath Goswami. Using notes taken down earlier from the lost manuscript copy, he arranged to have it published from the Sanskrit Press Depository in 1896.

The *Kadcha* became a controversial work almost instantly. Even so, a second edition was brought out by the University of Calcutta in 1926. This edition was edited by the literary historian Dineshchandra Sen and Banwarilal Goswami, a descendant of Jaygopal. In the meantime, an appreciative note by Haraprasad Sastri appeared in the *Calcutta Review* in 1898, further sharpening the controversy. A public meeting to debate and discuss the issue was called at the *Bangiya Sahitya Parishat* (Bengal Academy of Letters) on 7 November 1900 but proved inconclusive. Following a brief lull, the controversy was resumed with much intensity in the 1920s with a spate of writings flowing from Vaishnavas and lay scholars alike. Among these, we must take note of Dineshchandra himself writing in the *Calcutta Review*, one Amritlal Sil in the Bengali journal *Prabasi* (both in 1925), and an undated but sharply accusatory booklet by B.V. Dasgupta. Dasgupta's work also carried a preface by Jadunath Sarkar, evidently to reinforce the argument that many events connected with Chaitanya's tours and as described in the *Kadcha*, were historically untenable. Dasgupta even went to the extent of calling the work a 'Black Forgery'. Closer to our time, some well-known literary historians of Bengali literature such as Sukumar Sen and Asit Kumar Bandopadhyay have also dismissed the work as pure forgery. Dineshchandra Sen, who consistently stood by the authenticity of the *Kadcha*, was targeted by critics from various quarters. Contemporary Vaishnavas believed that his support of the work and its author had only led to the defaming of Chaitanya and Vaishnavism in general. Sukumar Sen took him to be a highly gullible figure and an incorrigible romantic to the core.

While the Gowamis in Calcutta, Nabadwip, and Santipur may have busied themselves over the question of whether or not the ascetic Chaitanya had condescended to extend his grace to public women, as claimed by Govindadas, lay writers and scholars noticed serious discrepancies in the text of a very different nature. First, of the 78 places Chaitanya is said to have visited, very few could be identified with existing sites. Second, the work betrayed a poor sense of history. Thus, the city of Purnanagar (modern Pune), which the *Kadcha* claims as one of the several sites visited by Chaitanya, did not exist in Chaitanya's time. Also inexplicable is the use of the word *janala* (for window), a word of Portuguese origin, at a time when the Portuguese are not known to have established significant commercial or political links with the region. There was reference also to a town called Russellkonda, founded only in 1837 and named after the British officer George Edward Russell (1787–1863). In 1925, Melville Kennedy, the author of an important work on the Chaitanya movement—*The Chaitanya Movement: A Study of Vaishnavism in Bengal*—puzzled over the fact that the *Kadcha* showed the sanyasi Chaitanya with matted locks. Some critics wondered how an illiterate man such as Govindadas, belonging to a ritually inferior caste (of blacksmiths), could have the skill to produce such poetry, while still others wondered if Chaitanya himself and his intimate followers would have at all allowed such a man to remain in his personal service, risking ritual propriety.

Since the 1920s, the general reading of this work has been clearly negative and Jaygopal Goswami himself was believed to have carried out the 'forgery'. After the second edition of the work came out in 1926, even a diehard supporter such as Dineshchandra Sen was heard admitting a certain degree of text torturing. In 1933, Satischandra Dey, the author of the classic *Gaurangadev O Kanchanpalli* (Chaitanya and Kanchanpalli [Modern Kanchrapara], 1923) and otherwise a stout defender of the *Kadcha*, admitted editorial manipulations in the 1926 edition by virtue of which the text was deliberately made to look archaic. In 1934–5, the *Gaudiya Vaishnava Sammilani*, an organization of Bengali Vaishnavas supported by some respectable residents of Calcutta, organized a protest meeting, altogether rejecting the work and the first full-length study of the issue by Nirmal Narayan Gupta (1984) also casts serious doubt on its authenticity. And yet, on another level, there remained some simmering doubt and discontent. Bimanbihari Majumdar, both as a Vaishnava or a lay scholar, refused to commit himself one way or another. For one, he stated that he could not figure out just what motives could have compelled Jaygopal Goswami to carry out the alleged forgery. Prima facie, Santipur Goswamis colluding to have a Shudra as Chaitanya's companion does seem unlikely, given the fact that other than Brahmins, they condescended to accept only Baidyas and Kayasthas as disciples. Going by the available evidence on Russellkonda, it could well be that the *Kadcha* was a post 1837 work and yet the question remains: how much after? And if the *Kadcha* was forged close to that time, why did it surface only after about 60 years? Assuming also that the forger was an educated man and well conversant with the life of Chaitanya, would it not been naive of him to have replaced the shaven head Chaitanya with a sanyasi with matted locks? It looks unlikely that Jaygopal himself was guilty of such naivety and oversight. One of the objections raised by orthodox Vaishnavas, as we have noted above, was to do with the ascetic Chaitanya's reportedly extending his grace to prostitutes. But this too does not defy explanation. Perhaps, the act of grace did not pose a threat to male continence and the Brahmin's ritual purity. The Bengali mystic Ramakrishna Paramahamsa (1836–1886) exhibited the same compassion and grace to prostitutes–turned-actresses of the Bengali stage. Upon hearing this, some of his followers—particularly reformist Brahmos—are known to have stopped patronizing contemporary Bengali theatre and calling upon the saint himself.

There is good reason to believe that Govindadas Karmakar was a historical character, for he is mentioned in at least two contemporary sources: in a verse (included in the anthology *Gaurapadatarangini* (An Anthology of Verses in Praise of Chaitanya, 1934) by *padabali* poet Basudev Ghosh) and by Jayananda in his *Chaitanya Mangal*. On the other hand, establishing his historical identity does not also prove his authorship of the *Kadcha*. What we have then is a missing biographer, or at least a biographer of whose identity we cannot be certain of. Perhaps the alleged act of forgery does not render every act or event connected with Chaitanya reported in the *Kadcha* as spurious. There might well have been a pre-existing narrative framework upon which the additions and accretions were tendentiously foisted.

The controversy around *Govindadaser Kadcha* had a significantly positive effect on the Karmakar community in Bengal. By 1921, they claimed Kshatriya status and thereafter held an annual commemorative festival at Kanchannagar, reportedly the birthplace of Govindadas. In independent India, memorials were built in his honour by the Sahitya Parishat and the Government of West Bengal in 1952 and 1983 respectively. During the same period, the neighbourhood has been a favoured settlement for refugees from erstwhile east Bengal, who have now built temples that house life-size statues of Govindadas Karmakar, besides those of Chaitanya, Advaita, and Nityananda. We have it on the authority of Jogendranath Bhattacharya, the author of a valuable ethnographic study on Bengal titled *Hindu Castes and Sects*, that there indeed existed in Dhaka an affluent Karmakar community who were goldsmiths by profession and Vaishnavas in religious following.

Govindadaser Kadcha has undergone at least two reprints in modern times, the first by Dey's Publishing of Kolkata in 1997 and more recently in 2013, by an organization that calls itself the *Kadcha Kavi Sangh*.

3 *The Life and Times of Krishna Chaitanya*

For a man who inspired pious and prolific poetry, profound scholasticism, and selfless renunciation, whose very persona and presence drew vast numbers of common men and women to his side and left an enduring impression on successive generations, the life of Chaitanya at first glance appears rather commonplace and unspectacular. He passed away when less than fifty, spending the last years of his life at Puri in a god-maddened, ecstatic state and virtually as a recluse. His death itself remains shrouded in mystery, with conflicting accounts offered by later day hagiographers. And yet, in the short span of his life, he left behind a rich spiritual and cultural legacy, both in his native Bengal and neighbouring Odisha, where his life and acts are still revered and celebrated. The movement he inspired survives even today in myriad forms, going beyond provincial and national boundaries.

Posterity has often associated Chaitanya with uncharacteristic acts or accomplishments in which he actually evinced very little interest. He was neither a scholar nor an active preacher or publicist; what he said or performed poured quite spontaneously out of his heart. His was a life ruled more by feeling than judgement, more by emotion than rational deliberation. Both in his time and thereafter, Chaitanya has been perceived or understood in very different ways. Some saw him as an ideal devotee, others as an avatar, as God Himself descended on earth in human form to redeem humanity in crisis. The growing and fervent belief in the miraculous descent of a *yugavatar* explains why, of all major saints or religious figures of medieval Bengal, hagiographic attention was most abundantly directed at him. Closer to our times, something similar was to happen with the Bengali mystic Ramakrishna Paramahamsa. Contrary to claims often made, Chaitanya was not the self-conscious founder or architect of an organized religious movement. However, as his contemporaries have testified, he did nevertheless transfer his energies and intent to chosen followers and devotees. This subsequently laid the foundations of a highly successful movement, now with a global presence. He was never known to hold public discourses, compose erudite texts, or campaign for social and religious reform. Rather, as his intimate disciple and poet Narahari Sarkar observed in his little known Sanskrit text, *Srikrishnabhajanmritam* (Devotional Verses Dedicated to Krishna, c. 16th century), he could reform human character merely by shedding tears of love and compassion; reportedly, his personal piety and purity alone would cleanse every soul of its moral blemishes or shortcomings. The biographer Kavi Karnapur has claimed that people would turn into devotees even without ever meeting him in person or receiving personal instructions from him. Interestingly enough, in the context of Chaitanya, we may justly speak of only devotees and followers, not disciples, since he did not formally initiate anybody into a life of *sanyas*, not even the famed Goswamis of Vrindavan.

About seven feet tall, Chaitanya would stand out in any crowd. He could be easily spotted amidst a milling crowd participating in a Vaishnava procession, defying the orders of the local Kazi. To cast him as such an imposing figure may not have originated in hagiographic needs, as some critics suspect. Krishnadas Kaviraj claims that Chaitanya's height equalled four times his own arm's length which would be in the range of 72–80 inches or about six feet eight inches.[1] He also had a

---

[1] The well-known modern Vaishnava scholar and commentator Radha Govinda Nath (1879–1970) puts this at 84 inches or fully seven feet.

lustrously pale complexion (hence also called Gora or Gauranga) with shoulder-length hair, a broad chest, long limbs almost reaching down to his knees. Raghunath Das Goswami, for some time his companion at Puri, describes him as 'Hemadri', a mountain of white gold, and this at a time when he had turned into a frail, self-denying ascetic with a shaven head, unmindful of even routine requirements or petty indulgences. Several contemporaries who met him in person testify to his extraordinary looks, which they called *devadurlabha*. Indeed, in his pre-ascetic days at Nadia, Chaitanya was the subject of evocative poetry, some of which go to erotic lengths in describing how the women of Nadia passionately coveted a man like him as a lover or husband.

His complexion, however, has also been the cause behind interesting conjectures and speculations. A recent work of fiction (Shaibal Mitra's *Gora*, 2013), which recasts his life and work quite radically, tacitly suggests that he was fathered by a man of middle-eastern descent. In Mitra's perception, evidently, Chaitanya's bodily features as described in contemporary works ill fitted those of an ethnic Hindu Bengali. The matter of complexion, incidentally, also proved to be something of an embarrassment for those devotees and theologians who fancied him as Lord Krishna descended on earth. There was a double problem here, as we shall later have occasion to examine. First, the *shastras* ruled out Krishna appearing successively in the *Dwapar* and *Kali yugas*. But more importantly, it was puzzling that the dark form of Krishna would inexplicably change into the paleness of Chaitanya. The ingenious solution which poets and theologians eventually struck upon was to construct an androgynous Chaitanya, combining the dark Krishna with the golden splendour of his mistress, Radha.

Apart from figuring prominently in formal philosophical discourse, the popularity of Chaitanya in public memory also rests on the way quotidian religious cults understood or celebrated his life and message. Many rural cults originating in 17th- and 18th-century Bengal accepted Chaitanya as their founding father and claimed to more faithfully interpret his life and message. Two features that are distinctive to these cults are: first, the tendency to privilege his social message, whether real or imagined, over the purely religious; and second, to treat Chaitanya more as a concept than as a historical figure. The Bauls, Sahajiyas, Kartabhajas, and a host of other rural cults in Bengal took Chaitanya to introduce a kind of religious democracy, overriding entrenched caste hierarchies and older conventions determining gender relations. By comparison, their acceptance of mainstream Vaishnava theology was rather selective and upon which they also foisted ideas and practices that were typically theirs. In numerous Sahajiya tracts, for example, Chaitanya himself is seen to have adopted sexo-yogic practices which required a female ritual partner other than one's wife. Clearly, theirs was a path of defiant dissent against the social conformism of orthodox Vaishnavism.

Chaitanya's Nabadwip

Nabadwip is said to have risen to prominence with the Sena kings assuming power in Bengal by the middle of the 12th century. This ruling house was later to establish another power base in eastern Bengal to which their last ruler, Laxman Sen, was forced to retreat in the wake of the invasion by Bakhtiyar Khilji in 1202–3. Thereafter, the province came to be ruled successively by Turks, Pathans, and Abyssinians, punctuated by a brief return of Hindu rulers. The man to first displace the reigning Muslim sovereign (of the Iliyas Shahi dynasty) in 1415, albeit only temporarily, was Raja Ganesh, who later took the name Danujamardana Dev. Three years later, one of his sons, Mahendra Dev, ascended the throne again. In the context of Chaitanya's life and work, this is an important factor to reckon with since contemporary accounts claim that following the successful coup by Raja Ganesh, the Muslim ruling classes remained in some fear of a Hindu backlash. In the closing years of the 15th century, coinciding with Chaitanya's adolescent life in Nadia, it was widely rumoured that there was soon to occur another coup led by a Brahmin upstart. Not surprisingly, some state officials connected this to the rising popularity of the Brahmin Chaitanya himself. We do know from available sources that the reigning ruler, Alauddin Hussain Shah (reigned between 1494–1514), who apparently took these rumours seriously, instructed his men to keep a close watch on Chaitanya and his movements. On his first visit to Bengal post *sanyas* (in early 1510), Chaitanya was advised by his close followers, some of whom were important officials of the sultanate, never to be seen at the head of a crowd for fear that this may cause misapprehension and bring about

some state reprisal. In Chaitanya's Nadia, there persisted some mutual
hostility and distrust between the two major communities, Hindus and
Muslims. Reportedly, Hussain Shah's predecessor in office, Jalaluddin
Fateh Shah, had been behind the persecution of non-Muslims, forcing
some such as the famed Nyaya scholar Vasudeva Sarvabhauma to flee
to the safety of the neighbouring Hindu Kingdom of Odisha. Further
down this chapter, we shall examine how such an environment contributed to the first major encounter between a watchful, apprehensive, and
distrustful state and a sensitized civic community that was keen to assert
its rights over that state.

We have vivid descriptions of early 15th-century Nabadwip in
early hagiographic writings concerning Chaitanya. Vrindavan Das's
Chaitanya Bhagavata found Nabadwip to be simply incomparable as a
human settlement, offering its inhabitants a life of peace and prosperity.
Even in the early 18th century, roughly three centuries after Chaitanya,
it was a spacious and well-populated site. *Bhaktiratnakara* by Narahari
Chakravarti mentions that it stretched for about 16 square miles, comprising a town and several villages. From this work, we also gather that
Nabadwip was so called on account of a cluster of nine islands which
made up its main land mass. However, critics have been also quick to
point out that the term 'Nabadwip' may just as well mean a newly formed
land mass (*naba+dwipa*), which could then put its acclaimed antiquity
in some doubt. Jayananda's *Chaitanya Mangal* too describes it as a well
populated settlement, boasting of brisk trade and commerce in rice, silk,
and cotton and as a clearing centre for merchandize arriving from upper
India en route to destinations in the near east. By Chaitanya's time, evidently, Nabadwip had replaced Satgaon (Saptagram) as an important
maritime centre.

The town could equally boast of extraordinary intellectual achievements. Even in the pre-Chaitanya days, it had come to be known as the
most developed centre—even on a pan-Indian scale—for the study of
Nyaya philosophy, overtaking neighbouring Mithila. By the late 15th
century, the new school of syllogism 'Nabya Nyaya' was almost exclusively the preserve of Nabadwip Brahmins. It was also the site where a
new genre of *smriti*—Hindu-Brahmanical social and legal codes (*Nabya
Smriti*)—was formulated and codified, reportedly in the face of both the
new threat from Islam and significant internal shifts in the ordering of

Hindu society. Arguably, contemporary Hindu Bengali society (and the situation in Nabadwip was no exception) was increasingly affected by three inter-related conflicts: first, the palpable loosening of the *varna* hierarchy and the 'indiscriminate' mixing of social classes and categories; second, a growing tension between upper caste—upper class Hindus and the new Indo-Muslim ruling class in Bengal; and third, new social aspirations visible in certain sections of Hindu artisanal and trading classes which had found some economic affluence but were consistently denied avenues of upward mobility.

Both Jayananda and Vrindavan Das freely complain of a visible decline in social norms and conventions. It was reported that the Shudras were no longer willing to serve Brahmins and women, their husbands, and the larger patriarchy. Allegedly, upper-caste Hindu widows now defiantly partook of flesh and fish, a situation only aggravated by the reported spread of 'false' and hedonistic notions of culture and religion. For contemporary writers, such features typically represented the *Kali yuga* syndrome in Hindu religious literature, characterized by degenerative time and a widespread inversion of established values and practices. It is quite possible that early Vaishnava hagiographers overdrew this picture somewhat so as to highlight the social and spiritual revolution ushered in by Chaitanya and to draw public empathy against persecution from both the state and orthodox Brahmanism. On the other hand, it seems reasonable to argue that scholasticism among Nadia Brahmins did breed formalism, arrogance, and scepticism. Allegedly, religion had been yoked to material considerations and the pursuit of power. Vrindavan Das reports that in contemporary Nabadwip, Shakti worshippers and Sakta priests were far better off since they catered to people who linked the act of god-remembrance to tangible rewards in everyday life. They worshipped only such gods or goddesses who would grant them coveted goals in worldly life, to the utter neglect of forbearance and piety. Vaishnavas, as Vrindavan Das further reports, were ridiculed for their modesty or moderation and for willingly embracing a life of abstinence and poverty. In his *Chaitanya Chandradoya Nataka*, Kavi Karnapur speaks of the presence of false ascetics, fearsome Kapaliks, and grossly corrupt Tantriks who ruled the roost since they and their followers took an entirely instrumental view of religion. This stood in sharp contrast to Chaitanya's message which spoke of 'ahetuki bhakti', pure and pious devotion, entirely unrelated to some cause or expectation.

A Precocious Child

Chaitanya was born in Nabadwip on 18 February 1486 as per the Julian calendar, or on 27 February as per the Gregorian. As though to suggest that he was no ordinary mortal, some accounts such as that of Vrindavan Das claim that he was in his mother's womb for as many as 13 months. It is difficult to be sure about the exact site of his birth since contesting claims have been made with regard to this for a very long time, flaring up into a major public controversy by the closing years of the 19th century. One reason for such contestations to have developed was the frequency with which the river Ganges changed its course, especially between 1572 and 1575. It is on record that during Chaitanya's time, it flowed to the east of Nadia town but subsequently shifted to its west. A major earthquake struck the region in 1762. In 1792, Diwan Gangagovind Singh, who made his personal fortunes in the service of the East India Company, constructed a temple at Ramchandrapur, a few miles off Nabadwip at the spot that he believed was the birth site of Chaitanya. This temple is known to have survived until 1821, when it went under water. In the 1850s, Rev. Lal Behari De, who has left behind some interesting accounts of Bengal Vaishnavism, also upheld this conclusion. Some 40 years later, Vaishnava theologian Kedarnath Datta actively propagated the cause of Mayapur, which was across the river from Nadia town, as the designated birthplace of Chanakya, much to the anger and disappointment of many lay individuals and Goswami lineages. Today, rightly or wrongly, it is Mayapur that enjoys greater attention both from local tourists and the larger international community of ISKCON Vaishnavas. Its spotless environment, well-ordered routines, and globalized presence helps support claims of adhering to a 'cleaner' religion.

All extant accounts agree on Chaitanya's birth coinciding with a lunar eclipse on a full moon night, which the local residents regarded as highly auspicious. There was much devotional singing and worship offered to popular deities to mark the significant astronomical configuration. Chaitanya was the second son born to Jagannath Misra, a Vaidik

Brahmin of Vatsya *gotra* from Sylhet, and Sachi, daughter of Nilambar Chakravarti, also from Sylhet. He was named Viswambhar, apparently to match the name given to his brother, Viswarup, older to him by about nine years. Seven daughters had earlier been born to the couple but each of them died either at childbirth or in infancy. Certain hagiographers have read some significance into these numbers. Anxious to uphold the identification of Chaitanya with Krishna, Jayananda observed how each was the eighth child born to his parents. In this, however, he was mistaken because as per available evidence, it was Viswarup and not Viswambhar who was the eighth child. In retrospect, the name Viswambhar appears to have been unpopular and the child was more often called 'Nimai', a name reportedly given to him by Sita Devi. She was the wife of Advaita Acharya, a neighbour and a close friend of the Misra family. There is some difference of opinion on just what led to that particular name being conferred on him. In one view, the name was a talisman meant to protect the child from ill health or misfortune and here, one can indeed sense the anxiety of a mother who had lost seven children successively or the feelings of a friendly neighbour who fully shared her sense of loss and grief. Alternatively, the name could have been given to the child since he was born under a neem tree. Whatever be the cause, the name Nimai stuck and was in vogue for a long time. Even down to the late 19th century, Bengali playwrights attempting to dramatize the traumatic episode of Chaitanya renouncing the world preferred to call it 'Nimai Sanyas'.

We are uncertain about just what occupation Jagannath Misra pursued. He does not appear to be a teacher–scholar who made a living by running a *tol*. There is no evidence of his tutoring either Chaitanya or his elder brother at any stage. On the contrary, Jagannath appears to have come to the conclusion that scholasticism bred irresponsible thoughts and false vanity in a man. His wife, Sachi, was convinced that it was the pursuit of a scholarly life that had led her elder son, Viswarup, to decline marriage or enter a householder's life. For this she blamed the veteran Advaita Acharya, his local teacher and a man who was known to have been partial to *Jnan Yoga* or the path of gnosis. Viswarup was to eventually renounce the world at the age of 16, accepting the monastic name Sankararanya, which suggests that he was initiated into *sanyas* by a monk of the Dasnami order. There is also a legend to the effect, though by no means substantiated, that his *dikshaguru* was none other than

Keshav Bharati, under whom Chaitanya himself was to later accept *sanyas*. Viswambhar is said to have been very fond of his brother and later in life, one of his declared purposes of touring south India was to locate him. In this matter, however, he was unsuccessful for it is generally believed that the ascetic Sankararanya had died by the age of 20, well before Chaitanya set out on his southern tour.

Hagiographies disagree on the material status of Jagannath Misra. The *Chaitanya Bhagavata* calls him 'su-daridra', a man with a paltry income. Perhaps Misra made a living by performing sundry services as a family priest and as a *kathak* who presided over public recitations from scriptures such as the *Bhagavat Purana*. It is also quite likely that Misra's hopes were pinned on his elder son finding a suitable vocation in life and supplementing the family income. The news of Viswarup accepting *sanyas* so upset him that he promptly had Viswambhar pulled out of his *tol* for fear that further education would only lead him away from his duties and responsibilities towards the family. Apparently, this has encouraged some scholars to speculate that meagre family resources frustrated Chaitanya's efforts to pursue higher studies and pushed him towards a life of renunciation. On the contrary, the *Chaitanya Charitamarita* shows Jagannath Misra to be affluent and not under any financial duress. In hindsight, the claims by both Vrindavan Das and Krishnadas Kaviraj appear to be somewhat exaggerated in their own ways and on account of varying ideological compulsions. On the whole, it seems reasonable to say that Jagannath Misra was a man of modest means and yet sufficiently endowed to keep his family in a reasonable degree of comfort. Judging by the fact that Chaitanya was not forced to seek a livelihood till about five years after his father's death in 1497, one would have to say that Jagannath Misra was never depressingly poor.

Jagannath, as we know, was one of the several Brahmins who had migrated from his native place Sylhet in east Bengal to Nabadwip, presumably in the early 15th century, and was a Vaishnava by religious persuasion. This list of migrants includes at least two other prominent companions of Chaitanya: Sribas, whose home in Nadia was to become the site for hosting a Vaishnava revival, and Advaita Acharya, who traced his descent from a politically influential family of the region. There is considerable difference of opinion as to the probable cause for such migration. This has been variously put down to recurring famines, political trouble in the region, and persecution from local Muslims swearing allegiance to the famed Sufi crusader, Shah Jalal. Perhaps it was Jagannath's ambition to be counted among the famed Nyaya or Smriti scholars of Nabadwip. What circumstances contributed to defeat these plans we shall never know. Quite possibly, he also had a certain share in ancestral land in Sylhet from which, presumably, the family was able to later derive some sustenance. Some accounts of Chaitanya's life suggest that his tour of east Bengal that occurred sometime in the year 1506 included a visit to the extended family which resided at Dhaka Dakhin in Sylhet so as to settle his share of ancestral property.

By the late 16th century, when Vaishnavism had come to be associated with pedantry and scholasticism, it became habitual on the part of hagiographers to project Chaitanya as a scholiast or, at any rate, as a deeply learned man. Jayananda states that he was equally conversant with the philosophical school of Nyaya, Smriti (Hindu law) and Alankar (rhetoric). However, such specious claims are not exclusive to older works. Kedarnath Dutta believed that Chaitanya read Smriti on his own and Nyaya in competition with friends. And if Dineschandra Sen is to be believed, Chaitanya was fluent in 13 or 14 languages including Pali, Prakrit, Persian, and Arabic! A modern work called *Pashanda Dalan*, to which we have referred before, reveals Chaitanya as a well behaved, highly committed student, not given to any childish pranks and who quickly completed his course of studies, much to the satisfaction of his parents. In his biographical writings on Chaitanya—chiefly in the multi volume Bengali biography *Amiya Nimai Charit* (The Nectar-Like Life of Nimai, 6 vols., 1975–8) and the English *Lord Gauranga* (1897)— Sisir Kumar Ghosh too grossly exaggerates the educational record in respect of Chaitanya. *Advaita Prakash* (The Life of Advaita, n.d.), a late work composed probably in the late eighteenth or early 19th century, even claimed that he had authored a *tika* on Nyaya as well as on the *Bhagavat Purana*.

Arguably, such claims originated in apocryphal stories narrated in certain late accounts about a very learned yet unassuming Chaitanya, a quality that was evidently expected to demonstrate Vaishnava humility. Chaitanya is reported to have rescued the famed Nyaya scholar Raghunath Shiromani from ignominy and embarrassment by selflessly casting away his own commentary on Nyaya into the waters of the

Ganges. He is also believed to be a contemporary of the founder of the
Bengal school of Tantra, Krishnananda Agambagish. Some accounts
press the claim that Chaitanya was instructed in Nyaya by none other
than Vasudeva Sarvabhauma. Evidently, such assertions or arguments
were meant to nurture and strengthen romantic perceptions about 16th
century Nadia witnessing an unprecedented flowering of intellectual
and cultural life, buttressed, no doubt, by the presence of Chaitanya
himself.

The fact of the matter, however, is very different. Going by modern
accounts, Raghunath Shiromani would have been born only around
1510 and Vasudeva Sarvabhauma, as we have earlier noted, is known
to have fled Nadia fearing Muslim persecution before Chaitanya was
born. Vasudeva was known to both Jagannath Misra and Nilambar
Chakravarti, and he did fondly recall his association with his friends on
the day Chaitanya met him at Puri, sometime in 1510. Importantly, he
had no recollections of having ever met Chaitanya himself at Nabadwip.
The *Chaitanya Bhagavata* does indeed mention a certain Krishnananda as
a fellow student of Chaitanya at the local *tol*. But this Krishnananda was
the son of Ratnagarbha Bhattacharya, an emigrant from Sylhet, whereas
Agambagish's father was Maheswar Gaudacharya. A great grandson
of Krishnananda Agambagish, Ramtoshan Vidyalankar authored the
Prantoshini Tantra (a tantric work given the name Prantoshini, c.18th
century) and by this reckoning, Krishnananda had to be born nearly a
hundred years after Chaitanya.

When at a propitious age, Chaitanya was admitted to the *tols* run
by Gangadas Pandit and Sudarshan Pandit. It was under Gangadas
that he mastered *vyakaran*, in particular the school known as Kalapa
Vyakaran, a trifle surprising considering the popularity of others such
as the Mugdabodha. Legend has it that he even produced a *tika* on
Kalapa which proved to be highly popular with students of east Bengal
and added to his earnings. Curiously, even an otherwise reliable account
such as Murari Gupta's suggests that Chaitanya taught *laukik satkriya
vidhi* to his students. This looks quite improbable given the fact that
Smriti was never taught to boys as young as the ones that Chaitanya had
in his care. As for Nyaya, we may refer to the remark appearing in the
Chaitanya Charitamrita wherein local residents of Nadia are reported to
have expressed some regret at the fact that a young man as talented as

Chaitanya had not taken to the study of Nyaya. The context in which this remark was made is significant. Apparently, this originated from critics who believed that Chaitanya had virtually wasted his life by losing himself in fits of bizarre Vaishnava ecstasy.

As a student, Chaitanya was inattentive and mischievous and was often reprimanded by both his teachers. For a while, learning did bring him a sense of vanity and argumentativeness for he once tried picking grammatical flaws even in the works of Iswar Puri, a Vedantin but also a pious Vaishnava who was destined to be his *shikshaguru*, the man who first aroused in him the sentiments of Krishna *bhakti*. Iswar Puri, however, was quick to call his bluff and this is about the only incident reported in the hagiographies of an audacious Viswambhar being humbled by another in a matter of academic disputation. Indeed this incident may have somewhat chastized the young man. Later, in the role of a teacher himself (beginning sometime in 1501), Viswambhar is known to have taught his students the value of unassuming humility. As a young boy, he was notorious for his childish pranks, teasing and tormenting young girls who would come by the riverside or playing a trick or two on the elderly. At home, too, he proved hard to control, often defying commonplace social or ritual conventions that were part of the daily life of a Brahmin. When angry or upset with his mother, he would smash pots and pans from the kitchen, shred garments into pieces, or seat himself upon a heap of rubbish, much to the alarm and revulsion of Sachi and their neighbours. Some accounts, indeed, speak of his being ill-tempered and impatient, even going to the extent of causing injury to his mother by angrily hurling brickbats at her. Interestingly enough, hagiographers who choose to honestly narrate such incidents, also derive much pious intent from them. Thus, when seated on the heap of rubbish, the infant Chaitanya is shown to lecture his mother on how only the ignorant made distinctions between the ritually 'pure' and 'impure'. Some other texts then go on to interpret this as a discourse on *Jnan Yoga*, the path of gnosis! On another occasion, when the infant Viswambhar ate a clod of earth, it was taken to be reminiscent of the acts of the infant Krishna. Krishna, having similarly devoured a lump of earth, opened his mouth to his foster-mother, Yashoda, only to reveal the entire universe. Several incidents are also reported about how Chaitanya would eat food offered to Krishna. Quite naturally, the Brahmins who offered such food were at first, mighty offended but later made to realize how their offer had indeed been rightly claimed by none other than the Lord Himself.

Not surprisingly, modern writers and critics found such explanations far from unexceptionable. Nirad C. Chaudhury observed how this was but a mockery of *Jnan Yoga*; J.C. Ghosh, whose work we have discussed in previous chapters, found it difficult to 'restrain his incredulous laughter' at the reply Chaitanya gave to his mother. It would be only fair to add, though, that some contemporary figures could still read positive meaning even into this mischievous playfulness. Educationist Iswar Chandra Vidyasagar (1820–1891) and, after him, poet Rabindranath Tagore (1861–1941) have both found in these acts the infusion of liveliness and creative energy. In what is now a classic statement, Vidyasagar was to remark how, with respect to children, he always preferred such vigour and joyous abandon to meekness and over disciplined docility. Also, Viswambhar's frequenting the bathing ghats also had a savoury side since it was there that he met and courted Laxmi, who was to soon become his first wife.

The suspension of Viswambhar's studies proved to be temporary, for Sachi convinced Jagannath that without learning and scholarship to support him, a Brahmin would find it hard to make a worldly living. It was thus that the young boy was able to resume his studies and, not-withstanding continuing distractions, emerge as an intelligent student. Most sources call him *shrutidhar*, who could reproduce verbatim what he had heard but once. Apparently, this was a quality that enabled him to humble visiting pandits of whom one in particular was known to be a formidable scholar, popularly known as the *digvijayi*. Legend has it that the *digvijayi*, when asked to compose verses in praise of the Ganges flowing by, promptly composed a hundred of these impromptu; but his pride was soon shattered when Viswambhar, having heard the verses just once, picked rhetorical faults in them with ease. The story then narrates how Saraswati, the goddess of learning, appeared before the humili-ated scholar, consoling him with the revelation that he had lost to none other than the Lord Himself! The 18th-century text *Bhaktiratnakar* identifies the *digvijayi* with the famed scholar of the Nimbarka school of Vaishnavism, Keshav Kashmiri. If this is true, the incident may well be a specious claim coming at a time when sectarian rivalries were at their sharpest. In any case, history puts these two figures reasonably far apart in time. Also, going by one modern account, the composition for the

Ganges attributed to Keshav Kashmiri was excerpted from Viswanath Kaviraj's 14th-century work, *Sahitya Darpan* (The Mirror of Literature, c.14th century).

It is difficult to be precise with the chronology of events that followed. Apparently, Chaitanya's marriage to Laxmi lasted only about six years. She lost her life due to a snake bite at a time when Nimai Pandit was away, touring east Bengal. Interestingly enough, Vrindavan Das found the snake bite to be only metaphorical, arguing that Laxmi actually died of *viraha*, the intense pain of separation from her husband. There is good reason to believe that Viswambhar, too, had great affection for his childhood love and her death cast a deep gloom on his life. There is a vivid description of his hanging his head in utter grief upon hearing of her death when he returned to Nabadwip. Prima facie, it does look odd, therefore, that Jayananda's *Chaitanya Mangal* depicts the grief-stricken Viswambhar dancing joyously upon receiving the news of Laxmi's death; and yet, this could only be Jayananda's way of telling us how he had already been consumed by Divine love and hence, he was indifferent to personal losses in worldly life.

Viswambhar married a second time on the insistence of his mother who, presumably, was still counting on him to settle down and raise a family. The bride on this occasion was Vishnupriya Devi, daughter of one Vallabha. Vishnupriya survived her husband by several years, becoming a key figure in post Chaitanya Gaudiya Vaishnava tradition. Numerous heart-rending stories and plays came to be written on the theme of Vishnupriya being heartlessly forsaken by a husband who took to *sanyas* at a time when she was in the prime of her youth. Incidentally, Vishnupriya Devi was also among those who contributed significantly to perpetuate her husband's memory. According to Murari Gupta, she was the earliest to install an image of Chaitanya, perhaps when he was still alive, and start its worship.

We are reasonably certain that Viswambhar's marriage to Vishnupriya took place sometime in 1507. Jagannath's death required Viswambhar to journey to Gaya to perform his obituary rites; but, for reasons unknown, this visit could occur only in 1508. It was at Gaya that a life-transforming event happened.

As per available evidence, it was at Gaya that Viswambhar met Iswar Puri for a second time, having met him earlier at Nadia. We know very little of Chaitanya's two gurus—the *shikshaguru* and the *dikshaguru*—except for the fact that they both belonged to the Dasnami order of monks instituted by Acharya Sankara and, for that reason, had to be *advaitins* in their philosophical orientation. And yet, they were also given significantly to the tradition of Krishna *bhakti* as was their own guru, Madhavendra Puri. This is an interesting development with regard to what may be loosely called the Hindu ecumene, a syncretic world view whereby competing sectarian loyalties and philosophical disputations between rival schools appear to lose some of their sharpness. One way or another, the critics of Sankara's non-dualist philosophy had all been Vaishnava-Vedantins, which is to say that they somehow grafted dualist *bhakti* theism related to the worship of Vishnu–Krishna upon that which was primarily a monistic view of the world, collapsing the possible distinction between the subject and object. In the post Sankara era, devotional compositions were even attributed to Sankara himself. By the close of the 14th century, thanks to Madhavendra Puri, philosophical perspectives had come to be heavily suffused with emotional *bhakti*; even among people otherwise known to be Vedantins: *bhakti* dualism was clearly gaining over a monistic view of the world. At the time, the Advaita tradition was but weak, seemingly unable to meet the challenges thrown by 14th- to 15th-century dualist philosophers such as Jayatirtha and Vyasatirtha and a new synthesis, under the late 16th-century scholar Madhusudan Saraswati (c.15th–16th century), was not yet in the offing. At Gaya, Iswar Puri is believed to have taught Viswambhar the *dasakshari* Gopal mantra, a ritual formula of 10 syllables, no doubt inherited from his guru, Madhavendra Puri, and which reportedly induced a transformative experience in Viswambhar.

Many of his friends and acquaintances failed to recognize the vastly changed man upon his return to Nabadwip in the early months of 1509. The haughtiness in Viswambhar had given way to uncharacteristic shyness and humility, and an acutely emotional attachment to God and his mysteries had replaced argumentativeness, vanity, and pride of learning. The name of Krishna was now constantly on his lips. Viswambhar suspended teaching immediately upon his return to Nabadwip and resumed it only around March, albeit only temporarily. Sources report that his students found it perplexing that their teacher should unmindfully dwell on the subject of Krishna *bhakti* while ostensibly instructing them in grammar. Eventually, this was to lead to an unpleasant altercation between Viswambhar and his students, in all probability pushing him closer to a life of renunciation. On that occasion, the teacher is reportedly said to have remarked that the potion he had tried to caringly administer to the sick was beginning to produce results quite contrary to that intended!

The most dramatic incidents of Viswambhar's life may be said to have taken place in the period between his return from Gaya (January–February 1509) and his accepting *sanyas* (roughly a year later). One major development that commenced soon after his return from Gaya was the holding of nocturnal kirtan sessions involving Chaitanya and his most intimate followers and companions. These were mostly held at the residence of Sribas, famously known in Gaudiya Vaishnava history as *Sribaser Angina* (Sribas's courtyard). Contrary to what may appear from this description, such sessions were held behind closed doors and certainly hidden from public view and soon became the subject of considerable local gossip. The orthodox society in Nabadwip alleged that Viswambhar and his companions secretly practiced sorcery and black magic in the name of *kirtan* singing. By all appearances, the participants in these *kirtan* sessions were keen to maintain strict privacy and would not allow the presence of people not considered a part of the group. During one of these sessions, Viswambhar sensed the presence of what he called an 'intruder', who happened to be none other than Sribas's mother-in-law who had hidden herself in one corner to watch the proceedings unnoticed. On Viswambhar's orders, however, the old woman was literally dragged out by her hair—a very un-Vaishnava act to say the least. Presumably, there was no dearth of curious onlookers. When a Brahmin keen to gain entry to the *kirtan* party was denied this, he reportedly cursed Viswambhar with separation from friends and family. To those hagiographers who saw destiny intervene at every important stage in Viswambhar's life, this was but the foretelling of his *sanyas*. For the orthodox though, the very act of community singing was fraught with mischief and represented a radical overturning of social norms, disregarding norms of *jati* and gender. The sight of ritually defiled or marginalized castes openly joining a congregation of upper-castes was, no doubt, threatening to established Brahmanical conventions and privileges. Reportedly, what neighbours also found irritating and unbearable was the noise that these night-long kirtan sessions made, presumably keeping many people awake all night. Some wondered why devotional expression and the act of God remembrance required such 'raucous' singing; after all, it was hitherto customary for people to do this privately and in measured silence. However, what made this especially objectionable to most people was the apprehension that this would invoke the wrath of the state which had been already known to come down heavily on public displays of the 'Hindu spirit' (*Hinduani*). Sources allege that the Kazi of Nadia, motivated precisely by such intentions, had ordered the destruction of drums that accompanied Vaishnava devotional singing and threatened local Hindu residents with serious reprisals if they defied his orders. Rumours were afloat that the Sultan had dispatched a boatload of soldiers in response to complaints lodged by some aggrieved residents, the bulk of whom were, ironically, Hindus. It was widely feared that the ways of Viswambhar and his close companions would get the entire community of Hindus into trouble with an already hostile ruling class. Some even attributed recurring illness and droughts that visited their locality to these 'bizarre' practices. It is against the backdrop of such growing tension that we may best understand the incident known to Gaudiya Vaishnavas as 'Kazi *dalan*' or the humbling of the Kazi.

The Kazi *dalan* episode has been quite significant for most hagiographers but more so with later day scholars who read contemporary meanings into it. The literary historian Sukumar Sen and the scholar–critic Girijashankar Raychaudhuri, who delivered a series of lectures on the subject of Chaitanya at the Calcutta University in the 1940s, referred to it as the first successful civil disobedience movement against an oppressive and unjust state. Also interesting is that authors such as Vrindavan Das and Krishnadas Kaviraj—who were among the first to report the incident in some detail—vary significantly in their descriptions, while some others such as Karnapur, Lochandas, and Murari Gupta ignore it altogether. Ipso facto this raises some doubt about the veracity of the incidents reported.

In its barest outline, the incident occurred as follows. Upon learning that Chaitanya and his companions intended to take out a *sankirtan* procession through the town that would involve public devotional singing, the Kazi of Nadia issued an order forbidding it. Reportedly, this order so irked Viswambhar that he defiantly exhorted his men to gather together for a procession, to the accompaniment of musical instruments and flaming torches. By all available accounts, the gathering was massive and proved quite intimidating for state officials who were preparing to take preventive action. The procession could not be stopped and, winding its way through Nadia town, it ultimately reached the residence of the Kazi at the village called Simulia. It is at this point that the accounts begin to differ. In Vrindavan Das's testimony, it was Viswambhar who ordered mob violence that resulted in the destruction of the Kazi's residential property and gardens. State officials, unable to control the crowd, reportedly fled the scene. Jayananda adds that following the incident, Muslim residents in the entire village of Simulia deserted their settlements in panic. The apologetic and visibly frightened Kazi was then accosted by Viswambhar and his party and reprimanded for his 'wrongdoing'. In Krishnadas Kaviraj's version, however, there is no palpable destruction of property and the violence, too, as we have observed earlier, is considerably scaled down. The impression carried by this version of the event is that the Kazi's and Viswambhar's followers came to an understanding before the situation got entirely out of hand. In an endearing gesture, the Kazi was heard reminding Viswambhar that since he and Nilambar Chakravarti had once been residents of the same village, it would be only befitting for him to call the Kazi 'mama'. What followed was a lengthy discourse on the impropriety of slaughtering cattle and the consumption of beef, at the end of which the Kazi was only too happy to admit that being relatively 'modern' in origin, the Koran and other related texts that sanction such practices must be in the wrong. In the course of the conversation, evidently, the Kazi did try to retaliate by bringing up the matter of beef eating by ancient Hindus; but this, in turn, produced the startling theory that at the time this was in vogue, sages and holy men had the power to bring back the slaughtered cattle to life! In his short tract, *Smaranamangal* (The Life and Precepts of Chaitanya), dated 1896, on the life of Chaitanya, Kedarnath Dutta Bhaktivinod, even claimed that at the end of it all the Kazi himself joined the sankirtan procession. This goes beyond the reportage of the *Chaitanya Charitamrita*, which suggests that having realized his folly, the Kazi promptly withdrew his orders and the Vaishnava enthusiasts of Nadia were henceforth left in peace.

Regrettably, there are no other contemporary accounts, and certainly not in Persian or Arabic texts, which might help us to more effectively scrutinize the veracity of the incidents as reported. At first sight, it does seem a little far-fetched to suggest that the state adopted such a soft, submissive, and conciliatory policy, especially given the large-scale destruction of property and the degree of violence reported.

Another incident that presumably occurred around this time was associated with two brothers popularly known as Jagai and Madhai, Brahmins by birth and law enforcement officers of the state. Fearsome and forbidding characters and notorious for drinking and debauchery, they were dreaded by most residents of Nabadwip. What *Chaitanya Bhagavata* found especially objectionable was their Sakta–Tantrik loyalties, even alleging that they had no scruples about consuming un-Hindu food. In hindsight, it would appear as though the brothers took exception to the way the Vaishnavas were trying build a community of devotees whose abiding quality was simply God-remembrance and the lack of ostentation in religious life. Also, their wrath was especially focused on the two chief evangelists appointed by Viswambhar—Nityananda, the Brahmin, and Haridas, the man with strong Vaishnava–Sufi leanings, of whom we shall speak later in more detail. One day, when Nityananda and Haridas were out in the streets trying to spread the message of love and devotion, the brothers, greatly under the influence of liquor, chased them vigorously all over the town. When Nityananda tried to reason with them, the irate Madhai flung a piece of a broken earthen pot on his face, causing him to bleed profusely. Upon hearing of this incident, Viswambhar flew into a rage. In Vrindavan Das's description, he soon assumed the posture of Krishna himself, angrily summoning his favourite weapon, the *sudarshan chakra* (discus), with which to punish the infidels. However, texts report that it was Nityananda and not Viswambhar, who revealed the true qualities of a Vaishnava on this occasion by graciously forgiving his assailant. Following the incident, Jagai and Madhai were greatly transformed men; a repentant Madhai even went on to construct a bathing ghat for local residents as an act of public charity.

What did the new devotional movement initiated by Viswambhar achieve? Kirtan singing was not new to Hindu Bengali culture. One may recall that on the full moon night when Viswambhar was born, there was much rejoicing and singing to mark an auspicious occasion. What Viswambhar added to this may be understood in both its social–psychological and theological aspects. Texts such as *Chaitanya Bhagavata* portray an untypically immodest Vaishnava in Viswambhar, ever keen to assert his divinity and avataric status among his close followers. He was mighty pleased when the veteran Advaita Acharya, the pious Vaishnava and a man reportedly older to Viswambhar by over 40 years, invoked the opening lines of the *Vishnu Purana* in his praise. To Murari Gupta, he revealed himself as the Varaha (boar) avatar of Vishnu, to Sribas as the four-armed Lord Vishnu himself, to Nityananda as the six-armed deity comprising Rama, Krishna, and himself. At Sribas's residence, he seated himself on the throne meant for an icon of Lord Vishnu, further insisting that all members of the family including Sribas's wife and children formally venerate him as the Lord. Vrindavan Das even shows him praising Sribas for taking him for what he actually was (an avatar) and not a pretentious upstart or one suffering from hallucinations. For a man who, in later life, would become visibly irritated at his followers for treating him as some divine being and would consistently shun public attention, such brazen immodesty prima facie belies explanation. It is entirely possible though that such acts were meant to instil a sense of courage and conviction among his followers at a time when they were numerically small and facing persecution from several quarters. For such people, it would have no doubt helped to believe that God had indeed descended on earth on purpose and was leading them on the path of piety and righteousness.

The other important component to Viswambhar's activities from this period was the ushering of a kind of spiritual democracy whereby distinctions of caste or creed were considerably eroded in favour of the devotional collective, internally undifferentiated. In the *Chaitanya Bhagavata*, Advaita is heard explicitly asking Viswambhar to propagate *bhakti* among the most marginalized communities of Shudras and women so that they too might lose themselves in devotional ecstasy and emerge as better men and women. However, even at a time when he remained self-adulatory, arrogant, and aggressive, Viswambhar was, in some respects, not orthodox in his habits. Even as a Brahmin, he was seen mixing freely with the marginalized communities in the neighbourhood such as the *malakars* (garland makers), *sankharis* (conch shell makers), *kansaris* (braziers), and *baniks* (traders and shopkeepers). Sons of *goalas* (milkmen) endearingly called him mama and even invited him home for lunch, an invitation hitherto unheard of, perhaps, in a Brahmin dominated Nadia. Chaitanya would often haggle over vegetable prices with a man named Sridhar and it is on record that immediately after the encounter with the Kazi, he condescended to drink water from an old and perforated iron vessel belonging to Sridhar. Understandably, some hagiographers have tried to distract attention from this instance of ritual violation by stating that Sridhar himself was a Brahmin. A closer examination renders this unlikely since Sridhar lived in one of the poorest parts of the town, inhabited by *tantis* (weavers). Moreover, if Sridhar was himself a Brahmin, as reported in sources, it would have made no sense for hagiographers to highlight this event.

In the movement initiated by Viswambhar, God-remembrance now had a socially levelling quality, at least in theory, and ornate ritual processes were discarded in favour of pure devotion. Undoubtedly, there was a certain magnetic quality to the man and in the movement that he led. This movement did not claim to be a social revolution radically dismantling older structures of power and everyday routines and yet, was able to successfully rework older elements of belief and practice into a new devotional praxis which did not insist on putting one's social status before religious faith. Instead of a mechanical reading of texts—to which only a few could relate to anyway—men and women found a new experience in spontaneously shedding tears of ecstasy. At least within the devotional community of Vaishnavas, the non-Brahmin could now look upon himself as the Brahmin's equal.

Sanyas and After

Viswambhar accepted *sanyas* under Keshav Bharati at Katwa, a few miles north of Burdwan, in January 1510, whereupon he assumed the name Krishna Chaitanya. It is entirely possible, however, that he was never a fully ordained *sanyasi*. As per traditions associated with the Sringeri Math to which the *sanyasis* of the Bharati order are affiliated, 'Chaitanya' was a title given to novices. There are also conflicting views about just why he chose to spend his ascetic life at Puri. While Lochandas claims that he did this on the instructions of his guru, *Chaitanya Charitamrita* comes up with a more cogent explanation. It suggests that he camped at Puri on the advice of his mother, who rightly drew attention to its geographical proximity to Bengal and to its standing as a pilgrim spot of all-India importance. Here, one might justly add that even as an ascetic, Chaitanya remained a dutiful son, always sensitive to the needs of his aging mother. When at Puri, he would depute chosen followers to take good care of Sachi Devi and at least on one occasion he appears to have rued the decision to abandon his mother in favour of *sanyas*.

In hindsight, the decision to embrace a life of renunciation remains puzzling in many ways. As the pioneering scholar of Vaishnava history Sushil Kumar De was to observe many years ago, the motives behind this were 'diverse and complex, best left obscure'. For one, in his everyday habits or behaviour, Viswambhar was far removed from an ideal *sanyasi*. When at Puri, he had to be constantly alerted by his vigilant companion, Swarup Damodar, about straying from duties enjoined upon the *sanyasi*. The *Chaitanya Charitamrita* frequently refers to his huge appetite, a quality unbecoming of an ascetic, and to the fact that even when hosted by his close companions, such as Advaita Acharya, he would be treated to the choicest dishes and condiments, expressly forbidden to a *sanyasi*. Upon meeting the Nyaya scholar Vasudev Sarvabhaum at Puri, Chaitanya reportedly asked him not to treat him as a 'true' *sanyasi*, arguing that it was only his love and devotion to Krishna which had pushed him to adopt this path. This is an unconvincing explanation given the fact that none of the six Vrindavan Goswamis, who were deeply devoted to Krishna *bhakti*, formally adopted *sanyas* even though they lived a life of extreme self-denial, asceticism, and frugality. At least three hagiographers—Vrindavan Das, Jayananda, and Lochandas—look upon his *sanyas* as faked (*kapat sanyas*). It might appear as though his decision to accept *sanyas* under Keshav Bharati appears to be a plan drawn up in haste and perhaps for lack of an immediate alternative. Both Sarvabhaum at Puri and Prakashananada, whom he subsequently met at Kashi, were to rule that the Bharati order to which Keshav belonged was not a particularly distinguished order and ideally not one that Chaitanya should have sought. Also quite extraordinary is the way Chaitanya was initiated. Reportedly, Chaitanya himself whispered into the ears of his guru the mantra that was meant to initiate him into *sanyas*, a seemingly bizarre case of a pupil initiating his own guru! However, the most radical breach of rules occurred at a time when Chaitanya was touring Bengal, immediately following *sanyas*. A careful scrutiny of sources reveals that during this time, Chaitanya met his mother at Santipur, not once (as is allowed to a *sanyasi*) but twice, and if Murari Gupta is to be believed, even his wife, Vishnupriya.

Since the manner in which Viswambhar accepted *sanyas* implies a degree of desperation, it might be worth speculating just what might have brought this on. A clue to the possible cause may be gleaned from what Viswambhar told his friends about accepting *sanyas* being the most practical method of overcoming the mounting opposition at Nabadwip. Reference has already been made to his altercation with students, sometime in the summer of 1509. The incident so stirred the Smarta-Brahmin community of Nabadwip that it rallied behind the students and threatened to socially boycott a seemingly unkind and intimidating teacher.

All the same, it seems a trifle unconvincing to attribute Viswambhar's *sanyas* solely to his desire to escape his critics, even if this seems to be his own explanation of the matter. Here one must also allow for the fact that the decision to accept *sanyas* was taken in the face of opposition from his close friends and family. The widowed Sachi was devastated and some of his close companions pleaded with him to reconsider his decision, justly citing the fact that the Vaishnavas in Nabadwip were not yet an organized community and that Viswambhar's desertion might seriously jeopardize what was already a precariously weak movement. If, therefore, Viswambhar still stuck to his decision, one would have to imagine that there was perhaps a greater consideration at work. Unlikely as it might appear, the decision to accept *sanyas* was, in all probability, a well thought out plan and not purely spontaneous or taken in undue haste. Arguably, accepting *sanyas* had the dual advantage of conforming to a conventionally respectable path (it was commonly held that a man accepting *sanyas* bestowed redemption upon his ancestors and successive generations) and to disarm opponents who were now hard pressed to speak ill of a man who had renounced the world. Some critics, however, have interpreted Viswambhar's *sanyas* in a very different light. This has been variously been put down to the trauma that he suffered on account of Laxmi's death or to an unhappy conjugal life with Vishnupriya. Neither of these explanations are convincing, for *sanyas* appears to be too radical a step to adopt under either of these circumstances.

Immediately upon his accepting *sanyas* at Katwa, Chaitanya made a short tour of Bengal where he was temporarily reunited with followers

such as Nityananda, Haridas, Murari, and Advaita Acharya, the last
hosting him at Santipur for a few days. The details of this journey are far
from precise as are those of his subsequent journey to Puri. Jayananda,
Karnapur, Vrindavan Das, and Krishnadas Kaviraj suggest routes that
Chaitanya might have taken on this occasion but these differ from
one another in vital details. This imprecision with details was to later
produce an exasperating remark from Bimanbihari Majumdar. He wondered how, with such lack of precision or faithful reporting, biographers
could ever be sure of Chaitanya's itinerary or movements, especially with
regard to his long tour of the south, which lasted nearly two years and
remains a contentious subject in Vaishnava literature.

Chaitanya reached Puri in the spring of 1510 and after spending about 18 days in the city, left for his tour of the south. The most
important part of this brief stay at Puri was his visit to the Jagannath
temple. Legend has it that he was ecstatic upon catching sight of the
insignia flying atop the temple even from a great distance. Entering the
temple in an emotionally charged state, Chaitanya's movements initially
raised the suspicions of the *pandas* present and, quite possibly, he would
have been turned out of the temple but for the timely intervention of
Vasudeva Sarvabhaum. Sarvabhaum, as we know, was a scholar of
both Nyaya and Vedanta, and his first response to Chaitanya's ways
was a mixture of awe and uncertainty. For one, he wondered why a
man as young and handsome as Chaitanya had taken to *sanyas*. He was
also intrigued, as we have earlier observed, by the fact that the young
Chaitanya had accepted a guru from a relatively inferior order. As
reported, the two were subsequently drawn into an extended theological dialogue, which, predictably enough, only highlights the erudition of
the young *sanyasi* interpreting chosen verses from the *Bhagavat Purana*
in multiple ways. Sources differ on just how long this exchange of views
lasted. Whereas *Chaitanya Bhagavata* reports that the dialogue lasted
a day, the *Charitamrita* stretches this to as many as 12. In the latter,
furthermore, Vasudeva's conversion from a Vedantist to a Vaishnava
is highlighted even at the cost of some anachronism. In persuading
Vasudeva Sarvabhaum to accept the superiority of the Vaishnava
view over the monistic, Chaitanya is seen using Rupa Goswami's
Bhaktirasamritasindhu (An Ocean-like Compendium of *Bhakti-rasa*,
c. 16th century), a classic text on Vaishnava aesthetics but which had

not come to be written just yet! In truth, Vasudeva, who authored the non-dualist text *Advaita Makaranda* (A Text on Advaita Philosophy, c.17th century), never came to accept Chaitanya as an avatar, nor did he think that avatars could at all manifest themselves in the degenerative *Kali yuga*. On the contrary, he may have taught Chaitanya a lesson or two in humility, which was to have important social and theological implications. His advice to the young *sanyasi*, for instance, was never to claim any special status, especially in a town in which Jagannath was the unrivalled deity.

Vasudev Sarvbhaum's intervention was important in the religious life of Chaitanya in two related ways. First, backing from an individual who had won the favours of the local state helped Chaitanya to gain greater public acceptance. Though sceptical of Chaitanya's *sanyas* or, for that matter, his particular interpretation of scripture, Vasudev nevertheless had ample respect for the renunciation and selflessness of the young *sanyasi*. Legend has it that he even composed a series of eight verses in praise of Chaitanya (*Chaitanyashtakam*) in Sanskrit, a Bengali translation of which appeared in the Vaishnava journal *Gauranga Madhuri* in 1928–9. In Puri, Chaitanya soon came to be accepted as 'Sachala Jagannath' (the living Jagannath) but this was also made possible by the reverence that he and his companions showed to the Jagannath cult itself. For several years in succession, it was common for Bengali followers and devotees of Chaitanya to undertake an annual pilgrimage to Puri on the occasion of the Rath Yatra. There was ecstatic dancing and singing by these men at the head of the Rath procession, which Chaitanya himself joined on occasions. That apart, he is also known to have personally performed the ritual cleaning of the Gundicha Mandira, an act that was said to carry great religious merit. The other reason why Vasudev's company proved important was because it was at his behest that Chaitanya met Ramananda Ray, governor of the Godavari districts, on his way to south India. The theological dialogue that he reportedly had with Ramananda, commonly known as 'Ramananda Samvad', comprises a key theological element within the Bengal school of Vaishnavism. Though earlier hinted by the *padabali* poets, the conversation between Ramananda and Chaitanya—more in the manner of a catechism—represents the first discursive treatment of Chaitanya's 'Radhabhava', an esoteric state in which he is said to represent the pious love and devotion of Radha towards her beloved Krishna.

Sometime in April–May, 1510, Chaitanya left on a tour of south India, returning to Puri only about two years later. The tour could be ascribed to several reasons. Some scholars have advanced the theory, based on the Madala Panji documents belonging to the temple at Puri, that fearing an imminent Muslim invasion from neighbouring Bengal, the Jagannath icon had already been moved from Puri to Chilika lakes; and with the presiding deity absent, religious life at Puri could not have been quite the same. On the face of it, this seems like a plausible theory, except for the fact that the Jagannath icon was very much stationed in Puri, even during the spring of 1510 when Chaitanya first visited it. It, therefore, needs to be determined if some significant developments occurred between the spring and summer of 1510 which encouraged Chaitanya to move out of Puri. As noted earlier, perhaps Chaitanya hoped that he might still meet his brother, Viswarup, who had become and ascetic and left home. It is not until the last leg of his journey, with his visit to Pandharpur, that he received the tragic news of his brother's premature death. Quite possibly, Chaitanya was also keen to familiarize himself with the older and vibrant Vaishnava traditions in the south, albeit sharply divided along sectarian lines. It is here that he eventually found two quasi-Vaishnava texts no longer available in northern India, the anonymous *Brahma Samhita* (a text glorifying the life of Govinda or Krishna, c. pre-15th century) and *Krishna Karnamrita* (devotional text in praise of Krishna, c. pre-15th century) by Lilasuka. Historian and a biographer of Chaitanya Amulya Charan Sen tells us that the first of these works was in the Marathi script and the second in Malayalam. If this be so, there had to be the practical problem of transliteration into Devnagari /Bangla scripts about which, however, sources are silent. Apart from camping at the important Sri Vaishnava site of Srirangam during the rainy season that year, he also subsequently visited the Sringeri Matha in Chikamagalur and the Madhva Matha in Udupi. Especially at the last two places named, he is reported to have been drawn into doctrinal disputations with fellow monks.

Chaitanya's tour of the south has remained contentious on broadly two counts. First, but for *Govindadaser Kadcha*, whose authenticity continues to be doubted to this day, there is really no full or first-hand account of the southern tour. Murari Gupta spent only two imperfect cantos on this event; Karnapur's account is sketchy at best; Vrindavan

Das overlooks this episode almost entirely; Jayananda and Lochandas have really nothing new to add; and Krishnadas Kaviraj is apologetic about not being able to narrate the episode in sufficient detail. Existing narratives of Chaitanya's tour of south India disagree on both the companion who reportedly accompanied Chaitanya on the tour and on the itinerary itself. Krishnadas Kaviraj states that the companion was one Kala Krishnadas (in the *Bhaktiratnakara*, this is Krishnadas Hod) who, however, has not left behind any account. This, as we have noted before, raises the important question of just what the sources of information might have been for accounts provided by the *Charitamrita* and those by Jayananda and Lochandas. After all, no well-known companion of Chaitanya or a chronicler accompanied him on this tour, thus making even hearsay evidence inadmissible. Also, there seems to be no concrete evidence to suggest that Krishnadas was by birth a Brahmin. This was to be an important issue subsequently since the credibility of *Govindadaser Kadcha* was doubted on the ground that the Brahmin Chaitanya would not have agreed to have a non-Brahmin as his companion. In the absence of reliable information, we remain uncertain about Chaitanya's itinerary.

What seems indisputable though is that Chaitanya's initial movement was along the east coast which ended in Rameswaram. Thereafter, he moved towards the north and north-west, travelling along the west coast until he reached Maharashtra. The *Charitamrita* endorses his tour of Maharashtra and Jayananda of neighbouring Broach and Saurashtra. It is not improbable that, as reported in the *Charitamrita*, Chaitanya met Ramananda Ray a second time on his way back to Puri.

The tour of south India proved to be valuable for Chaitanya and his movement in several respects. First, it is here that he met people who were to later become his intimate followers. Of these, we may readily mention Gopal Bhatta, who subsequently settled in Vrindavan and Paramananda Puri, again interestingly, a Vedantin *sanyasi* with strong leanings towards Krishna *bhakti*. Presumably, the tour also helped Chaitanya to more clearly define or delineate the broad contours of his theology. This, he would have done at Srirangam, Sringeri, and at Udupi, though the last of these is by far the more interesting given the fact that by the 18th century, Vaishnavas of the Chaitanya cult chose to affiliate themselves with the Madhva *sampradaya*, notwithstanding acute doctrinal differences.

Pining for a vision of Krishna and of his pastoral playground in Vraja had been a recurring feature in Viswambhar since his return from Gaya. This sense of separation from Krishna (*viraha*) is said to have increased manifold once he took *sanyas*. Immediately after his initiation at Katwa, Chaitanya is believed to have expressed a desire to visit Mathura and Vrindavan but was tricked into touring the area adjacent to the river Ganges by Nityananda, who gave him to believe that the Ganges was none other than the river Jamuna. On Vijaya Dashami day (September–October) of 1514, he set out a second time for a journey to the Vraja country but had to abort his plans upon reaching Bengal. Moving along the Ganges to Panihati, Kumarhati, Phulia, and Santipur, he finally rested at Ramkeli in north Bengal where, incidentally, he also happened to meet Rup and Sanatan—carrying the designations *Dabir Khas* (personal secretary) and *Sakar Malik* (chief minister) respectively—high ranking officers under Hussain Shah's regime who were later to settle in Vrindavan as the most venerated among Goswamis. The *Charitamrita* reveals that the two officers had secretly been corresponding with Chaitanya expressing their wish to join the devotional movement and it is not unlikely that it is from them that Chaitanya also learnt of Hussain Shah's intentions of launching a second attack on Odisha. What compounded matters is that anticipating an invasion by Hussain Shah, the Odiya king, Prataprudra, had already set in motion plans for a pre-emptive attack on Bengal. This created considerable political instability and turmoil in the region and put travel across borders at some risk. Reportedly, it was on Sanatan's advice that Chaitanya was forced to change his plans. He was advised to isolate himself from his numerous followers and to never be seen at the head of a gathering of people for fear that this might arouse the suspicions of the state. It is also quite possible that visiting Vrindavan was never Chaitanya's true intention on this visit. Rather, his plans all along had been to meet Rup and Sanatan and to suitably prepare them for taking the movement forward. This theory appears to be strengthened by the fact that immediately upon meeting Chaitanya (which they were forced to do at a very late hour one night), Rup and Sanatan decided to quit the service of the state. With this, Rup was considerably luckier than Sanatan. While the former went back to his ancestral home to make a settlement on his properties and, thereafter, prepare for a new life at Vrindavan, Sanatan was put under house arrest on the orders of the Sultan and had to eventually bribe his way out. Chaitanya returned to Puri before the onset of monsoon in 1515.

In October that year, Chaitanya finally set out on his pilgrimage to Vrindavan, in all probability arriving there in early 1516. Vrindavan takes its name after Vrinda, who, at some point in time, assumed the status of the local deity. Legend has it that the earliest religious shrine in the region was built in her honour, but is now untraceable. Vrinda is also taken to be synonymous with *tulsi*, a plant particularly sacred to Vaishnavas and, hence, Vrindavan may have also indicated a site for *tulsi* groves. Perhaps in later tradition, this feminine character came to be variously identified as a female companion of Radha and even as Radha herself. The *Gautamiya Tantra* identifies Vridnavan as the site of Radha's *sadhana* or spiritual praxis.

In early India, Vrindavan was not known to be particularly holy to the Hindus; very little is known about it between the 7th and 11th centuries. Vrajabhumi as a site sacred to the Vaishnavas is mentioned in at least five puranas—*Varaha, Skanda, Narada, Adi,* and *Padma*—but these are relatively late works and underwent several recensions. It is a reasonable guess, therefore, that the ascendancy and importance of Vrindavan rose at least two centuries after the compilation of the *Bhagavat Purana,* by when the Krishna cult had acquired a pan-Indian importance. Also interesting is the fact that Vrindavan was originally a site sacred to the Saivas and even modern anthropologists and researchers have noted the existence of at least four major Siva temples in the area. Vraj Parikrama or the pilgrim tour of the various holy sites of Vrindavan, a practice going back to the mid-16th century, starts by paying reverence to Gopeswar Siva, the Siva revered by the *gopas* or cowherds.

We have some evidence of a pilgrim trail between Bengal and Vrindavan even before the advent of Chaitanya. At the time Madhavendra Puri visited it, presumably sometime in the early 15th century, he met visitors from Bengal. As with the revival of Krishna *bhakti* in Bengal, Madhavendra Puri was a key figure in the recovery of Vrindavan as a sacred habitat. Legend has it that this dedicated Krishna devotee who had resolved to live by whatever unsolicited food he was able to obtain, was once visited by the Lord Himself dressed up as a young cowherd.

The cowherd offered the starving Madhavendra a bowl of fresh sweetened milk and, thereafter, reappeared in his dreams that night with the plea that he be rescued from the mound of earth under which he had been buried for long for fear of the *yavanas*. The following day, upon excavating the mound, Madhavendra and his companions found the image of Gopala (infant Krishna), which was then duly consecrated and set up atop Gokula hill. It is also known that with the tacit consent of rival Vaishnava communities in the region, the worship of this image was entrusted to Bengali immigrants until about the close of the sixteenth or the early 17th century when violent feuds broke out between the followers of Vallabha and Gaudiya Vaishnavas.

Chaitanya is credited with the discovery and rehabilitation of important Vaishnava sites associated with the cult of Radha and Krishna, but this needs to be qualified in at least two respects. First, the Vaishnava community which arrived the earliest in Vrindavan were followers of the Nimbarka sect and not the Gaudiyas. In later history, the Gaudiya numerical presence was visibly rivalled by the Vallabha order and the Radhavallabhis. Second, Chaitanya's intention with regard to Vrindavan was not so much to revive the pilgrim trail as to transform it into a major Vaishnava theological centre. It is for this purpose that he had sent his companion Lokenath Goswami to Vrindavan as early as 1510 and subsequently instructed Sanatan to revive and replenish local sites and artefacts. It was Sanatan Goswami (in some traditions, Rup Goswami) who recovered several holy sites through the diligent study of a particular section of the *Varaha Purana* known as the *Mathura Mahatmya*. Similarly, while Chaitanya is said to have rediscovered the Radha Kunda, also mentioned in the *Varaha Purana*, its rehabilitation and replenishment was possible only after Raghunath Das Goswami, the only non-Brahmin among Goswamis and a man who inherited a fabulous family fortune, personally took up this task.

On the journey to Vrindavan, Chaitanya was accompanied by one Balabhadra Bhattacharya and his domestic help. Perhaps to avoid any mishaps resulting from the political turmoil in the region, they preferred to travel through the longer and less frequented route passing though present day Jharkhand. Eventually, they halted at Varanasi and, on the request of one Tapan Misra whom Chaitanya had earlier met on his tour of east Bengal, camped there for about 10 days. Chaitanya's experiences at Varanasi were far from pleasant. He was virtually ignored by the Advaita scholars and sadhus who dominated religious life in that city. In Krishnadas Kaviraj's account, Chaitanya is seen regretfully confessing how he had utterly failed to sell his merchandize (*bhakti*) in Kashi. Except an anonymous Maratha Brahmin and two of his followers, Tapan Misra and Chandrasekhar Baidya, no one agreed to hear his discourse on Krishna *bhakti*. The time spent at Vrindavan itself also proved to be somewhat unproductive. For much of his stay, Chaitanya is known to have been in a God-intoxicated state; a first-hand acquaintance with the mythology surrounding Vrindavan and its sacred geography only intensified his sense of separation from Krishna, driving him into recurring fits of ecstasy. It was under one such spell that he jumped into the Jamuna and would have drowned but for the timely rescue by his companions. He was thronged by crowds wherever he went and this too proved an unwelcome distraction. Apprehensive of his health and personal safety, Balabhadra led him out of Vrindavan by a river route to Prayag, just in time for the auspicious bathing in the Ganges on the occasion of the winter solstice. It was at Prayag that Chaitanya was reunited with Rupa and his younger brother, Ballabha (also known as Anupama). It was also here that he reportedly met one Vallabha Bhatt at village Adail, who could well be the Telugu saint and scholar Vallabhacharya (1479–1521), the founder of the Vaishnava sampradaya named after him.

Travelling beyond Prayag, Chaitanya halted at Varanasi a second time and, according to the *Charitamrita*, used this occasion to instruct Sanatan in Vaishnava theology over a period of two months. Krishnadas Kaviraj attached great importance to this event, for in his narrative the discourse is spread over as many as six chapters. It would only be pertinent to add that as on other occasions, the author of the *Charitamrita* remains completely oblivious to the fact that Chaitanya is shown speaking on matters from Sanatan's own *Laghubhagavatamrita* (*Bhagavat Purana* in abridged form, c.16th century) and two out of Jiva Goswami's numerous works—*Sarvasamvadini* (a commentary, c.17th century) and *Tattwasandarbha* (Discourses on the Essence of Vaishnava Theology, c.16th century)—neither of which could have been known to Chaitanya. Compared to his previous experiences at Varanasi, the second visit proved to be relatively less disappointing. The *Charitamrita* is about the only text to refer to Chaitanya's winning over the *advaitin sanyasi*

Prakashananda, believed to be the author of the *Vedanta Siddhanta Muktavali* (Discourses on Vedanta and the Path to Liberation, c. 16th century). Unsupported by other contemporary texts, the veracity of this incident does remain open to some doubt. What compounds matters is Krishnadas mimicking Prakashananda and virtually poking fun at the theory of *vivartavada*, by virtue of which the world was only an apparent transformation of Brahman as different from its being actually *parinamavada*. Again, untypically for a non-dualist, Prakashananda reportedly perceives Shakti (Brahman's energy) as the *upadan*, the material cause of the world. Implicitly, this comes around to admit the theory of *bhedabheda*, which forms the backbone of Gaudiya philosophical discourse. The Prakashananda episode, whether real or imagined, leaves us with no doubt about the fact that by the time the *Charitamrita* came to be composed, doctrinal contestation between non-dualists and dualists had palpably sharpened.

By May 1516, Chaitanya was back in Puri and, going by all established evidence, did not venture out again until his death in 1533.

Sometime after the annual Rath ceremony (June–July) of 1516, the brothers Rup and Sanatan called on Chaitanya at Puri as per his instructions. For the next 10 months Rup received detailed instructions from Chaitanya on Vaishnava aesthetic theory before he went back to Vrindavan around the spring of 1517; these were later to be the foundation of his prolific literary production. A few days after Rup had left Puri, Sanatan appeared before Chaitanya, having contracted a malignant skin disease. Giving up all hopes of recovery, Sanatan was preparing to give up his life when he caught the attention of Chaitanya who dissuaded him from committing the act. Sanatan was then hosted by Chaitanya and his local devotees for about a year, during which time he was suitably instructed on his future tasks. He returned to Vrindavan by the time of the Holi festival of the year 1518, fully recovered from his illness.

Some claims regarding Chaitanya's travels are bound to remain contested. Bengali scholar Nirmal Narayan Gupta, for instance, lays claim to a second visit to Vrindavan in 1526–7, a tour of Kamrupa in 1528, and a meeting with the Assamese Vaishnava saint–scholar Sankardev (1449–1568). Bimanbihari Majumdar believed that Chaitanya had occasion to meet both Kabir and Nanak, a claim also reiterated by the recent work, *Gora*, which quite extraordinarily adds Portuguese naval commander Alfonso de Albuquerque (1453–1515) to the list. Prima facie this is not improbable, but it is unsupported by any trustworthy evidence. Even assuming that such meetings indeed took place, they seem to have escaped the attention of contemporary hagiographers belonging to the relevant traditions.

The Last Years

As can be imagined, few works on Chaitanya deal with his last years in sufficient detail. For one, it must have been painful and unsavoury for hagiographers to report on the self-inflicted suffering that Chaitanya underwent during these years, increasingly withdrawing himself from the public gaze and appearing visibly irritated when devotees took to his worship and adulation. It was at this time that he also began to deny himself even the barest of comforts, refusing a mattress and pillow to sleep on until some of his followers devised a makeshift mattress made from plantain leaves sewn together. At most times, he would keep crying out in ecstasy, expressing deep anguish at his continued separation from Krishna. Chaitanya himself and his intimate followers took this as the expression of *mahabhava* or the supreme state of pining and devotion that Radha revealed for her lover, Krishna. Indeed, Radhabhava, or the moods of the disconsolate Radha, came to dominate his life at Puri, just as those of Krishna had once done during his sojourn in Nabadwip. He would wander off in the dead of the night and be subsequently be found at odd places, completely oblivious of his movements. On occasion, his intense agony would lead him to violently rub his face on the jagged flooring of the pitifully cramped room (called the '*gambhira*'), resulting in profuse bleeding and sores. Such occurrences became so frequent that his devotees were constrained to engage a night watch who would keep a close check on his movements. What did give him some joy though was recurring devotional singing and theological discussions with Swarup Damodar, his constant companion during these years. Damodar, in fact, fulfilled three vital and interrelated functions. First, he kept constant vigil over Chaitanya's movements, alerting him of any possible departures from the norms of a *sanyasi* that might catch the public eye. Second, it was he who personally vetted any matter that was to be put before Chaitanya. In this, it would appear, he was gifted with a sense of foresight and astute judgement. Once, when a Brahmin from Bengal appeared at Puri and desired to present before Chaitanya a biography in verse that he had put together, this was promptly turned down on the grounds that, if made public, such a work might actually jeopardize Chaitanya's residence in Puri. Reportedly, what made Damodar wary was the author's elevating of Chaitanya above Jagannath. The astute Damodar obviously did not think that this would go down well with the local people, for whom Jagannath was the sole and incontestable deity. In hindsight, such decisions proved to be fortuitous; some sources clearly suggest that, envious of the influence that Chaitanya was wielding on the king and the people, a conspiracy by some priests of the Jagannath temple and some ministers was already afoot to cause him bodily harm. Third, as per available evidence, Swarup Damodar was also a gifted musician and percussionist and kept Chaitanya entertained with devotional songs suitable to his moods. He was certainly the chief proponent of Chaitanya's Radhabhava theory which found its best poetic expression in Krishnadas Kaviraj's *Chaitanya Charitamrita*. As we have noted elsewhere, it is indeed a pity that his *Kadcha* (notes) cannot be traced any longer.

Two other noteworthy events of these years were the death of Haridas and the *tarja* believed to have been sent by Advaita from Santipur in Bengal. Haridas, along with Nityananda, had been one of the two major evangelists of the Chaitanya movement in Bengal and further down this work, we shall have occasion to discuss further details of his life and work. For now, it is only appropriate to narrate the personal interest that Chaitanya took in arranging for his last rites on the beaches of Puri. The *Charitamrita* describes how he dug through the sand and gently laid to rest the body of a man who had endured much pain and humiliation for having taken to the life of Vaishnava. A *mahotsava* was then organized by inviting public charity. Going by the account given in the *Charitamrita*, one would have to say that even people who might have known of his Muslim birth did not let that come in the way of honouring a venerable saint.

Reportedly, no one but Chaitanya could make any sense of Advaita's *tarja*; even Swarup Damodar had failed to decode it. Its esoteric meaning is still a matter of dispute and a literal translation is not of much help either. Prima facie, it did carry a negative message, warning Chaitanya to desist from whatever he was doing and to rethink his future plans. Krishnadas Kaviraj reports that upon hearing the *tarja* read out to him, Chaitanya gave out a deep sigh and thereafter, his pining for Krishna became even more intense. Here, the cause and effect are difficult to correlate since the *tarja* made no reference to Krishna or to an issue that was theological in nature, at least not ostensibly. Most modern scholars are of the view that it was a guarded message to Chaitanya, possibly suggesting that the movement he had launched had come to naught and that there was really no justification for him to continue living any more. Coming from Advaita, this seems a rather morbid message, especially going by the widely held view that it was in response to Advaita's fervent prayer and pleading that Vishnu/Krishna had agreed to descend as an avatar in Nabadwip. But such advice makes sense otherwise. Within a few years of Chaitanya's final return to Puri, the community of Vaishnavas in Bengal had begun to be deeply divided along lines of sectarian loyalty. There now emerged what is popularly called *shakhas* or branches, each led by an important leader, some of whom even established independent theological centres (called *Sripat*) at several places, chiefly in the districts of Burdwan, Bankura, Hoogly, and Nadia. Differences over social ideology and methods of worship further accentuated sectarian loyalties. Thus, the ways of the bohemian Nityananda who had been a Saivite *avadhuta* in early life looked suspicious and objectionable to many. Nityananda was known for his habitual drinking as befitting only tantric *sanyasis* and for putting on ornate and expensive dresses with jewellery—a practice that Vaishnavas strictly shunned. Also, from being an ascetic, he turned to a life of domesticity with two wives, Vasudha and Jahnava, who happened to be sisters. This earned him the title of 'Bantasi' (meaning a ritually defiled man), a highly pejorative term. In Chaitanya's own lifetime, the Advaita branch too had split open, with some sons of Advaita refusing to venerate Chaitanya; apparently, Advaita himself was powerless to prevent this. It is quite possible, therefore, that a sense of gloom and failure came to affect Chaitanya in his last days, adding to his agony. Especially after the 1520s, his recurring bouts of dementia, self-inflicted injury, and agonized existence increasingly sapped his bodily energies and left a once healthy man of a large bodily frame, frail and extraordinarily weak from the inside.

There is indeed a mystical quality about death itself but the death of Chaitanya is shrouded in considerable mystery. Until recently, scholars and scribes could not quite settle on the date of his death. For Ramgati Nyayaratna, the early historian of Bengali literature, it is 1548; for scholar–saint Ambikacharan Brahmachari, it is 1557; and as per anthologist of Vaishnava verse Jagatbandhu Bhadra, Chaitanya died in 1535. That apart, four major hagiographers—Murari Gupta, Kavi Karnapur, Vrindban Das, and Krishnadas Kaviraj—did not describe his death in any detail, presumably under the belief that Chaitanya being *Swayam Bhagavan* (the Lord Himself) could not have died the death of an ordinary mortal. Significantly enough, whereas it was common practice to organize a *mahotsava* and a *malsa bhoga* on the death of a Vaishnava saint or a high-ranking *mahant*, an exception is made in the case of Chaitanya whose death is never commemorated and does not enter the Vaishnava ritual calendar. There is considerable difference of opinion, too, on the exact timing of the event. In the opinion of Lochandas and Jayananda, this occurred on 29 June 1533; in the *Vaishnava Lilamrita* (The Nectar-like Divine Play of Vaishnavas, c. 16th century) by Madhava Patnaik, who claims to have been an eye-witness, the date is pushed back to the new moon night of Baisakh (April–May) that year.

The manner in which he might have met his death is not undisputed either. Krishnadas Kaviraj and a work attributed to Narottam Das, *Sadhanabhaktichandrika* (Discourses on the Bhakti Praxis, c.16th century), hint at Chaitanya getting drowned at sea; at least three well-known contemporary poets and writers from Odisha—Achyutananda, Divakar Das, and Iswar Das—claim that he passed away at the Jagannath temple, with his body promptly merging with that of Lord Jagannath. Another Odiya work, *Chaitanya Chakda* (Biographical Notes on Chaitanya, c.16th century) by Vaishnava Das, claims that he fell unconscious at the Garuda pillar inside the temple premises, never to recover; and Jayananda reports that his death occurred on account of a wound he suffered on his left foot. Jayananda's claim, incidentally, is endorsed by *Vaishnava Lilamrita*, which adds that the wound turned septic, producing acute pain and high fever. Finally, there is also the theory, though yet unproven, that Chaitanya fell victim to a conspiracy hatched by one Govinda Vidyadhar, an influential minister who planned to usurp power in collusion with the temple pandas. In the 1920s, the best known spokesperson of this theory was Dineshchandra Sen. Modern scholars have taken Jayananda's account to be the most realistic one, which also explains why the Vaishnavas themselves disowned it entirely. One of Chaitanya's biographers and well-known devotees O.B.L. Kapoor, for instance, dismissed the work as inauthentic and unacceptable. What appears to have been overlooked here is the way Jayananda combines mythology with realism. For Jayananda, keen to establish the identity of Chaitanya with Krishna, the foot injury to Chaitanya simply invoked memories of Krishna himself dying from a similar injury inflicted by a poacher. Thereafter, Chaitanya is seen ascending to *vaikuntha* . In hindsight, the possibility of Chaitanya getting drowned at sea looks unlikely, given the fact that he was a powerful swimmer and would often swim (in the company of Nityananda) from Nabadwip to Santipur.

Jayananda and Ishan Nagar, reputedly the author of *Advaita Prakash*, were tabooed by the Vaishnava community for suggesting that Chaitanya died of an injury which could prove fatal to only ordinary mortals. However, it would also appear as though Bengali Vaishnavas equally disliked the idea of Chaitanya merging with Jagannath. This led them to suggest the site of death as a place outside the temple premises. Jayananda himself suggests that he died at the residence of Kashi Misra, his host at Puri; the poet Narahari Chakravarti indicated the temple of Gopinath as the possible site, a thesis also supported in recent times by Amulyacharan Sen. Apart from Odiya poet Iswar Das, all others agree on the fact that this was a death which did not leave behind a physical body. In his work, the *Chaitanya Bhagavata*, Iswar Das—who otherwise subscribed to the theory of Chaitanya's body merging with that of Jagannath—quite puzzlingly states that on the orders of Lord Jagannath himself, the *khetrapal* of the temple carried the body to be thrown into the river Praci, a few miles from the temple.

4 Chaitanya's Companions, Associates, Devotees, and Followers

While the revival of Vaishnavism in late medieval Bengal centred on the attractive religious personality of Chaitanya and was inspired by it in many ways, it might not have grown into a movement but for the enthusiasm and support of people who served him and his cause in various ways. Some late and apocryphal works such as *Bhaktichandrikapatala* (Discourses on Bhakti, c.17th century), *Vrihatbhakti Tattwasara* (The Essence of Higher Bhakti, c.17th century), *Bhaktiratnakara*, and *Vaishnavachara Darpana* (A Compendium on Vaishnava Rituals and Rites, 1897) project Chaitanya as the main organizer of the Gaudiya movement. Although there is good reason to doubt this, it could be reasonably argued that in some ways it was indeed he who paved the way for an enduring religious organization on a trans-regional scale. For one, he appears to have envisioned a plan of action whereby Krishna *bhakti* could be turned into a vibrant living faith. In hindsight, this may be said to have adopted perceptibly two different agendas. One of these was the creation of a discourse that followed traditional styles of literary production, philosophical specula-tion, and scriptural exegesis anchored in older forms of Hindu cultural consciousness and practices. It was with the recovery and rehabilitation of Vrindavan as a religious and cultural centre of pan-Indian importance that this particular purpose found its fruition. The other direction that this plan took was simple evangelism that produced a free flow of fervent devotional sentiment. The area where this proved to be most successful was rural Bengal, marked by swelling rivers, forests, swamps, and marshy lands, all of which were an integral part of a self-sufficient rural economy. Even though Bengal Vaishnavism of the 16th century begun in the quasi-urban environment of Nabadwip, its greater following eventually came from peasant and artisanal communities in south and south-west Bengal, comprising the districts Bankura, Birbhum, Burdwan, Hoogly, and Midnapore.

Chaitanya also had the discerning qualities of a gifted leader who chose his workers well or rather picked on men of different talents and temperaments who could be entrusted to perform a wide range of tasks. It is not fortuitous that for propagating Vaishnavism in rural Bengal, he settled on Nityananda and Haridas—the first, a widely travelled Brahmin ascetic with an utter disregard for social and ritual conventions, and the second, a devotee who stood at the cusp of Vaishnava *bhakti* and Sufi Islamic *dhikr* and presumably reinforced both. They were men of courage and conviction which enabled them to withstand hostility or oppression from various quarters. Haridas was flogged in public on the orders of an irate Kazi when he refused to give up his faith in Krishna *bhakti*. The choice of Nityananda, too, was significant. Notwithstanding his non-conformism, Nityananda was still a Brahmin and, historically speaking, dissent or departures from established conventions are known to find greater social acceptance when originating from a Brahmin. Sometime in 1516, Chaitanya instructed Nityananda never to return to Puri as part of the Bengali contingent that undertook a pilgrimage at the time of the annual Rath festival, but to exclusively focus on Bengal itself as the sphere of religious activity. Incidentally, both these figures also preferred a mode of *bhakti* which differed from the eroticized *shringara* or *madhura* moods that Chaitanya himself is consistently identified with. From this it is tempting to conclude that Chaitanya's decision was based

on the realistic strategy of avoiding the moral pitfalls of freely propagating a highly eroticized *bhakti* symbolism among ordinary people,
however innocuous such symbolism may have looked at first sight.

Arguably, Chaitanya's choice of scholiasts such as Rup and Sanatan
for both salvaging Vrindavan as a pilgrim centre and producing a textual
corpus for a newly emerging *bhakti* discourse was also born of tactical
considerations. Of the six Vrindavan Goswamis, as many as four had
ethnic and cultural roots in south India, which seems both a tacit
acknowledgement of the historical roots of Krishna *bhakti* and also, paradoxically enough, of its potentially trans-regional trajectory. Though the
Bhagavat Purana itself is known to be of southern provenance, the Vraj
country remained a sacred site of immense importance for Vaishnavas of
the region. It is an established fact that the older Vaishnava *sampradayas*
of Sri Vaishnavas, Madhvites, Nimbarkas, and Vishnuswamis, all of
which had originated in southern India, had made their presence felt in
Vrindavan much before Chaitanya visited it.

Murari Gupta's *Kadcha* and the *Chaitanya Bhagavata* report that at
the Rath Yatra of Puri (we cannot be sure of the year) as many as 66
leading Vaishnavas of Bengal acknowledged the divinity of Chaitanya.
The Gaudiyas, as we know, had no central organization even though the
Charitamrita gives useful information on their being divided into four
main *shakhas*. Of these, the *mukhya* branch of Chaitanya lists 159 followers, including major Goswami figures such as Rup, Sanatan, and Jiva.
Nityananda is shown to have 83 followers, Advaita 40, and Gadadhar
Pandit 32. It is important to note though that although Krishnadas
Kaviraj speaks of the Chaitanya *shakha*, there was really no spiritual
lineage specific to Chaitanya, since he was at best a *shikshaguru* and not
a *dikshaguru* to his followers. Rup and Sanatan, though instructed at
length by him, do not acknowledge Chaitanya as their guru, except in
a general way. In the case of Bengal itself, the people who most effectively carried out Chaitanya's religious mission also employed ideas and
strategies which were not always consistent with those propagated by
Chaitanya himself.

Over time, the Gaudiya movement also acquired a complex network
of offices and sub-offices. Thus, we have references to the 'Mahantas',
originally 64 in number—which Kavi Karnapur further subdivides into
four sub-categories in the *Gaurganoddesadipika*—and the 'Kavirajas',

originally eight in number but with a propensity to include more in the face of an increasing number of aspirants keen to hold office. By the 17th century, the office of the Goswami in Bengal had turned hereditary. Increasing recruitment of Vaishnavas also meant the creation of multiple tasks and responsibilities, some of which had no association with everyday spiritual life. The problem was increasingly compounded by the fact that this recruitment occurred on multiple levels: there were *grihi* or householder Vaishnavas, most of whom belonged to respectable upper castes and abided by accepted social conventions. But there were also recruits from lower and ritually defiled castes whose association with both orthodox Vaishnava theology and social practices was suspect and rather loose. This class comprised Boshtoms and Bairagis, mendicants who lived by begging and often lived in secluded settlements known as *akhras*. More difficult to socially define was the class of Jat Vaishnavas, which could include both respectable householders and people from marginalized castes with disreputable pasts. In 19th-century Bengali literature, all three categories mentioned above became objects of ridicule and were more often than not associated with unscrupulousness and moral laxity.

However, all through this time, the office of the Goswami waxed in power and prestige. They generally served as gurus to householders but also grew extra-ecclesiastical powers; this, in turn, helped them acquire new mechanisms of control. Colonial ethnographic records reveal how, confronted with an expanding social base, the Goswamis preferred to work within an operative framework of hierarchy, delegating some of their powers to men whom they themselves appointed. Goswamis were now assisted by the *Adhikari* (which corresponds to the status of a superintendent) and by *Faujdars* and *Chharidars*, both of whom were cane-wielding officers who had the power of physically punishing recalcitrant Vaishnavas. Over time, the office of the Goswami also acquired pecuniary rights: the Boshtoms, for example, who did not formally conform to the institution of marriage and were known to frequently change their female partners, had to pay a fixed fee to the *Chharidar* for every such change, a part of which was siphoned off by the Goswami. By the 19th century, some Goswamis were known to even run gambling houses and grog shops. In colonial Bengal, the term 'Vaishnava' did not always meet with social approval.

In Chaitanya's time, and even for some time thereafter, it would have been quite extraordinary to publicly identify Vaishnavas by their caste standing. This is not to suggest that the movement launched by Chaitanya had effectively dismantled social hierarchies based on birth or that there was a growing aversion to enumeration by one's caste standing. On the contrary, it seems reasonable to argue that while Chaitanya's religion opened up new social spaces for a wide variety of marginalized men and women, the movement was still effectively dominated by a collective of upper-bracket castes. In 1939, in a bold departure from established practice, Bimanbihari Majumdar identified 490 Vaishnava names appearing in various texts by their caste standing. Significantly enough, he would have failed in this enterprise had the texts themselves not revealed the caste status of the people so identified. However, this conclusion itself can be read in two opposed ways. On one level it could be argued that since the relevant texts made no serious attempt to conceal the caste identity of the individuals concerned, they were not oblivious of the importance of such social categorization even within a devotional culture that, at least in theory, considerably diluted them. It is just as possible, though, that the caste identities of converts to Chaitanya Vaishnavism were purposefully inserted in the texts so as to more dramatically bring out the palpable change of heart on the part of concerned individuals. The latter theory assumes significance when one recalls that of the 490 individuals identified by Majumdar, as many as 305 belonged to the upper-bracket castes of Brahmin, Baidya, and Kayastha. Of these 305, only Brahmins accounted for 239. Of the ritually marginalized castes, Majumdar mentions only Subarnabanik, Bhuimali, Sutradhar, Karmakar, and Modak, represented by one member each. The caste ranking of 96 individuals could not be determined. Majumdar's list includes 16 women, which cannot be said to be exhaustive since Jayananda provides us the names of another 27. Finally, among Chaitanya's followers were at least 49 sanyasis, of whom about 40 clearly belonged to the Dasnami Order instituted by Adi Sankara. This is intriguing, to say the least, since Advaita philosophy—which the latter adhered to—was consistently rejected by both Chaitanya and Goswami theoreticians. If anything, this ought to set us thinking afresh on the fuzzy boundaries that often seem to separate one theological or philosophical tradition from another in late medieval India.

Given below is a brief but analytical survey of the Chaitanya movement as carried forward by his major companions, devotees, and followers that enable us to understand just how Krishna *bhakti* took root in sixteenth-century Bengal and elsewhere. Of Chaitanya's companions or associates, however, I shall speak selectively of only Nityananda, Advaita Acharya, Haridas Thakur, and Gadadhar Pandit at some length, followed by a section on the Vrindavan Goswamis. This chapter will conclude with a brief account of second generation evangelists whose work proved critical to the successful expansion of Gaudiya Vaishnavism.

Nityananda: The Maverick *Avadhuta*

In Hindu-Bengali culture, it is customary to invoke the expression 'Gaur-Nitai', hinting at the closeness of the two figures, Chaitanya and Nityananda. Between them, the two created and sustained for a long time a religious movement of far-reaching significance. Nityananda was about nine years older than Chaitanya and survived him by 12 years. He has been described as an imposing figure, carrying the *kamandalu*, and a mace resting on his broad shoulders, his left ear pierced by a ring in the manner of Nath Yogis, and dressed in blue garments. He may have even had a physical resemblance to Viswarup, for Sachi Devi once mistook him for her older son. In Vaishnava hagiography, Nityananda is also taken to be an incarnation of Balarama—the elder brother of Krishna—which, no doubt, contributed to strengthen theories of his inseparability from Chaitanya, widely held to be an incarnation of Krishna himself.

In early life, Nityananda was a Saiva *avadhuta*, born in the village of Ekchakra in Birbhum to one Hadai Pandit (also called Hadai Ojha) and Padmavati. The district Birbhum is traditionally famed as a Saiva-Sakta centre. Of the 342 temples in the area surveyed by David McCutchion in the 1960s, at least 29 belonged to this category. When establishing his centre at Khardaha (North 24 Paraganas), Nityananda is known to have also set up the worship of the Tantric goddess, Tripurasundari. *Avadhutas* are, by definition, free floating ascetics, not bound by any social conventions; and widely circulating legends of Nityananda's fondness for female company, a penchant for adorning his body with lustrous silks and gold ornaments, or his consuming animal flesh and spirits may not have been entirely fabricated. Contrary to Dasnami ascetics, *avadhutas* made no distinction between *tyaga* (the path of abstinence or renunciation) and *bhoga* (the path of sensual indulgence).

Some scholars have alleged that Nityananda's father, Hadai Ojha, was by profession an *ojha* or shaman or else a priest to the ritually defiled *jati* of the Hadis. This ascription, however, is easily denied by citing the case of Krittibas Ojha, author of the Bengali Ramayana and a respected Brahmin. However, some texts do point to the fact that Hadai Ojha's ancestors had been ritually degraded in the past for marrying outside rules of commensality. Advaita Acharya, for one, remained consistently distrustful of Nityananda's ancestry, also often accusing him of indulging in socially disreputable practices. Vrindavan Das reports that some Vaishnavas of Nabadwip could not bear to even hear his name. Indeed, it is somewhat difficult to explain just how the Gaudiya Vaishnava community in Bengal could overlook Nityananda's radical non-conformism unless one attached symbolic meanings to some of his bohemian acts. Thus, Nityananda's drinking spirits could also have served to only strengthen his identity with the mythical Balarama, who is known to have indulged in drunken sprees. And when, reportedly, in the middle of an ecstatic devotional experience, Nityananda was heard crying out for *madira* to be served to him, the word could also have been construed to indicate intoxicating *bhakti*! His adorning gold ornaments have interesting parallels with the ways of Ramakrishna Paramahamsa, who is reported to have worn such ornaments only to remove them with an air of disgust. By so doing, reportedly, he only wished to demonstrate that true renunciation came not through the suppression of desires but by treating these with disdain and detachment.

Legend has it that Nityananda was separated from his parents at the age of 12 by a wandering ascetic (identified as Iswar Puri in some texts), who then took him on a tour of the country for as many as 20 years. There is some difference of opinion on just who his guru might have been. Certain traditions project Nityananda as 'Swarupa' (one who knows the self) who could dispense with the office of a guru, while others call him a disciple of Sankarshana Puri, or alternatively of Laxmipati, both of whom are known to be disciples of Madhavendra Puri. In all probability, Nityananda was affiliated to the community comprising Madhavendra's several disciples which included Iswar Puri and Keshav

Bharati—who, as we know, had a significant role to play in the religious life of Chaitanya.

Nityananda's formally turning into a Vaishnava figure occurred after 1509 when he first met Chaitanya at Nabadwip, even though, as a man situated in the spiritual tradition of Madhevandra, he would have already been familiar with devotional sentiments anchored in Krishna *bhakti*. Reportedly, the two figures took a liking to each other instantly, though it would also appear that Chaitanya was at times acutely embarrassed by the idiosyncratic ways of the *avadhuta*—who, on occasion, fancied himself as a child and had to be suckled by Malini, the wife of Sribas—or by his tendency to wander about naked in public. On the whole, though, Chaitanya is known to have great faith in the spiritual personality of Nityananda: just as the lotus leaf would never soak water, he ruled, no evil thought or deed could be attached to Nityananda. It was apparently on Chaitanya's instructions that Nityananda gave up the life of an ascetic and entered a householder's life. He was married to two sisters—Vasudha and Jahnava—the daughters of a Brahmin, Suryadas Sarkhel, the younger of the two sisters being reportedly given away as dowry. There could also be a different perspective to this story. It is quite possible that Nityananda helped overcome the plight of a hapless father and rescued Jahnava from a lonesome life. Judging by contemporary practices, it would have been difficult to find a suitable Brahmin groom for a woman whose sister had been married to a Bantasi, a man who had abandoned ascetic life in favour of the householder's (considered to be a derogatory title). Though frowned upon by orthodox society, Nityananda's marriage could also have been viewed as a positive move since it reinforced the idea of Vaishnavism being primarily a religion for the *grihastha*. While Vasudha remained issueless, Jahnava gave birth to a son, Birbhadra/Birchandra, and a daughter, Ganga. Interestingly enough, notwithstanding the revered religious status of Nityananda, Brahmanism may have had the last laugh. A late text called the *Nityananda Prabhur Bangshabistar* (The Genealogy of Nityananda, n.d.) reveals that the family spared no efforts to get Ganga wedded to a Brahmin of high pedigree.

The philosopher Brajendranath Seal called Nityananda the first 'true democrat' in Bengal and quite explicitly his reference was to the ways in which Nityananda disregarded distinctions of *jati* and gender when recruiting devotees. In the well-known Vaishnava anthology *Gaudapadatarnagini*, a verse attributed to Lochandas speaks of Nityananda as the saviour of women and the *patita*. Nityananda's evangelizing drive offered space for women, a development which may not have entirely pleased Chaitanya himself. If Jayananda is to be believed, Chaitanya once reprimanded Nityananda for allowing women to join *sankirtan* parties at the Panihati festival organized (sometime after 1516) with financial help from Raghunath Das Goswami. Nityananda's honest and courageous counter to this, as reported in sources, was to remind Chaitanya that degenerative time in *Kali yuga* was quite unsuitable for scrupulously adhering to older social conventions That apart, Nityananda was the first to attempt an organization of Chaitanya's followers under the institution known as Gopalas, which was a collective of some of the best known Vaishnava figures from contemporary Bengal. As a follower of the *sakhya bhava*, he saw such figures as reincarnations of Krishna's playmates in Vrindavan. This idea, as we know, was to find its exaltation in Karnapur's *Gauraganoddesdipika* (1576) which identified 15 contemporary Vaishnava figures as Krishna's playmates in mythical Vrindavan. But Karnapur's list was far from stable and, in course of time, 'Gopal-hood' became a greatly coveted position, forcing Goswamis and other Vaishnava leaders to settle at number 12. Thereafter, new claimants were accommodated under the office of upa-Gopalas or subsidiary Gopalas, also fixed at 12. Of the 12 Gopalas, four were from Hoogly and Nadia districts each and three from Burdwan, suggestive of their relative importance as Vaishnava sites. The more well-known Gopalas—as, for instance, Abhiram Ramdas, Gauridas Pandit, Kamalakar Pippali, Purushottam Das Thakur, and Uddharan Dutta—were influential figures who eventually established autonomous centres of power called Sripats. Of these influential figures, three were Shudras. Uddharan Dutta, for instance, belonged to the *suvarnabanik jati*, a community that was known to have been ritually downgraded in the 11th–12th centuries by Ballal Sen, who established the Sena dynasty in Bengal, replacing the Palas. Hence, Nityananda's movement may justly be associated with successful sanskritization movements in late medieval Bengal, a trend which was to gather considerable momentum by the 19th century.

The induction of the *baniks* who enjoyed material affluence but were denied higher social status was of some practical and pecuniary benefit to the community of Vaishnavas at large. According to the seventeenth-century text *Murali Vilas* (a text in praise of Bangshibadan Thakur, c.18th century) by Rajvallabha Das, it was Uddharan Dutta who materially helped to organize visits by Bengali Vaishnava leaders such as Jahnava (Nityananda's second wife) to Vrindavana, thereby forging a link between Bengal and Vraj that was to prove important in the days to come. Having said that, it is important to also acknowledge that Nityananda's laxness with social rules and conventions did not seriously threaten Brahmin hegemony of the time. As many as nine of the 12 Gopalas were Brahmins by birth, a fact that would encourage the view that they simply appropriated the institution to their advantage.

In Bengal, Nityananda was perhaps the greatest advocate of *Gaurparamyavada*, a theory conferring on Chaitanya a status comparable with that of Krishna himself, as against *Krishnaparamyavada* of the Vrindavan Goswamis which saw him as a manifestation or descended form of the Lord. This is also borne out by the fact that in one way or another, Nityananda was the inspiration behind all major hagiographies on Chaitanya. By the 17th century, though, Nityananda's influence in Bengal had considerably waned, partly because his successors—such as his wife, Jahnava, and son, Birbhadra—entertained ideas perceptibly different from his own. Also, by this time, thanks partly to the growing popularity of Sahajiya Vaishnavism, *sakhya bhava* had increasingly lost to the more eroticized practice of *manjari sadhana*, in which, typically, the *sadhaka* imagined himself as a female attendant of *gopis*, vicariously trying to augment the eternal passion-play of Radha and Krishna in eternal Vrindavan.

Advaita Acharya: The Vaishnava Patriarch

According to the *Chaitanya Bhagavata*, it was Advaita's cry of anguish that caused Krishna to incarnate on earth as Chaitanya. It is believed that this old Brahmin was so greatly distressed by the callousness and moral depravity among people surrounding him that he consistently prayed for the Lord's intervention and was, in due course, rewarded for his prayers. The Brahmo theologian Hemchandra Sarkar, who produced a short biography of Chaitanya, likened Advaita's relationship to Chaitanya to that of John the Baptist with Christ.

Older to Chaitanya by about 50 years, Advaita is said to have lived to the age of 125 years and in Vaishnava iconography, he is invariably portrayed as a stout old man with a flowing white beard. Originally called Kamalakar Bhattacharya, Advaita was the son of one Kuber Pandit, a man who served as a scholar to a ruling house of Sylhet. At the age of 12, he migrated to Santipur, a town few miles off Nabadwip. Like Nabadwip, Santipur was a centre of traditional learning and, presumably, it was here that he completed his course of studies and settled into a householder's life. He took two wives, Sri and Sita, who bore him six sons. Advaita and his wives were close friends of the Misra family and rejoiced at the birth of the infant Nimai. For some time, he was also an instructor to Viswarup, which later led Sachi Devi accuse him of encouraging her son to adopt a life of *sanyas*.

Vaishnava texts describe Advaita as a man partial to *Jnan Marga/Yoga* and a scholar of the quasi Vedantic text *Yogavasistha Ramayana*. One of his several biographies also claims that he authored a commentary on the *Bhagavad Gita*. Though not uncommon among his contemporaries or near contemporaries, this juxtaposition of Jnan and Bhakti was an important feature in the religious life of Advaita and it is quite likely that he never fully gave up his interest in gnosis, a tendency that once provoked Chaitanya to physically assault the old man, to be rescued only by the pleading intercession of his wife, Sita Devi.

In his social instincts, Advaita was conservative; but this too must be qualified by the fact that even as an orthodox Brahmin, he offered shelter to Haridas Thakur, a man believed to be of Muslim birth, even inviting him to the ritual observances for his departed mother. It is also widely held that it was Advaita who first requested Chaitanya to spread the sentiments of *bhakti* among women and Shudras. One may recall that he was also the author of a cryptic message sent to Chaitanya at Puri, which hastened Chaitanya's death. What this message was actually meant to convey we shall never know and yet, it is quite definitively established that this triggered a reaction in Chaitanya who, thereafter, became even more unmindful of his physical self and his daily routines.

Unlike Nityananda, Advaita has been the subject of several biographies, the authorship of which, however, is as yet uncertain. It is also significant that over time, Vaishnava Goswamis belonging to the Advaita branch of Santipur grew more conservative and selective in their recruitment. The colonial ethnographer L.S.S O'Malley noted that they would admit only Brahmins and Baidyas. Advaita himself is shown to have had 43 disciples, although, following his death, his *shakha* split into three contesting factions led respectively by his wife, Sita Devi, his eldest son, Achyutananda, and his other sons supported by one Kamdev Nagar. An event of some significance in which the Advaita branch was drawn into with the Goswamis based in Nabadwipa is the controversy over the 'Gaur Mantra'. Whereas the Nabadwip group claimed that there had to be two different mantras for purposes of invoking Chaitanya and Krishna respectively, the Santipur Goswamis, led by Nilmani Goswami, even produced a *vyavastha* disputing this. In his classic, *Chaitanya Chariter Upadan*, Bimanbihari Majumdar reports that the controversy even took a violent turn with Goswamis from the two rival camps actually resorting to fist-fighting!

'Yavana' Haridas: The Exemplar of Modesty and Forbearance

The term *'yavana'*, often prefixed to the name of Haridas, has two somewhat contrary significations. On one level, it is no doubt a way of affirming his Muslim ancestry or else of his conversion to Islam later in life; on the other hand, the persistence of the term may have also served to underscore, at least up to some point in time, the accommodative spirit of Vaishnavism which did not scruple to accept a devotee even outside the Hindu fold. Interestingly, there was equally an attempt to claim Hindu ancestry for Haridas, which might explain the popularity of the appellation 'Haridasa Thakur' in some traditions and texts. Jayananda, for instance, claims that he was born to Hindu parents called Ujjwala and Manohar. Some Gaudiya sources even claim that his conversion from Islam to Vaishnavism was a way of atoning for his past sins. Radically opposed to this view is the song attributed to the Baul poet and composer Duddu Shah which questions the very need for conversion, given the possibility that one could relate to God just as well in Islam as through any other faith. However, it would be reasonable to assume that few would have dared to call him a *'yavana'* in Chaitanya's lifetime. During his residence in Puri, it was part of Chaitanya's daily routine to call on Haridas and feed him the Lord's *prasada* since Haridas himself would not visit the temple premises or beg for his food for fear of offending orthodox susceptibilities.

There are several apocryphal stories about Haridas. He is said to have been born in Budhan village in district Khulna and subsequently moved to Phulia. Thereafter, he eventually found shelter at Santipur with Advaita Acharya. Our sources also indicate that he was persecuted both on account of his being a saint as well as a Muslim. A powerful Hindu landlord of this region named Ramchandra Khan, doubting his saintliness, successively sent concubines as enticement to which, however, Haridas would not succumb. The story further narrates how, when the bewitchingly beautiful women visited him at his hermitage, Haridas had them wait outside until he had finished with his daily chanting of the Lord's name, which he reportedly uttered three lakh times a day. On their first visit the women lost patience and left; and on the second, having realized the spiritual prowess of the man and his utter disregard for temptations of the flesh, they begged his forgiveness and became his disciples. A greater tormentor was the local Kazi who threatened Haridas with reprisals in case he failed to promptly return to the ways of Islam. When this was refused, the Kazi had him publicly flogged at twenty-two designated places. At the end of this inhuman act, the persecutors left him for dead and threw the limp body into a nearby river. The cool waters of the river revived him.

Haridas was part of the Bengali contingent which regularly visited Puri for the annual Rath Yatra and even accompanied Chaitanya on his first journey from Odisha to native Bengal. He settled down in Puri, where he eventually passed away, presumably not long before Chaitanya himself. On Chaitanya's instructions, his body was buried on the beach at Puri and a *mahotsava* organized to commemorate the occasion.

Haridas is not known to have initiated any followers and there is no reference to his *shakha* in Vaishnava hagiographies. He was nevertheless widely respected as a saintly soul who put self-control and renunciation before all else. Bengali author and researcher Girijashankar Raychaudhuri has aptly observed how forgiveness was the quintessential quality in Haridas, for he is known to have readily forgiven his persecutors. It was also Raychaudhuri's observation that even Chaitanya himself would have been incapable of such compassion. We may recall how, on the directions of Chaitanya, Haridas actively assisted Nityananda in propagating Krishna *bhakti* in rural Bengal, though there is little information available to speak of this in any detail.

Gadadhar Pandit and the Gadai-Gauranga Community

It is important to include Gadadhar Pandit (also known as Gadai) among Chaitanya's close companions and co-workers. For one, some Gaudiyas came to attach special theological significance to their relationship, projecting Gadadhar as Chaitanya's *shakti*. Predictably, this created problems for those who took his wife, Vishnupriya, to fulfil that role as also for those accepting the theory of an androgynous Chaitanya, best elaborated by Krishnadas Kaviraj in *Chaitanya Charitamrita*. In time, such differences in theological conceptions were to breed sectarian hostility between various Gaudiya sub-communities. Until about the 17th century, such differences also reflected, to an extent, the inner differences between Krishna-centric and Chaitanya-centric theologies. However, with the progressive dissemination of Goswami ideology in Bengal and with important Bengali Vaishnava leaders increasingly drawn into strategic ties with Vrindavan, such differences were eventually glossed over. Also, with Chaitanya increasingly assuming the moods of Radha when at Puri, Gadadhar's role as his *shakti*, one imagines, would have turned redundant.

Pandit Gadadhar is believed to have been born in 1487, which makes him an exact contemporary of Chaitanya. He was born in Nabadwip to Madhava Misra, a *kulin* Brahmin but who may have suffered a fall in ritual status. Tradition sees him as a follower of Madhavendra Puri but initiated by one Pundarik Vidyanidhi of Sylhet. This association suggests that the family's roots were in Sylhet, as was the case for many followers of Chaitanya in Nabadwip. In his early days, Gadadhar was known for his penchant for cross-dressing. In the dramatic performances that Chaitanya and his followers held in secret at the house of Chandrashekhara Acharya, Gadadhar took it upon himself to play the roles of Radha, Rukmini, and Laxmi. In Bengal, the community of Vaishnavas which most actively propagated the eroticized Gaur–Gadadhar relationship was the one located at the Katwa sub-division of district Burdwan, commonly known as the Srikhanda Vaishnavas. Their most outstanding spokespersons were the brothers Narahari and Mukunda Sarkar, physicians by profession and gifted poets. Narahari Sarkar, as we may recall, was also a strong advocate of *Gauranagarabhava* and the explicit eroticism in their poetry seems to have been only reinforced by association with the Gadai-Gauranga community. One of Narahari's eminent disciples, Lochandas, went on to describe Chaitanya's lovemaking with Vishnupriya on the night prior to his accepting *sanyas*, persuading even the modern biographer Sisir Kumar Ghosh to observe that on this night Chaitanya produced a 'huge outpouring of *rasa*'. However, *Chaitanya Bhagavata* and Kavi Karnapur's *Mahakavya* (Anthology of Poems, n.d.) claim that Chaitanya spent that night in the company of Gadadhar. The quite explicit homoerotic suggestion notwithstanding, Ghosh even goes on to suggest that on this occasion, Gadadhar occupied Vishnupriya's place and gently massaged Chaitanya's feet. On this issue, Ghosh was clearly an exception, since *bhadralok* sensibilities were deeply hurt at the suggestion that both Chaitanya and Gadadhar could have been gay. In 1925, Bimanbihari Majumdar led a campaign against a work called *Rasaraj Gauranga Swabhava* (an esoteric text on Gauranagaravad, c.17th century) by one Viswambhar Babaji of Srikhand that made this suggestion quite explicitly. By his own confession, Majumdar found this so outrageous that he sought the assistance of the public prosecutor and the influential zamindars of Kasimbazar to impose a ban on the circulation of this tract. Some later-day followers of the Srikhanda community are also known to have been deeply affected by Tantric practices. Raishekhara, a poet and disciple of Narahari's nephew Raghunandan, was known to indulge in ritual sex with a woman named Durgadasi. Evidently, a majority of Gadadhar's followers or disciples came from the Srikhanda Vaishnava community or those who broadly supported their views.

In some ways, Gadadhar Pandit served as an important link between Vrindavan and Bengal. Four of his disciples functioned as either custodians or priests of three of the best known temples in Vrindavan: Govindadev, Gopinath, and Madanamohana. Gadadhar followed Chaitanya to Puri and camped there until his death. He was also famed as a *pathaka* of the *Bhagavat Purana* and there is a legend to the effect that his talent persuaded the second generation Vaishnava evangelist Srinivas Acharya to seek instructions from him. However, this was an opportunity sadly denied. Reportedly, Gadadhar requested Srinivas to fetch a fresh copy of the *Bhagavata* text from Bengal, but passed away while his would-be pupil was en route to Puri from Bengal.

Creativity and Fertile Passion: The Six Goswamis of Vrindavan

The term 'Goswami', literally 'the lord of the cows', is a term ascribed to Vaishnava figures of eminence who also held positions of leadership. Judging by available evidence pertaining to the Chaitanya tradition itself, the term appears to have been widely used freely only after 1576—that is about four decades after the death of Chaitanya—by when notions of authority, hierarchy, and organization had become well entrenched within the Gaudiya community. In the post-Chaitanya period, the question of providing intellectual substance and theological leadership had to be determined with caution and care in the face of both internal feuds within and sectarian rivalry outside. This catapulted certain figures closest to Chaitanya to positions of considerable power and prominence and of these, the most venerated names after Nityananda and Advaita were the famed 'Shada Goswamis' (the six Goswamis of Vrindavan), an expression probably originating with Krishnadas Kaviraj. All of them, at some stage, made Vrindavan their home, never returning to either Bengal or to their place of origin. Of the six, as many as four were of southern provenance or ancestry and of these, Gopal Bhatta Goswami never visited Bengal, migrating directly to Vrindavan on the instructions of Chaitanya. But for Jiva Goswami, all others had personally met Chaitanya at some point in their lives, some of whom even chose to narrate their experiences in prose and verse. The Vrindavan Goswamis were gifted scholiasts, poets, dramatists, commentators, and rhetoricians and between them produced as many as 219 works, all of which were in Sanskrit and based on classical conventions governing language and literature. Of them, only one, Raghunath Bhatt, the son of Tapan Misra, an early follower of Chaitanya, did not contribute by way of scholarship or even as a poet or songwriter. Their choice of language and locale sets apart the Goswamis from the *padabali* poets of Bengal, who chose to commemorate the various incidents in Chaitanya's life in the vernacular and almost entirely in verse. Also, whereas the *padabali* poets dealt mostly with the pre-monastic life of Chaitanya, the Goswamis did not, since they encountered only the ascetic Chaitanya either in Bengal or in Puri.

The Goswamis were also successful institution builders in multiple ways. Acting on the instructions of Chaitanya, they not only contributed to restore and rehabilitate Vrindavan as a sacred pilgrim site but also acted as trustees and spokespersons for a dynamic and rapidly expanding religious tradition. They welcomed pious visitors from Bengal, often acting as their teachers and counsellors, liaised with local patrons and with the Mughal state which bestowed upon them both munificence and political protection, oversaw the construction of temples and specialized libraries, renovated important religious sites connected with the mythical lives of Radha–Krishna, and kept alive a community of pious Vaishnavas. It is reasonable to argue that, on the whole, their work demonstrated qualities of religious leadership and the delicate intertwining of intellectual vibrancy and ascetic self-control. It is also something of a mystery that they should lead the life of staunch ascetics and yet invoke the most eroticized ideas and imageries to convey their religious beliefs.

When discussing the Goswamis at length, it would only be appropriate to begin with the brothers Rup and Sanatan. Sanatan was the older brother and held the position of a principal minister under Sultan Hussain Shah as *Sakar Malik*. It is quite possible that Rup, who was given the name *Dabir Khas*, was the principal secretary to Sanatan rather than to the Sultan himself. We may recall that soon after meeting Chaitanya at Ramkeli, the brothers decided to give up service under the state and seek refuge in Krishna *bhakti* that Chaitanya was passionately preaching at the time. In the case of Sanatan, this transition proved to be difficult. On hearing of his intentions, the Sultan at once had him put under house arrest. It was only the offer of a lucrative bribe that allowed him to escape unseen one night and join Chaitanya at Kashi, where he received detailed instruction over two months. Chaitanya also instructed him to recover and replenish sites connected with the mythical lives of Radha and Krishna that had fallen into disuse. Such pioneering efforts enabled later-day Vaishnava writers such as Narahari Chakravarti (also known as Ghanashyam Das) to write detailed accounts of the sacred geography of Vrindavan and codify ritual practices that devout Vaishnavas were expected to follow when touring this sacred habitat. Sanatan was the author of several works but his natural inclination was towards *siddhanta*, just as his brother Rup's was towards *kavya*, *alankara*, and *rasa*. Among his several works are *Vrihatbhagavatamrita*, an original and brilliant exposition on the *Bhagavat Purana*, and *Digadarshini* (literally, The Pathfinder, c.16th century), a commentary on the massive Vaishnava ritual compendium, *Haribhaktivilas*. The authorship of *Haribhaktivilas* is contested. Whereas Jiva Goswami attributed both the work and the commentary thereupon to be the work of Sanatan himself, *Haribhaktivilas* is now acknowledged to be the work of Gopal Bhatta Goswami. It is not unlikely that the latter completed the text that Sanatan had begun to write. However, the reasons subsequently offered for the exclusion of Sanatan's name are quite contentious.

Both Dineshchandra Sen and Melville T. Kennedy have argued that this was done with a view to keep out the possible 'Muslim' antecedents of the brothers Rup and Sanatan. The social origins of the brothers were first discussed in the Bengali paper *Somprakash* in 1872 and following that, in the collection of essays called *Probandho Ratna* (Gem-like Essays, 1908). In the latter, we may recall, they are quite mistakenly shown to be Muslim courtiers under Akbar. Contemporary writer Durgacharan Roy even made the claim that Rup and Sanatan were actually names given by Chaitanya to the brothers who had been born Muslims. In 1934, one Basanta Kumar Chattopadhyay, writing in the Bengali journal *Bharatvarsha*, alleged that their father had been converted to Islam by one Pir Ali Khan of Jessore. Dineshchandra Sen and, after him, Girjashankar Raychaudhuri went to the extent of arguing—on the basis of surveys they claimed to have carried in the vicinity of Ramkeli—that local people still refused to drink water from the tank that the two brothers were known to have excavated. The evidence for such claims is at best sketchy. Jiva's *Laghutoshini* (an abridged commentary, c.16th century) which provides us with a useful account of the family tree makes it clear that Rup and Sanatan (as also their brother Ballabha) were Maratha Brahmins by birth, descended from a ruling house that ruled Karnataka between the late 13th and early 14th centuries. It is important to note though that scholars such as Sen and Raychaudhuri did not assert the Muslim ancestry of the brothers out of any malice. On the contrary, this was probably intended to demonstrate the openness and cosmopolitanism of the Gaudiya tradition which, apparently, had no scruples about recruiting even non-Hindus. In any case, what runs counter to the theories of a Muslim ancestry is the fact that Rup and Sanatan were taught by one Mahamahopadhyay Vidyavachaspati and that they organized *Bhagavat path*, neither of which would have been possible had they been indubitably Muslims. In hindsight, it could even be argued that their Brahmin birth may itself provide a clue to the way the ancestry of Rup and Sanatan came under some suspicion. Girijashankar Raychaudhuri has also alerted us to the possibility that for a Brahmin, service under a non-Hindu employer often met with social disapproval and the instance he cites is that of Maharaja Nandakumar, who, allegedly, was despised by fellow Brahmins for precisely this reason.

Jiva Goswami was personally tutored by Sanatan; Rup too considered his older brother to be his guru. Sanatan was also a man of extreme modesty and was deeply respectful of conventions. One reason why many came to doubt his Hindu ancestry was his refusal to be in the vicinity of the Jagannath temple at Puri, claiming that he had lost the *adhikaar* to enter the premises. Chaitanya, it is important to add, fully approved of this decision, as he also did with Haridas who similarly avoided the temple premises. Sanatan's self-understanding as a ritually defiled person may have been derived from the fact that he had served a Muslim ruling class for long. On the other hand, this does not appear to be standard practice since, judging by the number of Hindus who served the Indo-Islamic state in various capacities, many more would have been forced to adopt this line of thought.

Like his brother Sanatan, Rup was personally instructed by Chaitanya at Prayag and Puri. It is also possible that he had poetic talent even before meeting Chaitanya in person. In later life, he was to produce an anthology of poems known as *Padyabali* (An Anthology of Devotional Poems, c.16th century), which possibly includes some from his early life. Rup's outstanding contribution was in treating *bhakti* itself as a *rasa*, the best accounts of which are available in the works *Ujjvalanilamani* and the *Bhaktirasamritasindhu*. He was also an accomplished dramatist, having produced the plays *Vidagdha Madhava* (The Astute Krishna, c.16th century) and *Lalita Madhava* (The Charming Krishna, c.16th century). Such works are also rich in Vaishnava theology as we shall have occasion to see.

Rup and Sanatan are believed to have died in Vrindavan within a few years of one another, in all probability between the years 1554 and 1559.

Jiva Goswami, the nephew of Rup and Sanatan and the son of Ballabha, was a prodigious and prolific scholar. It is difficult to be exact about the number of works he produced but the list would quite easily exceed 20.

Most of these were learned commentaries and interpretation of earlier texts by Rup and Sanatan. Jiva is believed to have been born around 1515 and arrived at Vrindavan sometime in 1541–2, having already received extensive scholastic training in Kashi. The *Bhaktiratnakara* claims that his teacher was the *advaitin* Madhusudan Saraswati, but this looks quite improbable. The bulk of Jiva's works were produced between 1555 and 1592 and we do also know that he was in the habit of constantly revising his works, indicating a mind that took a dynamic view of his own thoughts as also of the scholastic tradition in which he situated himself. Understandably enough, he is not mentioned by early hagiographers such as Murari Gupta, Vrindavan Das, Jayananda, and Lochandas, which would also broadly indicate his chronological location within Gaudiya Vaishnava history.

In early life, Jiva is believed to have been a man who took some pride in his learning and there is an unverified story about how he volunteered to challenge a visitor to Vrindavan in *shastrarth* and effectively humbled him. The story then goes on to say that this incident so upset Rup that he banished his nephew from the community of Vaishnavas, forcing him to lead a life of disconsolate repentance. It is believed that Rup was upset at Jiva for flaunting his intellectual prowess, a quality held to be inconsistent with the innate humility of a Vaishnava. In this instance, it was Sanatan's intervention that eventually rescued Jiva, without which he might have met with a fate comparable to that of Haridas Junior in Puri, whom Chaitanya had banished for approaching a local woman for the gift of some rice.

Jiva's works could be classified into three categories: first, Vaishnava theology and philosophy; second, commentaries, manuals, and grammar; and finally, poetics and literary compositions. It would be reasonable to claim though that his penchant was for the first, typically represented by his *Shadasandarbha* (The Six Discourses, c.16th century), a book comprising six dense theological discourses. As a theologian he also had the courage and originality to counter older Puranic claims about Krishna taking birth only in three of the four *yugas*. For Jiva, Krishna could just as well descend on earth in degenerative *Kaliyuga* since everything was possible for the Lord.

Jiva was the most respected authority figure in Vrindavan, especially after the passing away of his uncles, Rup and Sanatan (whom he also considered his gurus), and his influence was not limited to the Gaudiyas alone since Vithalnath of the Vallabha *sampradaya* was a close friend. It was Jiva who personally trained the second generation of Vaishnava evangelists such as Srinivas, Narottam, and Shyamananda and entrusted them with the important mission of carrying Goswami theology outside the Vraj country. He had regular correspondence with such disciples, sending them suitable advice and directions from time to time, some of which is reproduced in the *Bhaktiratnakara*. It was he who courteously received Nityananda's second wife Jahnava and, if the *Bhaktiratnakara* is to be believed, also her son, the charismatic Birbhadra, on their visits to Vrindavan sometime after 1576. This subsequently led to the greater dissemination of Vrindvana theology in Bengal and brought the Gaudiyas closer to Vrindavan theology. Jiva's works appear to mark the culmination of the theory of *Krishnaparamyavada* that held Krishna to be the supreme object of all devotion and the relative decline of *Gaurparamyavada*. It is quite significant that his *Shadasandarbha* specifically includes a discourse on Krishna (*Krishnasandarbha*, c.16th century) but not on Chaitanya. All the same, one would be overstating the case somewhat by suggesting that Chaitanya ceased to be the theological reference point for the Vrindavan Goswamis at any given time.

Jiva was a respected figure with the Mughal state too, for his name appears in contemporary legal documents related to some major Vaishnava shrines of Vrindavan—as, for instance, Govindji and Madan Mohana. Akbar is known to have granted a substantial area of land in 1565–8 to one Gopal Das, an associate of Jiva.

Jiva died a natural death in or around the year 1608, and it is believed that by the time he died, his body had become so emaciated and deformed from self-denial and starvation that it could not be buried in a sitting posture, as was the accepted practice among Vaishnava luminaries.

Had it not been for Raghunath Das, we would know very little about the other two Goswamis: Ragunath Bhatta and Gopal Bhatta. Raghunath Bhatta was the son of Tapan Misra, whom Chaitanya had met on his tour of east Bengal and who had been advised to relocate to Kashi. He was famed as a *pathaka* of the *Bhagavat* which he appears to have regularly carried out at the Vrindavan residence of Rup. As noted earlier, he is also the only Goswami who did not produce any texts or formally initiate a follower, which suggests that he was the only major

Vaishnava figure not to leave behind a *shakha*. Judging by available reports, he was also an expert cook, a quality found also in the poet Narahari Chakravarti.

Gopal Bhatta was the son of Venkata Bhatta and the nephew of Prabodhananda, one of the several biographers of Chaitanya. It is reliably known that while on his tour of south India, Chaitanya met the family at Srirangam where he had camped for about four months of the *caturmasya*. According to *Bhaktiratnakara*, the family of Venkata Bhatta may have been Sri Vaishnavas who were persuaded by Chaitanya to accept Radha–Krishna worship. There is some reason to doubt this theory for a late 17th-century work by Manohar Das produced in Vrindavan by the name of *Anuragavalli* (a text in praise of Srinivas and his lineage, c.18th century) claims that Gopal Bhatta was initiated by a Vaishnava of the Sanaka (Nimbarka) *sampradaya*, a sect that also focused on the worship of Radha and Krishna. But be that as it may, there is every possibility of his hosts at Srirangam being impressed with Chaitanya's religious personality and the emotional intensity that he had brought to Krishna *bhakti*. For one, the theological presence of Radha would have been new to the Sri Vaishnavas. It is believed that Chaitanya instructed Gopal Bhatta to move to Vrindavan, a directive he had also earlier given to the Goswamis Lokenath and Bhugarbha even before he himself visited the site, as also to Rup and Sanatan. Prima facie, this points to the possibility of Chaitanya envisioning a religious movement that would surpass purely provincial base. Gopal Bhatta had already camped in Vrindavan by the time Krishnadas Kaviraj arrived, because, along with Raghunath Das, he appears to have been a major inspiration behind the *Chaitanya Charitamrita*. Gopal Bhatta was also the teacher of the highly successful Vaishnava leader and evangelist Srinivas Acharya.

In hindsight, the life and work of Gopal Bhatta may said to be representing the growing trend towards greater social orthodoxy and affirming the supremacy of the Brahmins. The ritual digest *Haribhaktivilasa*, which is generally attributed to him, projects the Brahmin as the ideal *dikshaguru*, capable of initiating *bhaktas* of all social ranks. The work also tends to circumscribe the religious or ritual rights of women and inferior *jatis*. Gopal Bhatta obviously survived Chaitanya since he is known to have expressed some anguish over the fact that his pupil Srinivas had opted to enter the life of a householder.

There is some biographical material on Raghunath Das Goswami, the only non-Brahmin among the Goswamis and Chaitanya's close follower at Puri. Along with Swarup Damodar, he is known to have served Chaitanya in the capacity of an *antaranga sevak*. The Gaudiya community believed that Chaitanya offered his personal *salgram sila* to Raghunath and the *gunjamala* that he habitually wore on his person. Seemingly, this would support the view that Chaitanya himself did not think that *smarta* rites or rules apply to Vaishnavas.

Raghunath Das was the son of a rich Kayastha landowner of Saptagram by the name of Goverdhana. Though married, he was disenchanted with the thought of settling down to a life of *grihastha*. It is reliably known that upon first approaching Chaitanya to lead him to a life of renunciation, he met with disappointment. At the time, Chaitanya identified such moods with *markat bairagya*, an urge for renunciation that had been synthetically and temporarily induced under the pressure of circumstances and, hence, was shallow or insincere at its core. Raghunath was thus advised to wait until the time when it might be relatively easier for his family to overcome or overlook his decision to renounce. This has significant parallels with the advice that Sri Ramakrishna Paramahansa would often give to young men who sought a life of *bairagya*. For one, he would discourage the oldest son or the only child in a family from accepting a life of renunciation for fear that, in such instances, *sanyas* would unjustly lead to neglecting one's duties to a wife, children, or aging parents. It appears as though Raghunath did await a more opportune moment to join his master at Puri, where he was to camp for about 16 years. He subsequently moved to Vrindavan after the deaths of Swarup Damodar and Chaitanya. His life at Puri was marked by extreme *bairagya*, denying himself all forms of bodily comfort and assiduously living on a starvation diet. It is said of him that at the end of the day he would feed himself on foul and rotten food that even stray cows had refused. Quite clearly, he did not expect such hardships to be extended to fellow Vaishnavas, for it was he who, at the behest of Nityananda, organized a *mahotsava* for Vaishnavas at Panihati, situated to the north of Calcutta, where invitees were fed on a delicious diet of yogurt and flattened rice.

Other than Rup and Sanatan, Raghunath Das is the only Vaishnava theologian of Goswami status who received personal instruction from

Chaitanya. Hagiographies record that the master conferred on him a set of interrelated instructions: never to hear *gramya katha* or ever utter them; to always meditate on the holy name of Krishna; and to devote one's life to the personal service of Radha and Krishna at Vraj. Raghunath Das was well tutored in Sanskrit and the classics. He was also an author of considerable repute. Among his better known works are *Danakelichintamani* (Verses in Praise of Radha and Krishna, c.16th century), a work based on the mythical sport of Radha and Krishna, *Gaurangastavakalpataru*, (an anthology of poems in praise of Chaitanya, c.16th century) and *Chaitanyashtaka* (eight verses attributed to Chaitanya, c.16th century), the latter two comprising verses in praise of Chaitanya. Legend also ascribes to him a *kadcha*, now regrettably lost. The *Chaitanyashtaka* carries interesting historical information on Chaitanya. The verses in this reveal how Chaitanya habitually wore a *kaupin* and an outer garment of *aruna* colour.

In Vrindavan, Raghunath Das lived and died at the Radhakunda.

Short Breath and Second Wind

By the close of the 16th century, the major Gaudiya Vaishnava leaders of Chaitanya's generation had passed away. Of the Goswamis, only Jiva lived to see the dawn of the next. Importantly enough, the movement never lost its momentum. The inspiration that had once been derived from the life and work of Chaitanya grew and proliferated in several ways, penetrating new spaces and cultures but also, quite significantly, winning new recruits from a variety of social classes. By the mid-17th century, Gaudiya Vaishnavism had managed to win over a sizeable section of the territorial aristocracy of Bengal, Odisha, and some states in north-east India, a class that had hitherto been known to be *shakti* worshippers. The patronage and support of the local ruling houses considerably expanded the Vaishnava constituency. The Malla rajas of Birbhum, who were converted to Vaishnavism by Srinivas Acharya, made it mandatory for the local population—largely comprising tribal communities—to worship Radha and Krishna. Fellow evangelists Shyamananda and Narottam secured powerful patrons in tribal Odisha and in the district of Rajshahi in east Bengal respectively. The Odiya work *Sunya Samhita* by Achyutananda claims that Chaitanya had no less than 12,000 followers in Odisha, though this was later affected by dissensions between Gaudiyas and the followers of five prominent proto-Buddhist Odiya figures collectively known as the Panchasakha. Closer to our time, the researches of Prabhat Mukherjee reveal that in Chaitanya's time, the average Odiya knew more about Gaudiya Vaishnavism than of the syncretic breed of Buddhist–Vaishnava ideology represented by the Panchasakha. Whereas he had heard of the *Chaitanya Bhagavata* by Vrindavan Das, he remained unaware of the fact that the Odiya Iswar Das had authored a work by the same name. During his tours of western India in the 1920s, Kshitimohan Sen discovered two Gaudiya *mathas* set up in Surat in Srinivas Acharya's time and heard Bengali Vaishnava *kirtans* being sung at Navasari and Bulsar at an institution run by one Nandalal Goswami of the Advaita lineage. The history of the Gaudiya settlements in Mathura–Vrindavan still awaits its historian but we have it on Bimanbihari Majumdar's testimony that he found 'Madrasi' devotees in Vraj speaking fluent Bangla. This was obviously not the case everywhere. Jnanendramohan Das's pioneering study of Bengali migration to upper India reveals how the Gaudiya Goswamis who settled in Jaipur under the patronage of the local ruling house progressively lost their Bengali identity, preferring coarse *bajra* chapattis to a diet rich in rice.

Some prominent Vaishnava families of Sylhet were able to convert the Hajong tribals of Mymensing and Sylhet and by the early 18th century, the ruling house of Manipur. King Bhagyachandra of Manipur was reportedly a disciple of one Ramnarayan Misra, a Vaishnava saint descended from one of Chaitanya's uncles settled in Dhaka Dakhin in Sylhet. Rajdhar Manikya of Tripura (who reigned from 1611–23), embraced Gaudiya Vaishnavism while two of his supporters also extended their support to the movement. Govinda Manikya (who reigned from 1658–60) went on a pilgrimage to Vrindavan and a still later figure, Birchandra Manikya, was instrumental in financing the publication of Gaudiya literature. It was also due to his intervention that Manipuri followers of Chaitanya could secure a safe presence in Nabadwip in the face of considerable hostility from the ruling family of Krishnanagar that originated with Raja Krishnachandra. By the late 17th century, Gaudiya Vaishnavism had penetrated Dhaka–Vikrampur. The initial thrust had come from Birbhadra's tour of eastern

Bengal, following which a disciple of Gadadhar Pandit set up a *sripat* at Pancasar. Colonial ethnographer James Wise noted that about 74 per cent of the local population worshipped Krishna in some form. In the district of Pabna, Gaudiya missionaries managed to convert fishermen of the Malo *jati*.

However, the greatest impact of the expanding Gaudiya movement was most visible in south and south-west Bengal. The successful spread of Gaudiya Vaishnavism for much of the late 16th and 17th centuries created a close knit community of believers, which, in turn, bred new structures of religious space. The creation of such new devotional space, in turn, led to considerable investment in local art and architecture, with upwardly mobile castes especially taking to the construction of temples and other religious institutions. In the 1960s, David McCutchion surveyed as many as 121 Vaishnava temples in Midnapore district alone, 64 in Bankura, 57 in Burdwan, and 55 in Hoogly compared to only four in Nabadwip itself. Evidently, this suggests that the social and religious base of Gaudiya Vaishnavism was shifting outwards in relation to its place of origin. More recent district-wise surveys of fairs and festivals held in west Bengal reveal the same trend: one such survey listed 116 Vaishnava fairs and festivals being held in Midnapore, 72 in Bankura, 33 in Birbhum, and 62 in Murshidabad. Even some 40 years earlier, there were over 600 villages in West Bengal alone which carried the name of Krishna or one of his several appellations. Commenting on the post-Chaitanya period, the historian Ramakanta Chakravarti was justly observed how 'slowly but surely, Vaishnavism became an essential element of the Bengali way of life'.

Also significant was the palpable transformation in the leadership of the movement. In the post-Chaitanya period, the most successful missionaries who operated in various regions of Bengal and adjacent territories were Narottam Thakur, Srinivas Acharya, and Shyamananda. Two of them were non-Brahmins, but did not suffer any disadvantages on that account. It is somewhat ironical though that while at one level this signalled the broadening social base of the movement, the method often employed to achieve evangelist goals was a conscious identification with Brahmanical culture. The Kayastha Narottam did indeed have Brahmin disciples, but this did not go unopposed. At an important Vaishnava congregation held in Kheturi (Rajshahi), no less a person than Birbhadra had to come to Narottam's rescue, ruling that notwith-standing his non-Brahmin status, he still qualified to be called a *dwija*, a title traditionally conferred on Brahmins. Shyamananda, who belonged to the inferior pastoral *jati* of Gopas, insisted on his followers putting on the sacred thread as a part of their initiation into Vaishnavism. Such ambiguities can be read in perceptibly opposite ways. On one level, the act of non-Vaishnavas putting on the sacred thread was a frontal assault on Brahmin privileges and yet, the very act of adopting the practice reflected an anxiety for securing upward social mobility. This was an attempt at reconstituting the social structure without seriously dislodg-ing accepted social norms. In colonial Bengal, thanks to the birth of new institutions and methods of social enumeration such as the census, social and cultural identities were even more sharply contested, drawing Vaishnavas and Brahmins in extended polemics over their respective social and ritual rankings. The Vaishnavas, incidentally, did not seek to overthrow the office of the Brahmin; they merely sought parity in status.

The lives and works of Narottam, Srinivas, and Shyamananda were obviously important enough to inspire several popular biog-raphies, of which *Narottam Vilas* and *Bhaktiratnakar* by Narahari Chakravarti, *Anuragavalli* by Manohar Das, *Premvilas* by Nityananda Das, Krishnacharan Das's *Shyamananda Prakash* (The Manifestation of Shyamananda, c.17th–18th century), and Gopijanaballabha Das's *Rasik Mangal* (a text in praise of Rasik Murari, c.18th century) are the best known. These accounts are not always reliable and yet they are useful source material for post-Chaitanya Gaudiya history.

Narottam was the son of one Krishnananda Dutta of Kheturi, a site about 13 miles away from the district town of Rajshahi in east Bengal. Some texts show him to have been born a few years before Chaitanya, but there are popular legends about how the pre-monastic Chaitanya, when on his tour of east Bengal, wistfully pointed to the coming of a new messiah from the east. This, no doubt, is an attempt at upholding the authority of a saint whose status and standing as a Vaishnava leader was consistently under some dispute. Even in his early life, Narottam is said to have revealed a strong attraction for the life of renunciation. Having fled home, he first camped at Kashi, from where he eventually moved to Vrindavan. Here, after patiently awaiting a call from the guru, he was initiated by Lokenath Goswami. It was in Vrindavan that he also met and lived in the close company of Srinivas and Shyamananda, who had both similarly arrived there in search of a spiritual initiation. In the context of Gaudiya evangelism, this event was to bear considerable significance.

According to the *Premvilas*, Narottam had 142 disciples of which as many as 58 were Brahmins. There is a popular legend to the effect that offended at such blatant violation of social conventions, the Brahmin community led by one Ganganarayan Chakravarti sought the intervention of the Raja of Pakkapalli (Paikpara). Predictably, however, even before they confronted Narottam himself, the entire opposition comprising learned scholars and *mahants* were humbled in a debate by his followers masquerading as common grocers and shopkeepers. This was a subterfuge that was evidently meant to demonstrate how deeply Narottam Thakur's learning and piety had taken hold of common people.

Narottam was a talented man with a keen sense of music. He is taken to be the founder of the Garanhati style of *kirtan* singing named after the Garanhata *paragana* in Rajshahi. This particular style was based on the classical Dhrupad style of the Vishnupur school of music. About 30 works are attributed to Narottam of which at least two—*Premabhaktichandrika* and *Prarthana* (Prayers, c.16th century)—are undoubtedly his, the latter especially famed for its spontaneous devotional sentiment. Narottam's theology reveals the increasing use of *manjari sadhana*, which we have discussed above. Quite typically, in one of his works, Narottam expresses a desire to be reborn as a woman in Vrindavan. Not surprisingly, therefore, he was one of the mainstream Vaishnava figures to be readily appropriated by the Vaishnava Sahajiyas with their penchant for esoteric sexo-yogic practices.

However, in the history of Gaudiya Vaishnavism, Narottam is best known for his capacity for organization. He was the moving spirit behind the congregation of Gaudiyas in Kheturi, an event financed by his cousin, Santosh Dutta. In hindsight, it is possible to argue that the idea of convening such a congregation was born in Vrindavan itself and under circumstances that required the smoothening over of ideological differences that emerged time and again between the Vaishnavas in Bengal and those in Vrindavan. It is just as likely that Kheturi also aimed at resolving differences that were internal to Vaishnavas in Bengal itself. It is difficult to date the event but there are ample indications of at least two such congregations being held at Kheturi. According to Ramakanta Chakravarti, one such congregation was held in 1576, or shortly thereafter, but this is too imprecise a lead on which to date an event of such importance. We also know from the work *Rasik Mangal* that Rasik Murari, the foremost disciple of Shyamananda, attended the festival. Now, Rasik Murari was born in the year 1590 and died in 1630 and therefore it looks quite probable that the festival that he attended was the second of the two festivals that were held in the early years of the 17th century. It is perhaps to this congregation that texts such as the *Premvilas* refer to in some detail.

The Kheturi festival proved to be important for several reasons. For one, it was indisputably the biggest Gaudiya Vaishnava congregation ever held in terms of attendance. The *Premvilas* and other contemporary texts inform us that there were as many as 29 important leaders from Khardaha alone including Jahnava Devi and poet Jnandas, an almost equal number from Nabadwip, nine from Santipur, and 37 each from Burdwan and Murshidabad. Several important decisions were taken at this festival. An image of Chaitanya was set up independently, but so also were five images of Krishna, each carrying a special name. Second, it was decided that henceforth Chaitanya would be worshipped in the *yugala* mantra used in Radha–Krishna worship, a decision that was clearly meant to affirm the theory of Krishna as the divine source of Chaitanya. On the other hand, Kheturi also launched the singing of Gaurachandrika, the practice of invoking the name of Chaitanya at the commencement of singing verses in praise of Radha and Krishna. Arguably, this was but a concession to Gaudiyas based in Bengal, most of whom were still fiercely loyal to the memory of Chaitanya. Kheturi was also a joyous occasion, as the Vaishnavas gathered there reportedly threw *phagu* at one another, replicating perhaps the celebration of Holi by Radha and Krishna in mythical Vrindavan. Jahnava Devi, often referred to as 'Iswari' (meaning goddess) personally took charge of cooking and feeding the devotees gathered. At the end of the festival, she reportedly left for Vrindavan.

Kheturi marked an easy and acceptable transition from a state of difference and distrust between Vrindvan and Bengal to that in which Goswami ideology palpably gained the upper hand. Srinivas is believed to have told Narottam that of the various Vaishnava theological centres in ethnic Bengal, three in particular had gained ascendancy: Kheturi, Jajigram, and Vishnupur, all of which, incidentally, were openly loyal to Vrindavan. Quite significantly, Kheturi also marginalized the community of Gadai-Gauranga and paid little heed to the ideology once associated with Nityananda. Although the Khardaha Vaishnavas were present in good numbers, they were now led by a leader who was keen to bridge the differences between Vrindavan and Bengal. By the 17th century, apparently, there was no pressing need for a more accommodative strategy for further recruitment. Narottam himself is known to have discouraged Vaishnavas from resorting to *panchopasana* which permitted an eclectic reverence to a collective of five Hindu deities. The Vrindavan Goswamis too increasingly frowned upon indiscriminate proselytization; Rup Goswami's *Bhaktirasamritasindhu*, in particular, advised greater caution with this. However, Narottam's overtures to Vrindavan by no means implied the visible slighting of the Chaitanya cult itself. He was perhaps the last great leader of that cult but alive to the new strategic concerns and changing requirements of the age.

In some traditions, Srinivas is taken to be Chaitanya incarnate and perhaps his Brahmin birth may have strengthened such perceptions. However, temperamentally and in his social life, Srinivas proved to be very different. First, he was a man of formal learning who could have easily taken to the vocation of a scholiast; the title 'Acharya' (meaning revered teacher) was conferred upon him at Vrindavan when he interpreted, to the satisfaction of everyone present, a verse from Rup Goswami's *Ujjvalanilamani* even better than Jiva had been able to do. Second, whereas Chaitanya abandoned a householder's life for *sanyas*, Srinivas moved in the opposite direction, marrying not once but twice. He had six children from these marriages. Of these, a daughter, Hemlata Devi, was to assume leadership qualities. His marriage, however, displeased his guru, Gopal Bhatta Goswami, and cost him the office of the priest to the Radharaman Temple in Vrindavan. However, going by a more pragmatic assessment, it is doubtful if Srinivas would have preferred to spend his life as a priest at Vrindavan to the munificence showered upon him by the Malla rulers of Birbhum.

This brings us back to the dramatic episode concerning the alleged theft of precious Vaishnava manuscripts at Bon-Vishnupur by men in the service of the local ruler, Vir Hamvir (who reigned between 1596

and 1622) and their recovery by Srinivas Acharya. The *Premvilas* narrates the incident along the following lines. Keen to propagate Vrindavan
theology in Bengal, Jiva Goswami had arranged for the transportation
of some precious manuscripts among which were *Haribhaktivilasa*,
the works of Rup, Sanatan and Jiva, and, reportedly, also *Chaitanya
Charitamrita* by Krishnadas Kaviraj. The task was entrusted to the three
young Vaishnava apostles—Narottam, Srinivas, and Shyamananda—
who accompanied the bullock carts carrying the manuscripts. The entry
of two bullock carts, apparently laden with goods, aroused the suspicion
of men serving Vir Hamvir, who himself lived by brigandage. Assuming
that the carts, escorted as they were by up-country sentries, contained
precious merchandise, the robbers looted them one night. On inspecting
the material so robbed, Vir Hamvir was quite crestfallen and seized by
remorse. Getting wind of the events, Srinivas then approached the local
court and, before long, won over the apologetic king, initiating him into
Vaishnavism. Vir Hamvir henceforth took the name 'Chaitanya Das'
and was even known to compose poetry, some of which are included in
Vaishnava anthologies. Importantly enough, his initiation did not lead
to his relinquishing his royal duties; on the contrary, as we have earlier
noted, the king used his royal powers to enforce a Vaishnava way of life
among his subjects. This was to meet with some ridicule from contemporary poets such as Vijay Gupta who bemoaned the exaggerated emphasis
on self-control and abstinence, turning the active and the vigorous to a
life of meekness and docility. It also emerges that such moves also met
with some cultural resistance from the local tribes who were reluctant to
give up their own established religious beliefs and practices.

As with many other events in Gaudiya Vaishnava history, it is difficult
to precisely date this event and there remain nagging doubts. For one, it
is difficult to believe that the manuscripts being so transported were so
numerous as to take up the space of two bullock carts. Second, if at all
the dramatic robbery did occur, it would have happened sometime after
1596. This date is borne out by two independent sources: Vir Hamvir's
accession to the throne and Srinivas's visit to Vrindavan. In all probability, Srinivas reached Vrindavan around 1591–2 and lived there for
roughly six years. Also controversial is the claim made by *Premvilas* that
upon hearing of the theft, a senile Krishnadas gave up his life in agony,
jumping into the waters of the Radhakunda. Modern researchers have

come to treat this episode as apocryphal. In the first place, it cannot be affirmed if the manuscript of the *Charitamrita* was among the manuscripts being transported; but even more importantly, we are not at all sure if the work had even been completed by then. It is now reasonably well established that the work was not finished until the early years of the 17th century, even though 1615—as suggested by Tony K. Stewart— appears to be late by at least a couple of years.

Srinivas, as we have noted, was initiated by Gopal Bhatta Goswami, but he was also fairly close to Narahari Sarkar who encouraged him to visit Vrindavan. There is a legend to the effect that it was Srinivas who cautioned Jiva Goswami about the growing 'menace' of *parakiya sadhana*, in which spiritual practitioners engaged in a form of esoteric mental worship which relied on the services of female co-practitioners. This, importantly, was premised on the extramarital relationship between Radha and Krishna, widely accepted in popular folklore and legend. Orthodox Vaishnavas, however, were quick to realize that operatively, such practices often went beyond the purely mental—especially among the numerous dissenting quotidian cults—and posed serious moral problems for genteel society. Jiva is believed to have responded to Srinivas's cautionary words by encouraging the greater dissemination of the work *Gopal Champu* which projected Radha and Krishna as married partners. Understandably, Sahajiya or quasi-Sahajiya works took a very different view of Srinivas and his ideology. The quasi-Sahajiya text *Karnananda* (a text in praise of Srinivas and his lineage, c.18th century) by Jadunandan Das was quick to note the Acharya's closeness to the Srikhanda Vaishnavas and naturally presumed that the Acharya himself too was a practitioner of *parakiya sadhana*.

A little known work called *Srinivasashakhanirupanam* (The Genealogy of Srinivas, c.18th century) lists 42 disciples of Srinivas, but more detailed lists are available in the *Premvilas* and the *Karnananda*. Srinivas himself organized festivals at Katwa and Srikhanda, the first in honour of Gadadhar Das and the second in honour of Narahari Sarkar. A third festival was held in Jajigram, in which a mandate was reportedly passed on scrupulously abiding by the Goswami reading of the *Bhagavat Purana*.

Shyamananda, the youngest of the three evangelists, was born into an influential Sadgop family in the tribal territories of Midnapore. He is taken to have been born in 1556 and died in 1630. He was initiated in early life by one Hridaychaitanya, belonging to the Nityananda lineage. This later became a contentious issue when he also sought initiation under Jiva at Vrindavan. This was contentious since, by convention, a man was allowed multiple *shikshagurus* but only a single *dikshaguru*. A 17th-century work called the *Abhiram Lilamrita* of Ramdas reports that the Mahantas of Bengal collectively raised their voice against this startling departure from practice. However, a still later work, *Bhaktiratnakar*, suggests that tensions were somehow overcome to the satisfaction of both parties. In hindsight, it might be observed that in his day, Jiva was too important a figure for the controversy to have lingered for long. It is no less significant that even as a Vaishnava recruit from a relatively inferior *jati* and from an area not particularly known as a Vaishnava stronghold at the time, Shyamananda's personal preference was still for Vrindavan and Jiva. In this instance, at least, the connection often drawn between the 'democratic' movement launched by Nityananda and the successful recruitment of marginalized tribes and castes is fraught with some problems of explanation.

Like Srinivas, Shyamananda accepted the life of a householder upon returning from Vrindavan and after his death, his three wives bitterly fought each other for gaining control of his movement which had rapidly expanded in Midnapore and neighbouring Odisha. The success of Shyamananda's movement owes much to the efforts of his chief disciple, Rasik Murari, also a man of aristocratic origins. *Rasik Mangal*, a hagiographical account of his life and work, lists 203 disciples, as against only 31 for Shyamananda. It is also important not to overlook the fact that *Rasik Mangal* pays respect not to Chaitanya, Advaita, Nityananda, or, for that matter, to the close companions Shyamananda, Narottam, and Srinivas, but to the six Goswamis of Vrindavan. This suggests that notwithstanding their closeness to the Goswamis, Narottam and Srinivas were not quite taken to be fully attuned to Vrindavan ideology by the Midnapore Vaishnavas. On the other hand, the Vaishnavas of central and south-west Bengal appear to have retaliated by ignoring Midnapore and Odisha as important centres of Vaishnava presence. This certainly appears to be the case with the well-known text, *Premvilas*.

The most significant development associated with the Shyamanandi movement was its open encouragement to neo-Brahmanism as a tool for upward social mobility. Initiated Vaishnavas were expected to put on the sacred thread and not surprisingly, the Kayasthas of Balasore in Odisha and some communities in Midnapore are known to have significantly improved their ritual status by taking to such directives. An even greater measure of success in this matter came in the colonial era. By the late 19th and early 20th centuries, Midnapore alone had a sizeable number of Shyamanandi Vaishnavas. In Vrindavan, it was widely rumoured that Shyamananda had come upon the anklets worn by Radha and over time, this alone led to the Shyamanandis wearing a distinctive sectarian mark on their body.

Jahnava Devi and Birbhadra

Of female saints in the Gaudiya tradition, we hear of Hemlata Thakurani, daughter of Srinivas Acharya, and Madhuri Devi, sister of the Odiya Vaishnava Shikhi Mahiti. However, such figures stand in no comparison to Jahnava Devi, Nityananda's second wife, who enjoyed far greater popularity and following.

Jahnava Devi seems to have led a double life. In Bengal, she was primarily known as the wife of Nityananda and the spiritual preceptor to some important Vaishnava figures of her day. These included her own stepson, Birbhadra, poets Jnandas and Nityananda Das, and Ramchandra of Baghnapara, grandson of Bangshibadan Chattopadhyay, an intimate follower of Chaitanya. Outside Bengal, she was taken to be a facilitator who brought Bengal and Vrindavan closer in terms of ideology and ways of life. Jahnava's rise to power occurred rather late in the day and of the well-known texts, only Jayananda's *Chaitanya Mangal* and Ishan Nagar's *Advaita Prakash* mention her. It is interesting that *Chaitanya Charitamrita* itself does not at all refer to her, notwithstanding the fact that as Nityananda's wife, she would have been an object of veneration for Krishnadas. Her absence from the *Charitamrita* also revives the question of just when this work came to be completed since Jahnava was certainly active only in the closing years of the 16th century. However, there are also doctrinal differences between her and Nityananda that cannot be overlooked. For one, she did not quite approve of the *sakhya bhava* of Nityananda and the institution of Gopalas, nor did the Gopalas collectively approve of her leadership. Only two of the

12 Gopalas (Parameswar Das and Uddharan Das) consented to remain disciples of Jahnava and only two attended the festival at Kheturi where she played the role of a leader. Differences also appeared between her and Birbhadra. Birbhadra did not accompany his stepmother on her tour of Vrindavan and Jahnava did not accompany Birbhadra on his tour of east Bengal. In all probability, Birbhadra absented himself from one of the two festivals successively held in Kheturi.

Quite significantly, Jahnava's rise to power coincides with perceptible shifts within Vaishnava *sadhana* and modes of worship. Rajballabha Goswami's *Murali Vilas* shows her instructing her pupil Ramchandra in *manjari sadhana*, which, by this time, had come to be widely accepted in Vrindavan. Following her death in Vrindavan, Jahnava came to be known as 'Ananga Manjari', a name that uniquely combined the roles of a *sakhi* (female companion to Radha) and a *manjari* (who was expected to serve the *sakhis* themselves). That apart, she is not known to have produced any theological novelty herself, unqualifiedly accepting all of Rup Goswami's *rasa shastra*. Her association with *manjari sadhana* and with Ramchandra, a man who exhibited Sahajiya influences, has led some scholars to speculate that Jahnava too may have made some overtures towards popular theological radicalism. On the other hand, Premdas's *Bangshishikha* (a text in praise of Bangshibadan Thakur, c.18th century), which first suggested this association, has been taken to be a non-Sahajiya work by no less a figure than Kedarnath Dutta Bhaktivinod, who clearly represented a conservative voice within Bengal Vaishnavism. Interestingly enough, the *Bangshshikha* strongly disagreed with the title of Ananga Manjari being conferred on Jahnava, arguing that such exalted spiritual status could not justifiably be given to a woman. Evidently, what was prioritized here was not the role that a woman could more naturally play as a female companion or servitor to Radha and the *gopis* but the prospect of a male mentally assuming the role or functions of a woman.

Birbhadra, also known as Birchandra was the son born to Nityananda's first wife, Vasudha, and remains one of the enigmatic figures in late Gaudiya history. Birbhadra had to have been born after 1533 since, somewhat in the manner of Srinivas, he too was taken to be an incarnation of Chaitanya. Historian Amulyacharan Sen writes that he was illiterate and far removed from the world of Vaishnava learning and scholarship. Birbhadra's power and importance was essentially drawn from his association with both Nityananda and Jahnava, even though he himself carried a powerful persona. There is reason to believe though that his relationship with his stepmother was not always cordial. Apart from inheriting some of his father's charisma and social radicalism which Jahnava herself did not approve, Birbhadra clearly disliked Ramchandra, Jahnava's foster son. Apparently, Birbhadra was reluctant to share his paternal seat at Khardaha with Ramchandra, which then forced the latter to set up a rival theological centre at Baghnapara. As its very name suggests, the area may have once been overrun by tigers.

Like his father, Birbhadra married and raised children, one of whom—Ganga Devi—appears in late Gaudiya texts. At the second congregation in Kheturi, as we have earlier noted, Birbhadra was to dramatically uphold the *dwija* status of Narottam. He argued that in the case of a Vaishnava as pious as Narottam, the sacred thread, rather than being worn externally, was an invisible but integral part of his body itself. Prima facie, it would seem as though Birbhadra did believe in Vaishnava piety potentially overcoming differences in social status for he once whipped Gatigovinda, the son of Srinivas Acharya, for speaking pejoratively of the 'Shudra' status of Raghunandan, the nephew of Narahari Sarkar. Apocryphally, though, his fame rests on recruiting 1,200 *nedas* (literally shaven head) and about the same number of *nedis*, in all probability male and female practitioners from some form of corrupt Buddhism, into the Gaudiya fold.

Given his departure from social conventions, it looks quite ironical that Birbhadra insisted on getting his daughter married to a *kulin* Brahmin and even more so for objecting to the Baidya Raghunandan of Sripat Srikhanda taking to the ways of the Brahmin Gatigovinda. Such contradictory qualities are consistently visible in Birbhadra. Though otherwise claiming to be a true Vaishnava, he was also known for his ostentatious habits. When visiting the house of a disciple, he would travel on horseback. Once, during a festival held in his honour at Malda in north Bengal, a disciple reportedly gifted him two horses and 2,000 silver coins. His successful missionary tour of Dhaka is described in some detail in the work *Nityananda Prabhur Bangsha Bistar* (The Genealogy of Nityananda). There is an interesting story that narrates how Birbhadra was able to use his magical powers to persuade the local ruler to part with a block of beautifully polished granite out of which were carved three beautiful Krishna icons named Nandadulal, Vallabahji, and Shyamsundar. Of the three, the second possibly reveals some Pushtimargi influence, while the third, installed at Khardaha, continues to be highly revered to this day by Gaudiya Vaishnavas and even those standing outside that community.

For much of the latter half of the 16th century, the world of Gaudiya Vaishnavism acquired both an expansive material base and ideological vibrancy. The *sadhana* and the scholarship of the Goswamis attracted considerable attention from both ruling houses and common people at large. It is a reasonable guess that just as Nabadwipa itself had once become the centre of classical learning for Hindus even outside the province of Bengal, so did Vrindavan as a Hindu pilgrim site of pan-Indian importance and the centre of a new scholastic culture that was not limited to the study of Vaishnava scripture. Few libraries in north India could have rivalled the one put together by the Goswamis over time. This joining together of piety and culture may have resulted from the belief that the recovery of Vaishnavism as a religious or cultural system was best effected at a site with which it was also mythically associated.

5 Chaitanya in His Times and in Ours

The religious history of Bengal abounds in very many important figures of which, however, two have acquired iconic status: Krishna Chaitanya and Sri Ramakrishna. While separated in history by about 400 years, their lives and teachings reveal remarkable parallels, though obvious differences are not hard to detect. In good measure, the importance of such figures springs from the fact that they represent the two most popular and significant religious traditions to have been historically experienced in Bengal: Vaishnava devotion and Sakta-Tantric praxis respectively. Both appeared at critical junctures in Bengal's provincial history and were instrumental in reviving a religious culture in some crisis. Some texts and traditions attach much value to the fact that in both instances, this recovery or revival of Hindu religious life and culture occurred under conditions of alien rule—in the first instance under Turks and Pathans and in the second, British colonialism. Such perceptions were to prove creative and powerful since the abundant literature that celebrates the two lives also associates them with the liberation of a nation under siege, the freeing of a people hitherto held captive by alien and oppressive ways of life.

At least two well-known authors and commentators from the colonial period—Brahmo poet and songwriter Trailokyanath Sanyal alias Chiranjiv Sharma (1868–1915) and writer–scholar Girijashankar Raychaudhuri (1885–1965)—have advanced the claim that but for Chaitanya's unleashing of a religious revolution, creating a new social space, and bringing an easy and unencumbered spiritual life to the common people, the Bengali–Hindu community would have failed to survive the 'tyranny' of Islam and the Muslim ruling classes. The Bengali literary historian Dineshchandra Sen proudly designated a certain period in the history of medieval Bengal as 'the age of Chaitanya' and similarly, some others—for instance, D.S. Sarma (1883–1970)—have identified the advent of the renaissance in modern India not with the coming of the new episteme from the West or the birth of the English-educated intelligentsia, but with the old-world charisma of the barely literate Ramakrishna. In 1885, the Viswavaishnava Sabha, an institution founded by modern followers of Gaudiya Vaishnavism, launched the Chaitanya era that stood in competition not only with the Gregorian calendar but also with the Saka era and the Vikram Samvat. It is also important not to overlook the fact that both Chaitanya and Ramakrishna have inspired movements now with a global presence and which, in interesting ways, have reworked older Indian traditions in order to effectively meet modern day challenges.

In keeping with the tendency common in colonial Bengal, there were recurring attempts to draw analogies between the life of Chaitanya and those of well-known contemporaries from Europe with whom Anglophone Hindu Bengalis had grown sufficiently familiar. A similar strategy was employed to read developments occurring in India in the light of those occurring in early modern Europe. The Indian Civil Service member Romesh Chandra Dutt (1848–1909) believed that there occurred in 16th-century India an 'Enlightenment' and found Chaitanya to be its most remarkable product. In his introduction to Kavi Karnapur's *Chaitanya Chandrodaya Nataka*, Indologist Rajendralal Mitra found Chaitanya's social message comparable to that of the protestant reformer Martin Luther. Dineshchandra Sen was quite upset with French Indologist Sylvain Levi's (1863–1935) unwillingness to favourably compare Chaitanya to the Buddha, hastening to add that as a Bengali it was but natural for him to reveal a passionate and even fanatical devotion to Chaitanya. Sisir Kumar Ghosh, the author of a multi-volume biography on Chaitanya, argued that in Chaitanya's time, converting to Vaishnavism required the courage and conviction comparable to abandoning parental Hindu society in favour of the rebellious Brahmos of the 19th century. On one occasion, such enthusiasm drew him into a controversy with Mahadev Govind Ranade (1842–1901) and Sakharam Ganesh Deuskar (1869–1912), well-known figures from contemporary Maharashtra who strongly resented Ghosh's insinuation written in the *Vishnupriya Patrika* (1895) that it was the Brahmin Chaitanya's grace that transformed Tukaram, allegedly a 'lower-caste' man, into a pious and respectable poet–singer. Interestingly, whereas in our colonial history there soon developed considerable friction between social reformers or agitators and those who were political, this was strategically glossed over when it came to projecting the historical standing or relevance of Chaitanya. Only a few years after its foundation, the Indian National Congress refused to allow the Social Conference to hold its annual meetings at venues chosen by the Congress itself. The Congress argued that meddling with social issues only divided the nation, whereas focusing on the common enemy, the British colonial state, unified it.

Such formulations do not appear to hold true for 19th-century readings of the life and message of Chaitanya. Several anti-colonialist political mobilizers who had little claim to either understand or advance the cause of social reform chose to read Chaitanya primarily as a social reformer. In this category, we may include Surendranath Banerjee (1848–1925), Sisir Kumar Ghosh (1840–1911), and, to an extent, even Bipinchandra Pal (1858–1932). Speaking with the advantage of hindsight it could be argued that their interest in so projecting Chaitanya originated in the politically informed dual premise: first, that the act of social reform by Chaitanya ipso facto represented the weakening of established hierarchies of caste, leading to the greater enfranchisement of the lower classes into a growing community with a shared common ideology; second, such work contributed towards the formation of a nascent nationhood, even in Chaitanya's day. In this instance, evidently, the expanding frontiers of a social community were made to overlap with those of the political. Closer to our time, Nirad C. Chaudhury found Chaitanya to have uniquely revolutionized contemporary Bengali life, significantly shaped its present, and futuristically prepared it for greater challenges. A closer scrutiny, however, puts such presumptions under considerable doubt.

Chaitanya's Religion

In the 1920s, among the many significantly revisionist claims that he made, Melville T. Kennedy ruled out the possibility of Chaitanya being a social reformer. This offers an interesting contrast not only to modern-day Indian perceptions—which, under the spell of a nationalist rhetoric, saw him as an active crusader against caste—but also to conclusions arrived at by colonial ethnographers who had no cause to be influenced by such rhetoric. W.W. Hunter, for example, argued that but for its opposition to caste, which he deemed to be progressive in character, Chaitanya's movement was essentially passive in character and even reactionary in its advocacy of abstract meditation and asceticism. Serious reflection on both these statements will, however, persuade us to qualify these in some important ways. First, Hunter seems somewhat off the mark in suggesting that Chaitanya was actively opposed to the institution of caste but no less so in claiming that the Gaudiya movement was quintessentially marked by an emphasis on abstract meditation and asceticism. We shall briefly return to the question of Chaitanya's attitude to caste; for now suffice to say that Hunter's characterization collapses the distinction between the two broad levels of Vaishnava religious life, one that was essentially based on high textuality and complex processes of mental cognition and the other that was more spontaneous, emotionally charged, and largely free of textual references. As with other religious orders, the Gaudiyas too were divided into renouncers and householders; and renunciation itself came in two forms: that which was purely mental and that which combined mental acts of renunciation with the physical and the formal. Even the famed Goswamis of Vrindavan were not ascetics in the strict sense of the term, even though they led lives of reclusion and extreme renunciation. Many important Gaudiya leaders of both Chaitanya's generation and thereafter, among which the names Nityananda, Srinivas, and Shyamananda readily come to mind, travelled in the opposite direction, giving up the life of *sanyas* to turn into householders. It would also be an error to think that Goswami theology was unqualifiedly accepted by the ordinary Vaishnava, even more so if, within our definition of the 'Vaishnava', one were to also include Boshtoms and Bairagis, quite numerous by count, but following a social and religious life perceptibly different from that found among upper-caste Vaishnavas. For the former it was not so much the religious ideology that mattered as the new social space that was created, somewhat by default.

Kennedy's thesis poses a different kind of problem. First, we are left wondering just what he might have meant by the terms 'reform' and 'reformer'. Going by Kennedy's reading, if one was to take Chaitanya to be a 'religious reformer', it would be only reasonable to ask just what elements of contemporary Hindu religious ideas or practice did he wish to reform. There are a variety of problems embedded in the conceptual categories of the kind Kennedy chooses to use. For one, it could be quite justly claimed that 'reform' and 'reformers' are terms of quite recent origin which ill-fit Chaitanya and his times. In modern Hinduism, the act of reform was a perceptibly self-conscious act that originated in new concepts of history and society. To put it briefly, the urge to 'reform' was derived from a greater emphasis on human initiative and instrumentality and nurtured by new notions of time, in some ways quite untypically Hindu. By the mid-19th century, the Western-educated Hindu had begun to reckon with linear notions of time as against the circular or cyclical, which was traditionally known to Brahmanism, and took positivist history itself as the chronicle of linear and irreversible human progress. A deistic world view, which is what influenced the earliest 'reformers', spoke of an idle Creator God who took no further interest in his creation, leaving the responsibility entirely to human mediation. Generally speaking, the Hindu-Brahmanical view of time and change was cosmic, not historical, and it really did not allow ample space for human initiatives to regulate human life and existence. Pre-modern Hindu culture did acknowledge the need for change but did not see it as born of human will and agency. Hence, while an urge for changing or correcting irrational ideas or practices did constitute a part of pre-modern Hindu self-understanding, this was not necessarily understood as an act of self-conscious reform. To the best of my knowledge, there are no terms in the pre-modern vernaculars of south Asia that truly capture the essence or import of the terms 'reform' or 'reformer' as these came to be understood in modern India. It was the modern historian or scholar who called figures such as Kabir, Nanak, or Chaitanya 'reformers' or their work as 'reform', not their contemporaries.

Kennedy's error also appears to lie in associating Chaitanya with institutionalized reform, whether social or religious in nature, resting on a carefully prepared agenda and distinctly new notions of an anthropomorphic, man-centred universe. Organized work aiming at human welfare and a this-worldly concern for a democratic brotherhood appear to be less his aims when compared to the ultimately transcendental and other-worldly nature of Krishna worship. Chaitanya was neither a preacher nor a publicist and, in hindsight, his true aim appears to have been to regroup men and women united by some common but elementary religious principles and practices. It was more a religious phenomenon that he created, rather than religious ideology.

Contrary to what is often claimed, Chaitanya did not specifically aim at contesting popular, non-Vaishnava religious traditions. A common perception appearing in several texts is that he helped combat Sakta-Tantrik 'excesses'. The Jagai–Madhai episode, to which we have referred before, is sometimes seen as the typical Vaishnava chastisement of Sakta debauchery. On the contrary, though ecstatically absorbed in Krishna worship and solely preaching Krishna Bhakti, Chaitanya showed an ecumenical reverence for other Hindu deities and divinities. In Nabadwip itself, while dramatically re-enacting the sports of Krishna in the company of his followers, he is known to have paid respect to the Sakta-Tantrik Goddess. In later life, too, when touring south India, Odisha or Mathura–Vrindavan, he stopped by important religious shrines, paying reverence to a host of local deities, gods, and goddesses falling outside the Vaishnava pantheon. *Chaitanya Charitamrita* reports Chaitanya specifically instructing Sanatan never to speak ill of other divinities or religious traditions. This is quite consistent with *Chaitanya Bhagavata*'s warning that one who made an arbitrary distinction between divinities or avatars was the true sinner.

In his classic history of medieval Bengal, Jadunath Sarkar listed the following positive changes produced by the Chaitanya movement: decline in Sakta-Vamachar practices and the drinking of intoxicating spirits, the spiritual advancement of the lower classes, a greater prestige for Sanskrit, and closer links between Bengal and the rest of India. None of these, however, directly followed from Chaitanya's work even when he is cast in the image of a crusading reformer. On the contrary, Chaitanya and his religion had to put up with a degree of hostility from local ruling houses. We are reliably informed by Diwan Kartikchandra Ray in his *Khitish Bangshabali* (A Genealogy of the Ruling Family of Nadia, 1875)—an account of the ruling house of Krishnanagar—that Maharaj Krishnachandra (who reigned between 1728 and 1782), a powerful potentate of 18th-century Bengal, though otherwise indifferent towards Vaishnavism, remained so hostile to the Chaitanya cult itself that images of Chaitanya had to be hidden from public view in his kingdom.

The problem with delineating the religious views of Chaitanya is that other than the *Ashtaka* (eight verses) that he is said to have composed, all else comes to us through tendentious reporting in hagiographies. In the case of *Chaitanya Charitamarita*, there are practical difficulties in separating the views of Krishnadas Kaviraj from those of Chaitanya. Thanks to some careful textual comparisons made by modern scholars, we now know that much of what Kaviraj claims to have been the words of Chaitanya himself are actually reproductions from works later produced by the Goswamis or from other sources. Thus, Chaitanya's instructions to Sanatan Goswami are partly taken from *Brahma Samhita* and the *Krishna Karnamrita* (Devotional Verses in Praise of Krishna, c.pre-14th century), texts discovered by Chaitanya in the south, and the rest from the following works: *Laghubhgavatamritam* (short commentary on the *Bhagavat Purana*, c.16th century) and *Bhaktirasamritasindhu* by Rup Goswami, and *Sarvasamvadini Tika* (commentary on the six *sandarbhas* by Jiva Goswami, c.16th century) by Jiva Goswami. Similarly, Chaitanya's exchange of views with the Vedantin Prakashananda is essentially derived from Jiva's *Tattvasandarbha* (Discourses on Metaphysics, 16th century). Modern scholarship has found Krishnadas Kaviraj also guilty of misrepresentation; whereas he claims Ramanand Ray's 'Ramananda Samvad' (a dialogue that took place between Ramananda and Chaitanya) to have been derived from Swarup Damodar's *Kadcha*, Bimanbihari Majumdar has sufficiently established this to be a plagiarized version of Kavi Karnapur's *Chaitanya Chandrodaya Nataka* (14 verses from Act VII). The *Samvada* also uses the works of Rup and Sanatan and Krishnadas's own *Govindalilamrita*. The 'Ramananda Samvad', however, is not wholly a fabrication. We know from extant sources that some years after the dialogue took place, Chaitanya's emissary to the south, Pradumnya Brahmachari, requested Ramananda to repeat it to him.

It could be argued that on one level, passing off Goswami theology as Chaitanya's own is essentially not misreporting since the source of that theology was none other than Chaitanya himself. On close reflection, even this does not quite seem to be the case. In his *Vrihatbhagavatamritam* (extended commentary of the *Bhagavat Purana*), Sanatan Goswami does not acknowledge having received direct theological instruction from Chaitanya; rather, the work projects Chaitanya not as the Supreme Deity identifiable with Krishna as Nabadwip devotees would have it, but only the ideal Krishna devotee. It is quite noticeable that Goswami literature is, on the whole, somewhat reluctant to acknowledge Chaitanya as a direct source of Gaudiya theology. Other than making *namsakariya*, the Goswamis seldom refer to his personal religious views or teachings. In some cases, as in Rup's *Ujjvalanilamani* or Jiva's *Danakelikaumudi* (a play on the love sports of Radha and Krishna), even this is conspicuously absent. Raghunath Das Goswami, who knew Chaitanya quite intimately at Puri, devotes to him only three verses out of 20 in his *Stavabali* (Prayer Verses, c.16th century). The Gaudiya ritual compendium, *Haribhaktivilas*, has no special instructions for worshipping Chaitanya, for, in theory, there could not possibly be two Bhagavatas (Supreme Lord), as Krishna already occupied that place.

Chaitanya's *Ashtaka* (also called the *Sikshastaka*), which appears in the Antya Khanda (Part III), Chapter 20 of *Charitamrita*, makes for interesting reading. Of these, those listed as numbers five to seven are particularly significant. Verse number five, perhaps the best known of these, advises Vaishnavas to inculcate certain religious–ethical values and attitudes, not dogma. The ideal Vaishnava is expected to be as humble as the blade of grass which is perpetually trampled by foot or as tolerant and forbearing as the tree which does not protest the fact that its products are exploited so widely and gratuitously. Further, he is expected to respect those who have not been treated respectfully, but, above all, always engage in singing the praise of the Lord. In verse number six, Chaitanya is seen declaring that he coveted neither riches nor mass following or beautiful worldly objects; all that he sought was the grace of Krishna. The following is a loose translation of verse number seven which is especially interesting:

> O son of Nanda, I have always been your slave but caught up in the whirl-pool of successive births and deaths. Rescue me from this (condition) and treat me as a mere particle of dust of your lotus-like Divine Feet. (*Chaitanya Charitamrita*)

It is worth noting how in this verse, Chaitanya appears to be associated with two qualities which are conventionally not associated with him: first, the palpable desire to serve Krishna not in the capacity of a lover (*madhurbhava*) but that of a servant (*dasyabhava*). This suggests that the idea of an androgynous Chaitanya anxious to savour Radha's love for Krishna was an idea later foisted upon older sentiments of *dasyabhava*. The other feature, no less surprising, is the desire for attaining *mukti* or salvation, to be altogether freed of the karmic cycle of births and deaths. It is commonplace that even an ordinary Vaishnava, much less Chaitanya himself, preferred perpetual Bhakti to *mukti*. Verse eight (numbered 10 in some versions) resorts to the idea of feminization but with a difference.

> I know of no other God but for Krishna: whether he holds me in his embrace or kicks me away from Him is entirely His Will. He who is involved in amorous play with many women is free to treat me the way he likes. Regardless of what he chooses to do, he will always remain my God. (*Chaitanya Charitamrita*)

The above evidently represents the gendering of devotion and reinforces a woman's servitude to a male God. We are not even sure if this typically indicates Chaitanya's 'Radhabhava' or that of an ordinary *gopi* (*gopibhava*) since this alone does not exhaust the range of moods associated with Radha in Vaishnava conventions which include jealously, pique, and offended anger. An argument often offered in explanation is that 'Radhabhava' in Chaitanya was primarily associated with his life in Puri. This casts some doubt on the chronology of events, for Chaitanya is said to have revealed his identity as Radha to Ramananda Ray very early into his ascetic life (sometime in 1510). Going by the account in the *Charitamrita*, this was also the only instance of Chaitanya himself revealing the moods of Radha to a devotee (Ramananda); the others seem to have come upon this by inference.

It is quite evident from a perusal of our sources that Chaitanya did not make Bhakti contingent on the observance of everyday rites and usages. The socially or ritually inferior man was just as entitled to the adoration of Krishna as the respected Brahmin. Krishna worship admitted no distinction between men and women on the basis of their birth; the distinction, if any, was between those who worshipped Krishna and those who did not. On the occasion of the first Rath Yatra at Puri (1512) that he attended, Chaitanya described himself as a faceless *bhakta*, stripping himself of all social or vocational identities.

> I am not a Brahmin, nor a Kshatriya king, not even a Vaishya or Shudra. I am not a *brahmachari* nor a *grihastha*, a *yati* or a man who has retreated to the final stage of *vanprastha*. I am but the servant of those who look upon themselves as Krishna's servitors. This Krishna, the paramour of the *gopis*, represents Universal Bliss, the very Ocean of Supreme Delight.
> (*Chaitanya Charitamrita*)

In Chaitanya's perception, sincere devotion to Krishna constituted the primary foundation of faith. There is a particularly instructive episode recorded in *Chaitanya Charitamrita* about Chaitanya's encounter with a Brahmin at Srirangam, who was devotedly reciting verses from the *Bhagavad Gita*. This Brahmin lacked learning and could not comprehend the import of what he was reciting; by his own admission, he was simply following the orders of his guru. And yet, tears of ecstasy flowed down his cheeks as he read aloud descriptions of the rival armies facing each other in the battlefield of Kurukshetra. When asked just what had produced in him such fits of ecstatic delight, the Brahmin said that even as he carried on with the narration, he could clearly see the warrior Arjuna mounted on his chariot and the Lord Himself standing beside him as the charioteer. Chaitanya comforted the Brahmin by calling him an *adhikari*, a man who truly deserved to be blessed by such godly vision. There are other interesting episodes too of Chaitanya discouraging his followers from taking to a routine religious life. Murari Gupta narrates the instance of a follower named Shuklambar Brahmachari who remained dissatisfied even after completing a tour of major pilgrim spots such as Mathura and Dwarka. To this, Chaitanya is said to have responded by pointing out that even jackals were known to roam around in those places; the important thing, therefore, was to arouse Krishna Bhakti within oneself.

Murari also informs us that Chaitanya was displeased with his following a strict spiritual regimen and that he had little regard for adhering to a religious life governed by the *shruti*. While engaged in a theological debate with Madhvite ascetics at Udupi, Chaitanya is known to have ruled that those who followed the paths of Karma (ritual activism) and Jnan (gnosis) could not possibly be *bhaktas* or devotees. Prima facie, this appears to run counter to the tendency gathering momentum since the 14th century of bringing about a creative fusion of Jnan and Bhakti or, for that matter, the concept of *jnankarmasamuccaya* by virtue of which the pursuit of ritualism had been integrated with a path of speculative meditation. Chaitanya's *paramaguru*, Madhavendra Puri, as we may recall, was by initiation an *advaitin* and yet strongly drawn to Krishna Bhakti. Chaitanya himself may be said to have inherited the mystical qualities of Madhavendra for whom dark bellowing clouds in the sky would evoke thoughts of Krishna himself. Sridhar Swami, the author of the most popular commentary on the *Bhagavat Purana* and to whom Chaitanya remained consistently loyal, was both an *advaitin* and a worshipper of Narasimha, an emanation of Vishnu. Without there being some overlap between Jnan and Bhakti, it would have been practically very difficult for Chaitanya to attract several Dasnami monks, as he is known to have done. The Goswamis, however, were quick to seize upon the progressive reconciliation between the two streams. In his *Bhaktirasamritasindhu*, Rup Goswami appears to question the possibility of salvation following from spontaneous grace alone. In this view, Bhakti itself was a *sadhana*, a spiritual praxis that required some degree of self-disciplining. After him, the philosophical works of Jiva aimed at attaining a synthesis that may be aptly called 'Vaishnava Vedanta'.

Three other popular conceptions about the life and work of Chaitanya need to be suitably qualified. First, that the religious democracy such as the one Chaitanya tried to bring about was matched by an open disregard for social conventions; second, that Chaitanya himself put a philosophical gloss to his religious teachings; and third, that he had no capacity for organization and leadership. The third view was first put forward by Sushil Kumar De and has been contested quite often since, not without justification. In the earlier discussion on the life of Chaitanya in its historical context, we have noted how Chaitanya was successfully able to pick on the right men to carry out chosen missions or tasks without seeming to put much thought and effort to matters. There is, thus, the instance of Chaitanya sending two of his early acquaintances, the Goswamis Lokenath and Bhugarbha, on a reconnaissance mission to Vrindavan, well before he himself visited it. Modern scholars have similarly read tactful intentionality behind Chaitanya's recurring imperious and, at times, violent mood swings while at Nabadwip.

Going by extant sources, Chaitanya himself was no less instrumental in propagating the idea that he was indeed an incarnation of Krishna. It is quite plausible that such declarations were made quite deliberately and not in a state of unmindful religious ecstasy. Taken together, *Chaitanya Bhagavat* and Murari Gupta's *Kadcha*, the most authoritative sources on Chaitanya's early life in Nabadwip, list at least six such instances. Further, Vrindavan Das lists 10, Murari seven, Krishnadas Kaviraj four, Lochandas five, and Jayananda two instances of Chaitanya placing his feet on the heads of his devotees and followers, some of whom (like his mother and Advaita Acharya) were much older in age. This would have constituted gross violation of social conventions but for the possibility that Chaitanya was performing these acts only to instil in his followers faith and confidence in his leadership which was, in some ways, trying to counter both Brahmin orthodoxy and hostility from the state. Some hagiographic works also reveal a very audacious and immodest Chaitanya, instructing his followers to set up his images and icons to be revered and worshipped; reportedly, he did so to his wife, Vishnupriya, Pandits Gadadhar and Gauridas, and to one Jadav Kaviraj of Kulai village in Burdwan. The idea of the residents of Nabadwip anxiously awaiting the arrival of a redeeming avatar and Chaitanya's eventually being seen as one fits rather well into this argument. Also, this is worth contrasting with his attitude in Puri or Vrindavan where he was reportedly embarrassed by people regarding him as an avatar. It may be reasonably argued that by the time he visited or was actively settled at these sites, Chaitanya had already won a huge following and had been widely proclaimed as the Divine descended on earth. There is an interesting episode that occurred while Chaitanya was visiting Mathura and Vrindavan, narrated by Krishnadas. Some local people who claimed to have seen strange lights appear on the surface of the water in Kaliya Lake, a site connected to the miracle plays performed by the child Krishna, proclaimed that these indicated yet another avataric descent of Krishna. Ironically enough, Chaitanya is believed to have dispelled their belief with the argument that this was some hallucination and that Krishna could not be expected to incarnate in the age of Kali. Arguably, this somewhat shakes the very foundation of Goswami theology.

Historian Amar Nath Chatterjee has suggested that Chaitanya inaugurated the doctrine of *acintyabhedabheda* (inconceivable unity in difference) around the year 1510, which we are more apt to associate with the likes of Jiva Goswami. The year 1510, as we have earlier noted, coincides with Chaitanya entering the life of *sanyas*, but more importantly, in order to settle on this date, one has to assume not only his thorough grounding in metaphysics but also the penchant for putting a philosophical gloss on his teachings, neither of which Chaitanya appears to have had. Krishnadas Kaviraj, as is only too well-known, claims that on his tour of southern India, Chaitanya strongly disputed the philosophical positions of both the non-dualists at Sringeri Math and the dualists at Udupi. We also know from Chaitanya's reported meeting with Prakashananda at Kashi that the former firmly rejected Sankara's theory of *vivartavada*, which took creation to be merely an appearance and not a real act of transformation (*parinamavada*) occurring in the Brahman. This looks unlikely, to say the least. In all probability, this was more Kaviraj's personal reading of the matter than faithful reporting. That the Bhakti theology of Chaitanya was ill at ease with Sankara's reading of the Creator and creation cannot be doubted, but this need not have arisen in some acute philosophic disputation. Bhakti dualism is very likely to have quite spontaneously reacted to the monistic views of the *advaitins* which dissolved the hiatus between the subject and object of devotion.

Here, I cannot think of a better parallel than the one located in the life of Sri Ramakrishna himself whose dissatisfaction with non-dualism was not tantamount to an outright rejection, but was practically tied to the question of *adhikaar*: natural predispositions and the state of spiritual preparation in an individual. Here, again, the discomfiture with Advaita was not born of any philosophical debate or disputation but sheer spontaneity. I am willing to hazard the guess that Chaitanya's unhappiness with a monistic view of the world resulted not so much from philosophical reflection as from the instinctive anxiety of the devotee keen to practically separate the adoring human self from the transcendental object of adoration. There is ample reason to believe that Chaitanya had no formal training in philosophical studies or disputation, even though he may have been personally anxious to acquire this. If biographer Murari Gupta is to be believed, Chaitanya issued stern warnings to his disciples against taking to speculative discourses; it is only apt to recall that veteran Advaita Acharya was assaulted for persisting with the path of gnosis.

It is important nevertheless not to overlook persistent attempts at reconciling the views of Sankara with those of his subsequent critics. The researches of Bimanbihari Majumdar refer to an anonymous, late medieval tract by the name of *Sarvasampradaya Bhedasiddhanta* (a text determining the differences between various Vedantic sects or communities, n.d.) which attempts to locate meeting points between mutually conflicting philosophies and shows Chaitanya to be a follower of the *dvaitadvaita* philosophy of Nimbarka. Admittedly, the philosophy of *bhedabheda* which, like that of *dvaitadvaita*, juxtaposes duality with non-duality, was known to the followers of both Nimbarka and Bhaskara, and the term 'achintya' too had been adopted earlier by Nimbarka himself. On the other hand, sources do not reveal any significant influences on Chaitanya's life from Nimbarka sources, though such a lack may have also resulted from sectarian rivalry.

It is quite evident that one way or another, every critic of Sankara had to operate within the framework of reference set by him and Chaitanya's differences with the non-dualist view of Reality is but a continuation of an older trend. After him, it was not so much the *bhakta* who tried to address the problems raised by the non-dualist, but the non-dualist who tried to synthesize Jnan and Bhakti—meditative cognition and emotive devotion. The *advaitin*-turned-*bhakta* Madhusudan Saraswati, believed to have been a native of Bengal itself, best exemplifies this trend. It is important also not to lose sight of the fact that as a school of thought, pure dualism did not really develop after Madhva.

In his *Chaitanya Charitamrita*, Krishnadas Kaviraj appears to have captured, in essence, Chaitanya's instinctive dislike of both pedantry and philosophical disputation. Krishnadas sounds extremely unhappy at the fact that hitherto philosophers had merely engaged themselves in polemic, always seeking to substitute the views of others with their own. This took them away from reflecting adequately on the *parama karana* (first cause). Krishnadas concludes, in a manner that perhaps echoes Chaitanya's own sentiments, that he would rather go by what the *mahajans* had to say. The perpetually warring schools of Hindu philosophy had no practical value for him.

Finally, it is only apt to recall that in his ascetic days at Puri, Chaitanya fully endorsed the importance of abiding by social conventions, in respect of both himself and his followers. He supported Haridas and Sanatan, both of whom considered themselves to be ritually polluted and made the decision to not enter the Jagannath temple. Personally, he shunned even the smallest indulgence, disappointing many a follower who had lovingly brought him gifts. Also, he appears to have been extremely careful about following the conduct expected of a *sanyasi* and in this matter, relying greatly on the vigilant Swarup Damodar. Chaitanya would agree to be hosted by a non-Brahmin but always ate food cooked by a Brahmin. In Puri, he lived with the 'Shudra' Chandrashekhar but dined with the Brahmin Tapan Misra. The only exception he is known to have made was when he agreed to be fed by a Sanodiya Brahmin of Vrindavan, notwithstanding the fact that the Sanodiya Brahmin community was taken to be ritually inferior, despite being Brahmins. In this instance, Chaitanya agreed to make the exception on account of the fact that this particular Brahmin had once served the venerable Madhavendra Puri. This raises an interesting issue with regard to the ritual life or status of a *sanyasi*. In colonial India, the Vedantin monk Swami Vivekananda (1863–1902) is known to have defended his defiance of all taboos related to food and drink arguing that as a *sanyasi*, he ceased to be governed by rituals and social rules. The interesting issue at stake here is whether in the intervening historical period, rules of *sanyas* had appreciably changed or whether there were different standards applicable to the Brahmin Chaitanya and the Kayastha Vivekananda.

That the devotee need not be known by his *jati* standing was a view that Chaitanya insisted upon, to be repeated by Ramakrishna in his time. But this also conceals certain realities. For one, given the fact that a life of devotion was typically associated with the householder, it is quite safe to presume that this is also where rules of *smarta* ritual commensality applied the most. In the context of Gaudiya Vaishnavism, the *Haribhaktivilas* was a text for the domesticated Vaishnava, not the renouncer or the ascetic. Ramakrishna, too, warned his devotees that laxness with social rules or ritual conduct was permitted only for the *jnani*, not the *bhakta*. With both Chaitanya and Ramakrishna, devotional life within the community of devotees who shared a religious emotion was only a part-time release from the structured, routine-bound, and ritualized quality of everyday life. Spiritual democracy was hardly, if ever, meaningfully complemented by the social.

Sexuality, Women, and Chaitanya

In his classic study of biographical sources on Chaitanya, Bimanbihari Majumdar claims that there were at least 16 women among the followers of Chaitanya and Jayananda's *Chaitanya Mangal*, as we have noted, adds another 27. Since these women cannot always be identified by names, it is difficult to guess what their exact relationship may have been Chaitanya. It is quite possible that among the 16 identified by Majumdar were fig-ures such as Malini Devi, wife of Sribas, and Sita Devi, wife of Advaita, who were respectful of Chaitanya or the Vaishnava way of life without formally converting to Vaishnavism. For instance, we do not know if they sought initiation, which would be an acceptable clue as to whether or not they were formally counted among the Gaudiya Vaishnavas.

In hindsight, it would appear as though Chaitanya related to women in various ways, depending upon their age or social standing. At the residence of Sribas in Nabadwip, Chaitanya insisted that his wife and children pay formal obeisance to him, and it may be assumed that Malini Devi was present at some of the dramatic enactments carried out by Chaitanya and his close followers. At Santipur, he was feasted by Sita Devi and at Puri, hosted by the wife of Vasudev Sarvabhaum. There is no reason to believe that these women did not make themselves visible before Chaitanya, as might have been the case with other male strangers. Presumably, therefore, Chaitanya had no inhibitions about socializing with women considerably older in age. Especially from the *Chaitanya Bhagavata*, we also know of the pranks that the young Viswambhar played upon girls of a comparable age, tormenting and teasing them in various ways. The problem, apparently, was with adult women, especially at an age when Chaitanya himself had attained adulthood. Vrindavan Das tells us that the young Viswambhar would scrupulously avoid even sighting a *parastree*, far less fall into a conversation with them. This may have partly arisen in a growing sexual self-awareness but equally due to the Brahmanical fear and disdain for female sexuality. Arguably, this has little to do with his accepting *sanyas* which occurred only towards the closing years of his life in Nabadwip. While the Srikhanda Vaishnavas led by Narahari Sarkar made him the subject of explicit erotic attention from the local women of Nabadwip, Chaitanya himself is not known to have returned such feelings. It has been suggested by scholars such as Tony K. Stewart that Chaitanya almost instinctively turned away from women and was actually troubled and embarrassed by them.

On the other hand, we have some reason to believe that even after several years into his *sanyas*, rather than 'turn away' from women, Chaitanya feared that he had still not fully conquered his own sexuality. *Chaitanya Charitamrita* reports his confessing to a devotee, Pradyumna Misra, that the temptations of the flesh still affected his mind and body, subsequently adding that it was but a rare man who would remain unaffected by the sight of a woman. We have noted how Chaitanya remained quite sensitive to public perceptions of his life and teachings as a *sanyasi* in Puri. There is the instance reported by Krishnadas Kaviraj of how Chaitanya had grown very fond of a young boy who happened to be the son of a beautiful widow. Perhaps this became the subject of some local gossip since, having got wind of this, Swarup promptly advised Chaitanya to stay away from the boy for fear of a public scandal. Especially if Chaitanya's chastisement of Haridas Junior had preceded this episode, there was all the more reason for him not to be accused of following double standards. Haridas Junior, it may be recalled, had been permanently banished from the presence of Chaitanya for simply having begged some rice from a woman and ended his life at Prayag, having failed to win the forgiveness of Chaitanya.

And yet, there was something rigidly ascetic about Chaitanya's later life. Though many are inclined to dismiss *Govindadaser Kadcha* as a reliable source, there is something interesting that this text reveals. In the course of his meeting with Ramananda Ray, Chaitanya is reported to have told him that a man's passionate longing for a woman was not love and that true love would arise only in a state of mind which made no distinction between a man and woman. Some sub-traditions within Vaishnavism have chosen to call this state *sahaja* or natural.

This brings us to the related issue of just how popular and dissenting cults read or understood the religious world of Chaitanya. Many of these, especially those originating in the district of Nadia, took Chaitanya to be their founding father. Two instances that readily come to mind are those of the Kartabhaja sect—who take their founder, Dulalchand, to have descended from Krishna and Chaitanya—and the Balahari sect, who have conferred a similar status on their founder, Balaram. Sudhir Chakravarti, who has spent a lifetime researching popular cults in Bengal, tells us that even Muslim Marfati Fakirs equated Chaitanya with Allah/Rasul. In popular perception, Chaitanya proved attractive to such dissenting cults since he represented a strong challenge to Brahmanical orthodoxy. Historically speaking, however, this view is more romantically inclined than real. It would be more accurate to say that in the post Chaitanya era, many quotidian social groups read the life and teachings of Chaitanya as tendentiously as upper-caste members within mainstream Vaishnavism. To reiterate a point made before, the former were drawn far more powerfully to the seemingly rebellious idea of detaching one's caste standing from the question of religious entitlement than by theology alone. They also found some hope and legitimacy in the fact that a Brahmin himself (Chaitanya) should uphold this social rebellion, at least in principle.

There is a common tendency in academic scholarship and outside, to identify linkages between the *parakiya sadhana* of mainstream Vaishnavism—essentially a mental exercise but which could involve a female ritual partner—and tantric *deha sadhana* of the Bauls, Fakirs, and Sahajiyas based on sexo-yogic practices. Prima facie, it would seem as though dissenting and deviant popular cults drew upon the laxness and ambiguities underlying mainstream Vaishnavism and interpreted these to their own advantage. There are many Sahajiya tracts that portray not only Chaitanya himself but some of his closest followers such as Narahari Chakravarti, Paramananda Puri, Swarup Damodar, Pundarik Vidyanidhi, and Jagadananda Das as active practitioners of Sahajiya *sadhana*, albeit concealed from public view. Bengali literary scholar Ahmed Sharif, writing in the *Bangla Akademi Patrika* (1964), found Chaitanya himself to be one such practitioner. A recent study on Chaitanya (Tuhin Mukhopadhyay's *Lokayata Chaitanya*, 2014) confirms this perception. The view that Chaitanya may have been bisexual in his habits does not seriously challenge this perception since sexo-yogic practices could, apparently, also be practised between two people of the same sex. It is also well-known that Sahajiya tracts have similarly viewed pre-Chaitanya figures such as Jayadev, Vidyapati, Chandidas, and Lilasuka, each of whom has been associated with a designated female ritual partner. With regard to Chaitanya specifically, reference is often made to an incident that occurred in Puri. Reportedly, when invited to a meal by his host Vasudev Sarvabhaum, Chaitanya consumed a quantity of food that would have sufficed to feed as many as 10 to 12 men put together, at least that was the view of an eye witness, Amogha, the son-in-law of Sarvabhaum. In Krishnadas Kaviraj's account, on hearing Amogha complain thus, Sarvabhaum's wife is said to have cursed her daughter, Shati (Shashthi?) to a widow's life, for she could not bear to have an honoured guest such as Chaitanya treated so disrespectfully. However, Bimanbihari Majumdar tells us how a Baul acquaintance of his narrated a radically different version of the same story. In this version, the curse was provoked not by Amogha's rudeness but the suspicion that he was beginning to view with jealousy Chaitanya's secret liaisons with his wife, Shathi, in *yugal sadhana*. This version of the story also occurs in the Sahajiya tract *Chaitanyaprematattwa Nirupana* (A Discourse on the Theology surrounding Chaitanya, n.d.). Predictably, Majumdar found this interpretation utterly ruinous of social norms.

And yet, taking such appropriation or ascriptions at their face value tends to overlook some important doctrinal and psychological differences between mainstream Vaishnava practices and their popular variants. For one, Gaudiya Vaishnavas and Sahajiyas understand love and lust (*prem* and *kama* respectively) quite differently. For the Gaudiyas, the difference was qualitative, as between iron and gold; for the Sahajyas, this was not quite so. Rather, through an alchemic process which is taught only to the initiated, *kama* progressively turned into *prem*. Sahajiyas, furthermore, have no gods and for them, Radha–Krishna are but abstract principles to be mentally realized, not deities to be externally worshipped. Unlike what is done in *manjari sadhana* of the Gaudiyas, Sahajiyas do not seek to vicariously serve Radha and Krishna; on the contrary, they create or reconstitute a meditative body that makes it possible to feel their com-bined presence in them.

It would be an error if we assume that the idea of Chaitanya leading a secret sex life emanated from the Bauls, Sahajiyas, or other dissenting cults alone. Jayananda, though never a part of the Gaurnagari group of Narahari Sarkar, would have us believe that even when Chaitanya was in Nabadwip, women of virtually all social classes called upon him in the dead of the night and would pleasure him, assuming the mood that *gopis* had once adopted towards their paramour, Krishna. On the other hand, both *Chaitanya Bhagavata* and Kavi Karnapur's *Mahakavya* state that on the night immediately preceding his accepting *sanyas*, Chaitanya was in the company of Gadadhar. An anonymous verse in the anthology *Gaurapadatarangini* refers to Chaitanya as the *grihastha* and Gadadhar as the *grihini*, a relationship which early *padabali* poets such as Murari Gupta and Sivananda Sen also endorse. In his *Amiya Nimai Charit*, Sisir Kumar Ghosh describes Gadadhar occupying Vishnupriya's place and massaging Chaitanya's feet. In *Chaitanya Charitamrita* too, Gadadhar is referred to as Laxmi and Pandit Jagadananda as Satyabhama, the wed-ded wives of Vishnu and Krishna respectively.

Not all quotidian cults took to the Vaishnava ways of life or specifi-cally to the teachings of Chaitanya. In the late 19th century, the Matua cult was a notable exception. Historian Tanika Sarkar also narrates the case of the Balakdasis, a rural cult that principally included peasants, petty traders, artisans, and fishermen. When compared to the Gaudiyas, the Balakdasis appear to have adopted a more realistic and pragmatic strategy, assuring devotees of tangible benefits following from an unflinching devo-tion to the cult and its leadership. Thus, boatmen were assured of a safe passage through turbulent rivers, peasants from failing crops, and, more generally, protection from ill health and disease. Anthropological research reveals how peasant and tribal communities preferred to go by a religion that yielded the coveted results. Surajit Sinha's study of the Bhumij tribal communities in Chota Nagpur reveals how the local population preferred a Sahajiya practitioner over a Gaudiya preacher of the Nityananda clan. While the latter preached a somewhat abstruse doctrine, the former also taught the secrets of prolonged sex. At least for rural cultures or communi-ties, the Gaudiya insistence on devotion for the sake of devotion (*ahetuk*) does not appear to have carried much appeal.

Chaitanya himself had little to do with the two controversies that affected the Gaudiya community after him. First, there was the recurring debate over whether Radha's relation to Krishna was *parakiya* or *swakiya*. Was Radha the wedded wife of Krishna or the wife of another man with whom Krishna had developed an illicit relationship? From the perspective of *rasa* theory, doctrinally important to Gaudiya theoreticians, both aesthetic pleasure and the passionate fulfilment of love could be better derived not from sanitized relationships but from the wilful abandonment of social conventions and structures. There is a popular Sahajiya story which narrates the tale of two lovers who fell out of love once wedded. In substance, even Gaudiya theology agreed with this view. In some Bengali traditions, Radha was even taken to be Krishna's maternal aunt, thereby implying both scandalous promiscuity and incest. It is generally believed that Goswamis Rup and Jiva were persuaded to switch their preference from *parakiya* to *swakiya*, following considerable resentment among Vaishnavas in Vrindavan, especially those outside the Gaudiya sect. However, the supporters of *parakiya* appear to have grown stronger with the advent of early 18th-century theoreticians such as Viswanath Chakravarti, a resident of Vrindavan, and his Odiya pupil, Baldev Vidyabhushan. The doctrinal aspects of this issue were debated twice successively at the court of Jaipur in 1719 and 1723, but apparently with no practicable solution. Clearly dissatisfied with this turn of events, Raja Jai Singh Kachwaha of Amber sent an emissary, Krishnadev Sarvabhaum, to Bengal in the hope that he might be able to establish the *swakiya* position there. However, as available evidence reveals, Krishnadas was defeated by a team of local scholars headed by one Radhamohan Thakur, the guru of Maharaj Nanda Kumar, who was later to compile an early Vaishnava anthology, the *Padamritasamudra* (An Anthology of Vaishnava Verses, c.18th century).

Chaitanya himself had no reason to be embroiled in this debate, for his intensely ecstatic 'Radhabhava' would more strongly postulate a *parakiya nayika*. His position, it might be quite justifiably argued, comes alive in a song by the modern Bengali poet Kazi Nazrul Islam (1899–1976), in which Radha reminds Krishna that the *viraha* that separates them was not confined to one life but doomed to remain in perpetuity.

Baldev Vidyabhushan was implicated in yet another controversy concerning the issue of a formal affiliation for Chaitanya Vaishnavas.

The Kachwaha ruler, Jai Singh, was keen to assume the position and posture of a righteous Hindu king at a time when Mughal authority was visibly on the wane. So he insisted that the Gaudiyas bring about some self-discipline by affiliating themselves with any one of the traditionally acknowledged four Vaishnava *sampradayas*—Sri, Rudra, Sanaka, and Brahma, associated with Ramanuja, Vishnuswami, Nimbarka, and Madhva respectively. Perhaps he was also persuaded by rival *sampradayas* who had the Raja's ear. This required Gaudiyas to produce an independent commentary on the *Brahma Sutra* (a fundamental text on the metaphysics of the Brahman in sutra form, 5th century BCE–3rd century BCE), establishing their own philosophical position. Up to that point in time, the Goswamis had resisted the idea of an independent commentary since they took the *Bhagavat Purana* itself to fulfil that necessity. All the same, Baldev's decision to affiliate the Gaudiyas to the Madhva *sampradaya* is surprising, to say the least, on account of visible doctrinal differences separating the two. For one, the Madhavites were plain dualists as against the *bhedabheda* position of the Gaudiyas, but even otherwise, they paid no attention to Radha. Even assuming that this affiliation was more strategic in nature than doctrinal, we are still not clear as to what strategic advantages this might have brought to the Gaudiyas. The Madhvas, after all, are not known to have wielded any special influence at the Amber court. The decision is all the more surprising on account of the fact that while on the tour of south India, Chaitanya himself is reported to have contested the philosophical position of the Madhvas at Udupi. On the other hand, it would be useful to remember that such an affiliation had been earlier suggested by Kavi Karnapur in his *Gauraganoddesdipika* and that Baldev himself had been a Madhva follower in his early life.

The Colonized Bengali and Chaitanya

When seeking to explain the continued appeal of Chaitanya and his teachings in colonial India, the dominant thesis today is that this was but a function of colonialism itself and the visibly altered social and intellectual environment that it produced. Such explanations rightly draw attention to the typically Evangelist–Orientalist–Colonialist perceptions of Chaitanya, of the larger religious world of Vaishnavism, and to the discursive influences that these produced in the minds of the Western-educated Hindu intelligentsia in Bengal, for whom a convenient and popular shorthand is the term *bhadralok*. This discourse established certain views about Vaishnavism and Chaitanya which proved hard to shake off, since these readily met certain contemporary discursive needs.

By the late 19th century, there was a growing appreciation of Vaishnavism as a religious system in comparison to other faiths of indigenous origin such as Saivism and Saktaism. John Beames (1837–1902), writing in the journal *Indian Antiquary* (1873), found it to be 'a great improvement on the morbid gloom of Siva worship, the colourless negativism of Buddhism and the childish intricacies of ceremonies which formed the religion of the ordinary Hindu'. Subsequently, Sir Monier Monier-Williams (1819–1899) found Vaishnavism to be the only religious system that possessed the 'elements of genuine religion', for in his perception 'there could be no true religion without personal devotion to a personal God'. Sir Monier's judgement was, in good measure, determined by his own religious convictions, for he was also to write quite condescendingly about how—notwithstanding signs of superstition and hideous idolatry—Vaishnavism came closest to (Protestant) Christianity and hence, was the only religion capable of laying claims of being the 'real' religion of Hindus. This stands in some contrast to the unqualified vilification of Vaishnavism by the early missionaries in ethnic Bengal as, for example, by William Ward (1769–1823). A third related idea, also articulated by Sir Monier, was that a god such as Krishna was most required in India for he clearly evinced an interest and sympathy with the mundane and the suffering. In Indian writings of the period as well, Krishna does often emerge as a playful, compassionate, less demanding god. In an important study, historian Krishna Sharma draws our attention to how some Orientalist scholars, particularly Horace Hayman Wilson (1786–1860), wrongly took Bhakti as an undifferentiated system of beliefs and practices, equating it typically with the *saguna*, emotive *bhakti* of Chaitanya.

From such discourses, it might be argued that it was also possible to derive two other influential and enduring tropes: first, the thesis of an unmitigated degeneration and 'decline' within the world of Bengal Vaishnavism and second, the propensity to separate Chaitanya as an exemplary religious leader from the movement that grew around him and after him. Evangelists, Orientalists, or colonialist ethnographers had praise for Chaitanya but a strong dislike for his spiritual successors, particularly for the social world of post-Chaitanya Vaishnavism which they took to be tainted by corruption, moral laxness, and promiscuity among lower-class recruits, as well as ecclesiastical tyranny imposed by an upper-caste religious leadership. In his two-volume work, *Bharatvarshiya Upasak Sampraday* (The Theistic Communities of India, 1871, 1883), the quasi-Brahmo author and educationist, Akshay Kumar Dutta (1820–1886) even anticipated W.W. Hunter's ethnographic observation that degenerative Vaishnavism in Bengal was entirely a post Chaitanya phenomenon.

In an influential work published very recently (Varuni Bhatia's *Unforgetting Chaitanya*, 2017), the significance attached to Chaitanya in colonial Bengal is sought to be mapped on two related and yet palpably different registers: the romantic–nationalist and the religious–reformist. In both cases, Chaitanya's life and teachings are seen to be crucial for the 're-imaginings' of Bengal and of India that was to constitute the emerging *bhadralok* rhetoric in the 19th century. It was thus that Chaitanya was identified with the quintessential upper-caste Bengali, whether in terms of his speech patterns, food habits, or sartorial preferences. Arguably, this helped the 'recovery' of an older and exemplary cultural icon and rescued the naively remiss Bengali from the sins of collective amnesia. On a related level, he was taken to be the quintessential social and religious reformer who disabused his countrymen of a blind faith in gross superstition and non-egalitarian practices. For the reformist *bhadralok*, this amounted to imagining a longer and more continuous history of reformism by reading back into a prominent religious figure from the past but more importantly, to restore agency for the colonized themselves. In 19th-century Bengal, several members of the Hindu intelligentsia were heard saying that Indians had to give back to the West in equal measure what they had taken from it. In Swami Vivekananda's perception, an advanced knowledge of material civilization that had been learnt from the West had to be reciprocated by India's spiritual excellence; for Vaishnava author and publicist Sisir Kumar Ghosh, it was more specifically a matter of answering Christ with Krishna.

Bhatia also makes two other interesting points about how *bhadralok* appropriation of Chaitanya and Ramakrishna, occurring in and around the same period, differed subtly in some respects. First, whereas the life and teachings of Ramakrishna appeared discursively useful and attractive to this class as the 'other', Chaitanya was constructed in the mirror image of the *bhadralok* themselves; and second, while Ramakrishna's appeal lay essentially in his identification with the pre-modern world of innocence and folk culture, Chaitanya was seen carefully steering a middle course between the 'high' culture of Sanskrit scholasticism and the 'low' tradition of folk religion.

Its intrinsic merits notwithstanding, there remain certain conceptual and methodological problems embedded in Bhatia's formulation. While the continuing appeal of Chaitanya and of the Vaishnavism he preached could well be explained in the light of the heuristic categories Bhatia employs, such categories nevertheless appear to be largely valid for the specific community of the Western-educated, politically sensitized Hindu intelligentsia of colonial Bengal. In my earlier study of Ramakrishna and his urban devotees in colonial Calcutta, I have argued that while the preaching and parables of Ramakrishna were often twisted out of their contexts by some of his politically self-conscious *bhadralok* followers, this does not also explain his popularity with a wide cross section of visitors and devotees, not all of whom would have been drawn to an anti-colonialist rhetoric. I have argued instead that they were attracted to the saint for a great variety of motives, some of which were purely existential. It is important also to acknowledge that the social and cultural category of the *bhadralok* is itself sufficiently amorphous or ill-defined to be represented by the English-educated alone. To me, its social constituency appears to be undoubtedly larger and certainly growing to also include intermediary castes who had also begun taking to English education or even the non-English-educated gentry of which the rural Brahmin would certainly be an important component. Within the world of colonial social ordering itself, it would be hard to imagine a Western-educated Hindu holding public office but denied the status of a *bhadralok* simply on account of his not belonging to the upper-bracket castes Brahmin, Baidya, or Kayastha.

A typical instance which readily comes to mind is that of Deputy Magistrate Adhar Lal Sen, a man belonging to the ritually inferior *jati* of Suvarnavaniks but a close friend of the Brahmin Bankimchandra and among Ramakrishna's well-known devotees. An important limitation within current studies related to the social and intellectual history of colonial Bengal is precisely the failure to engage with the class that was semi-literate, not located in the urban metropolis of Calcutta and yet a part of the power structure that visibly determined the functioning of daily life in villages and *mufassil* towns. It would be an error to imagine that in colonial Bengal, the fate of Gaudiya Vaishnavism was in no way influenced by these classes. More importantly though, within the framework of a work such as the present one, the history of Gaudiya Vaishnavism has to be equally explained in terms of the pre-colonial times not familiar with European theories on egalitarianism or of the burgeoning nationalist sentiment. At this point, it would be worth asking just what led Muslim poets and scribes of Sylhet and Chittagong, the Bauls, Fakirs, or Sahajiyas spread more spatially throughout Bengal to speak so effusively of Chaitanya and of his religion or, for that matter, for several respectable people to volunteer for a life of poverty and mendicancy. Of the numerous Vaishnava saints and *mahants* listed by Haridas Das in his biographical sketches, most lived in a state of self-denial and penury. Lokenath Goswami, to whom we have referred often before, had to sell off all his family assets before commencing that journey.

The problem with Bhatia's categories is also that, at times, they split open into mutually incongruent segments. Thus, the compounded category of 'religious–reformist' would rarely hold true for a Vaishnava individual or for a designated class of Vaishnavas. Within this complex conceptual category, there would appear to be reformers who were not religious enthusiasts and religious enthusiasts who did not quite take to institutional reform. In the former category we may put the school teacher and political worker from Barisal, Aswini Kumar Dutta (1856–1923). Dutta was initiated by Bejoykrishna Goswami (1841–1899) of the Advaita lineage and yet his *Bhakti Yoga* (1897) is essentially a set of moral instructions delivered to his students, emphasizing caution in food habits and male continence. In the latter category one may include both Sisir Kumar Ghosh and Bipinchandra Pal. Ghosh and Pal spent a good part of their lives in political work and journalism; both also had Brahmo antecedents. But here, the similarity ends. Ghosh, unlike Pal, was not formally initiated into some form of Vaishnavism, even though he contributed substantially to its propagation, even composing some *padas* of his own under the signature Balaram Das. However, unlike

Ghosh, Pal's interest lay not so much in specifically representing the Vaishnavism of the kind taught by Chaitanya but to situate his life and teachings within the broader, resurgent Hindu cultural identity, trying to ideologically combat the Christian West. Pal produced several articles and at least two important works in this genre: *An Introduction to the Study of Hinduism* (1908) and a work published posthumously, *Europe Asks: Who is Krishna?* (1939). Importantly, Pal exhibits none of Ghosh's penchant for an emotively charged Bhakti. It occurs to me that he is indeed the first and, perhaps, the only quasi-Vaishnava theoretician for the Gaudiyas in colonial Bengal to write in English and interpret the deity Krishna not in the light of traditional Vaishnava canon but Hegelian philosophy. In Pal's understanding, deeply influenced as it was by Hegelian idealism, the absolute realized itself in and through the world-process. Interpreting the theology of an androgynous Chaitanya, he was to write thus: 'The Enjoyer goes out of Himself to the object of His Enjoyment and taking it up, He comes back to Himself—to be Himself and to fulfil Himself.'

Bhatia's formulation needs to be qualified in two other respects. First, the work of 'reform', as determined by her, is internal to Gaudiya Vaishnavism alone, as one might typically find in the work of Kedarnath Dutta Bhaktivinod. Bhaktivinod was primarily concerned, as were some other Vaishnava spokespersons of the time, with the weeding out of 'spurious' Vaishnavas, and his reformist efforts established new social and religious hierarchies and new structures of power instead of eliminating such structures entirely. In substance, Dutta's work took Bengal Vaishnavism back to a renewed veneration for the upper-caste guru instead of dispensing with this office altogether. This is perceptibly different from the general reformist discourse of the 19th-century *bhadralok*, shared by Brahmos and Hindus alike, and which, under the influence of Anglican Protestantism, frowned upon the offices of both the ritualist and the guru. Second, there is the fact that by the 1890s, 'reform' itself—whether in its passage through a legislature controlled by 'alien' and 'unsympathetic' bureaucrats or championed by non-Hindus such as Behramji M. Malabari (1853–1912)—came to be viewed with deep suspicion by the politicized Hindu intelligentsia. Quite significantly, the question of social legislation itself came to be linked to the growing demand for greater Indian representation in legislature. In 1890–1, upper-class Hindu society in Bengal arose in near revolt against introducing even minor legal amendments to the age of consent, even drawing some ire from reformer and philanthropist Iswar Chandra Vidyasagar (1820–1891) who took this to be unduly interventionist. Vivekananda found initiatives of reform as taken in contemporary India to altogether overlook 'grass root problems' and prove wantonly 'destructive' of the social order. By the close of the 19th century, both reform and the reformer were visibly under some cloud.

There is little reason to doubt that for some *bhadralok* ideologues, reading political messages into the life and teachings of Chaitanya, however tendentiously framed, was symptomatic of a new self-understanding. Inasmuch as cultural resources of the past had to be tactfully employed to reinforce the present, there did not appear to be as comparable a figure as Chaitanya, who could be creatively integrated into contemporary needs. We have earlier noted how episodes from Chaitanya's life—as, for instance, his combative encounter with the Muslim Kazi of Nabadwip—were given contemporary political meanings. However, this tends to overlook the fact that the valorization of Vaishnava religion and culture in the larger context of a growing nationalist rhetoric was not always contingent in acknowledging the mediating role of Chaitanya. While Ramakanta Chakravarti claims a direct co-relationship between a growing nationalist discourse and a weakening criticism of Vaishnavism or of Chaitanya, there is good reason to argue that a certain species of contemporary *bhadralok* writing remained uncomfortable with ideas and values associated with both.

Perhaps the most important exception here was Bankimchandra himself. Bankim was associated with a Vaishnava family and even his popular fiction abounds in characters who take to Vaishnava devotional singing. Importantly, however, Bankim also invokes at some important places a deity that resembles the warrior Krishna more than the playful pastoral hero of Vrindavan. In the novel *Anandamath* (1882), the valiant *santans* who seek to overthrow oppressive and unjust rulers, sing the glory of the four-armed Vishnu, the slayer of the wicked demons, Madhu and Kaitabha. The same novel critiques Chaitanya for spreading an enervating sentimentality and unmanliness in men expected to engage with the enemy in open combat. The theory associating the Chaitanya cult with effeminacy appeared in diverse contemporary and near contemporary sources, sometimes with ironical results. Tagore, who disapproved of the excitable and hysteric sentimentality in popular Vaishnavism was himself critiqued for aiding and abetting it. Vivekananda once warned his favoured disciple, Sister Nivedita, to stay off the Tagore family (read Rabindranath) for fear of spreading 'erotic venom' among people who actually needed to be awakened by the martial call of the bugle, not put to sleep by the soft sounds of the *khol* or the *kartal*. In his *Banglar Itihas* (1914, 1917), archaeologist and epigraphist Rakhal Das Banerjee (1885–1930) strongly supported the thesis of Vaishnava effeminacy, only to be repeated more recently by Mayadhar Mansingh in his history of Odiya language and literature (*Odiya Sahityer Itihas*, 1962). Interestingly enough, Sisir Kumar proves something of an exception here. In an article that first appeared in *Sri Sri Bishnupriya Patrika* in 1893 and now appended to his *Amiya Nimai Charit*, Ghosh admits that his first response to the teachings of Chaitanya was that its effusive sentimentality better suited the woman rather than the man. From this position, however, Ghosh appears to have progressively transitioned to a devotional culture heavily suffused with sentimentality. In his quasi-dramatic work, *Kalachand Gita* (1888), of the several characters who seek the grace of Krishna, only Sajalnayana (literally, the woman with welling tears in her eyes) attains Him. It is not at all improbable, as Bhatia argues, that through his writings, Sisir Kumar was able to forge linkages between a nationalist rhetoric and a devotional tradition. On the other hand, there is not enough evidence to claim that the Vaishnava devotional community proved to be an inspirational and effective model for nationalist integration.

The life and teachings of Chaitanya was a subject that frequently appeared in the modern Bengali press; these were also a matter of animated discussion among some contemporary social and religious groups as for instance, the Derozians, Brahmos and Indian Christians.

Some of the positive assessments of Chaitanya and his religion came from Derozians. Thus, Kissory Chand Mitra (1822–1873) and Shoshee Chandra Dutta (1824–1885), both products of the Hindu College, wrote in the *Bengal Magazine* (1872) and *India Past and Present*

(1884) respectively, to claim that this religion was indeed a new idea in Hinduism that repudiated caste and did not insist on renunciation. However, there were also more critical voices. Bholanath Chunder (1822–1910), also from this college and born into a Suvarnabanik Vaishnava family, found the public obsession with Krishna worship to be incompatible with the intellectual reputation that Bengal as a province or the Bengalis as a people carried: 'On the streets of Calcutta,' he complains, 'there are more images of Krishna and the emblems of Sita than perhaps the whole length of the Doab—and this in Bengal which is at the intellectual leadership of India.' Chunder's extensive tours of north India took him to Mathura and Vrindavan, enabling him to leave behind an absorbing, if also a somewhat puritanical, account of Vaishnava life in that region.

The reaction of early Christian evangelists to Chaitanya and Vaishnavism is too well-known to be repeated here. Suffice to say that much of this was a complex combination of ideological predispositions and acute observation. For instance, we gather from the Baptist missionary William Ward (1769–1823) that a substantial percentage of the Hindu Bengali population in Bengal was Vaishnava by faith even though the exact constituents of that faith are not very well defined. Ward also tells us how women of 'ill fame' in colonial Calcutta commonly professed the faith of Chaitanya so that they may be allowed decent funeral rites at death. Early educational surveys of Bengal conducted between 1835 and 1838 by William Adam (1796–1881) reveal that Vaishnava women were among the most literate, an accomplishment that appears to have been encouraged by an increasing turn from orality to textual culture over time. Missionary accounts of this period also vitally shaped Hindu public opinion, even among the upwardly mobile and neo-educated *jatis*. That Chaitanya should be associated with the morally suspect Radha–Krishna cult was an embarrassment for both evangelists and Hindus deeply impressed with their cultural reporting. Ward was scandalized upon discovering that in popular Hindu temples, Krishna was invariably found in the company of his mistress, Radha, and not his wives. By the mid-19th century, Hindu converts to Christianity were to echo such perceptions. Rev. Lal Behari Dey (1824–1894), also from a Suvarnavanik Vaishnava family, has left behind captivating accounts of quotidian Vaishnava life based on actual observation. Dey was both amused and a trifle concerned at how among 'lower class' Vaishnavas—Boshtoms, Babajis, and their female companions—raucous singing and hysterical emotional outbursts were taken to be a measure of spiritual perfection. In theological matters too, he had reason to be dissatisfied with Vaishnavas. For one, he doubted if Chaitanya could qualify to be called an avatar at all since his descent was clearly not foretold by any divine mandate. A true incarnation, Dey was to argue, would have been heralded by some prophecy, as was the case with Jesus. A tract published by the Church Missionary Society in 1892 titled *Chaitanyatattwabodhika* (Determining the Essence of Chaitanya's Theology, n.d.) by one Haradhan Mukhopadhyay reinforces this perception. Mukhopadhyaya's critique focused on the alleged shortcomings of character and temperament in Chaitanya, particularly on his tendency to quickly fly into a rage, often leading to perpetrating violence on others. Such qualities, Mukhopadhyay observed, ill fitted an avatar. A more penetrating accusation and one which may have offended the Vaishnavas even more was the theory that Chaitanya's disregard for *jati* was born not out of any genuine ideological conviction but only a clever ploy devised to attract lower-class recruits. In his 1925 study of the Chaitanya movement in Bengal, Melville T. Kennedy devoted an entire chapter to a didactic comparison between Vaishnavism and Christianity, which one of his reviewers chose to completely ignore. Outside this didacticism, Kennedy's pressing concern was that Chaitanya Vaishnavism did not develop the concept of the sinner nor did it speak of the ways in which men might work towards redeeming their sins. Such matters, he argued, were quite unreasonably left to God's grace.

Of the Indian converts to Christianity in 19th-century Bengal, only the poet Madhusudan Dutta (1824–1873) was enthused by the Vaishnava tradition and even admitted as much. Best known for his creative retelling of a story from the Ramayana, the *Meghnadh Bodh Kavya* (The Slaying of Meghnad, 1861), and for his pioneering experiments with blank verse, Dutta also exhibited a keen appreciation and understanding of Vaishnava mythology and literary canons. After he had produced the dramatic poem *Brjangana Kavya* (Verses Based on Life at Vraj or Vrindavan 1861) based on Radha–Krishna lore from Vraj country, a Goswami from Shantipur came visiting him one day at his Khidirpore (Calcutta) residence and was quite devastated to find the author to be a Christian. Reportedly, the Goswami went back a deeply saddened man, comforting himself with the thought that he had indeed sighted a pious Vaishnava who had been for some reason cursed to lead the life of a Christian. Dutta himself had the presence of mind to chide the veteran Brahmo leader Rajnarayan Basu (1826–1899) for his failure to separate literary ideals from the social or the religious. On 29 August 1861 he wrote thus to Basu:

> I think you are rather cold towards the poor lady of Braja. Poor man! When you set down to read poetry, leave aside all religious bias. Besides, Mrs. Radha is not such a bad woman after all. If she had a 'Bard' like your humble servant from the beginning she would have been a very different character. It is the vile imagination of poetasters that has painted her in such colours. (*Madhusudan Granthavali*, the Collected Works of Madhusudan Dutta)

As a sympathetic understanding of Krishna's much abused lover, this perhaps stands unparalleled in 19th-century Bengali literature. Dutta was also to confess that whereas he cared 'two pins' for the religion of the Hindus, the 'grand mythology of his ancestors' moved and inspired him.

The Brahmo reaction to Chaitanya and Vaishnavas is said to have begun with Raja Rammohun Roy (1774–1833). In hindsight, though, this looks more a matter of the pre-existing sectarian rivalries between Vaishnavas and Saktas. There are apocryphal stories in circulation about how an orthodox Vaishnava would not condescend to use the term 'kali' for ink because it was reminiscent of the fearsome Sakta goddess Kali, preferring to use the Persian word, *syahi*, instead. There is also the celebrated and quite instructive exchange between the well-known Sakta-Tantrik practitioner Ramprosad Sen (1717–1775) and his Vaishnava contemporary Aju (Ayodhya) Gossai (Goswami). Reportedly, while Ramprosad bemoaned the world and world-processes as a gigantic hoax wrought upon man by beguiling Maya, Aju Gossain saw the phenomenal world as an abode of *ananda* or pure bliss; put more bluntly, it is a place where one might enjoy some revelry and fun. This perceptible difference in approach and understanding was quite characteristic of the Sakta and Vaishnava views of Hindu metaphysics and soteriology. The former produced more polarized perceptions of life, swinging between life affirmation and negation, and its overarching approach to life was often marked by a depressing obsession with the sheer 'fragility' and 'meaninglessness' of all life or the utter helplessness of man before the capricious and mysterious play of the Divine, which could neither be understood nor foretold. Rammohun's *Brahma Sangit* (Brahmo prayer songs) repeatedly speak of *bibek* and *bairagya*, withdrawal and renunciation, and adopt an almost alarmist approach to the inevitability of death. By contrast, the Vaishnava attitude was more life-affirming and it fancied that sensuality and love which one human being showed towards another could more effectively grow into a love for the Divine. There are at least three known instances of Chaitanya himself or one of his important followers substituting names denoting a morose concern with human unhappiness or suffering by those that indicated mirth and contentment. Chaitanya changed the name of one of the female attendants at Sribas's house from Dukhi (unhappy) to Sukhi (happy). Similarly, Jayananda was the name given to one who was previously called 'Guiyan' (in all probability, a pejorative term). In Vrindavan, Jiva Goswami renamed Dukhi Krishnadas as Shyamananda.

Rammohun's critique of Vaishnavism was grounded in both ethical and theological objections. Referring to the episode of the infant Krishna stealthily stealing butter and cream, as narrated in the *Bhagavat Purana*, he once complained to his Baptist friends at Serampore of how even the sweeper of his house would not dream of committing such a dastardly act. His theological objections, in particular, were directed against Vaishnava idolatry, towards the high reverence for the guru, and implicitly, perhaps, towards the tendency to freely recruit lower-class men and women into spiritual life. Rammohun's own penchant for Vedantic *jnan* effectively ruled out the possibility of recruiting lower castes and for a long time into its history, as we may justly recall, the Brahmo Samaj was identifiable as both an upper-caste constituency and a male-centric organization. Rammohun's debates with Gaudiya Vaishnavism are memorialized in two successive tracts called *Goswamir Sahit Vichar* (Polemics with the Goswami, 1818) and *Pathyapradan* (Prescribing the Right Course of Treatment, 1823) in which he plainly ridiculed the veneration of figures such as Krishna and Chaitanya. The latter work also brings out the polemical side to his writings. Sometime around 1822–3, Nandalal Tagore, son of Haramohan Tagore of the

Pathuriaghata branch of the Tagore family, engaged an employee of the Fort William College in Calcutta, Pandit Kashinath Tarkapanchanan (1788–1851), to produce a tract contesting the 'heretical' religious views of Rammohun. The tract was called *Pashandapidan* (Persecuting the Heretic). To this, Rammohun promptly replied by way of his *Pathyapradan*, citing the Tantric work *Tantraratnakar* (a relatively modern Tantric text, n.d.), to state that the Vaishnava trio of Chaitanya, Advaita, and Nityananda were actually demons reborn as humans! It appears to have escaped Rammohun altogether that his religious views agreed with those of the Vaishnavas in two vital respects: first, in its emphasis on monotheism and second, in its life-affirming quality.

The Brahmo Samaj after Rammohun reveals an ambivalent position towards the Gaudiyas. On the one hand, an effusion of Bhakti sentiments is known to have gripped the Brahmos under Keshab Chandra Sen (1838–1884), with Keshab himself assuming the moods of Chaitanya (*Chaitanya-bhava*) at Monghyr in 1868. Bipinchandra Pal once wrote to say that but for Keshab, modern Bengal may not have adequately respected Chaitanya. The Brahmos were the first group in modern Bengal to actually organize *sankirtan* processions, anticipating even the neo-Vaishnavas themselves. One such event was organized on 24 January 1868 with as many as 400 Brahmos attending. On 16 Aghrayan 1792 (Saka era), corresponding to the months of November–December in 1870 CE, the *Dharmatattwa*, a Bengali journal started by Keshabchandra, began serializing a feature called 'Life and Religion of Chaitanya' (*Chaitanyer Jeebon O Dharma*); one of his loyal followers, Trailokyanath Sanyal alias Chiranjiv Sharma, produced in 1884 a two-part narrative on the life and times of Chaitanya titled *Bhaktichaitanyachandrika* (a quasi-dramatic text in praise of Chaitanya, 2 vols., 1884). Sanyal's work employs an interesting narrative strategy wherein the author poses himself as a contemporary of Chaitanya in Nabadwip and claims to provide eyewitness accounts of major episodes occurring in the life of the saint. The rapid effusion of Bhakti, however, also contributed to split the Brahmo Samaj a second time in 1878 since it allegedly encouraged personalized Bhakti, with Keshab increasingly assuming the position of the venerable saint and guru, and authoritarianism that was resented by the younger, politically more sensitized Brahmos. Sibnath Sastri (1847–1919), one of the major architects behind the schism of 1878, speaks approvingly of devotional collectives such as the *nagar sankirtan* but not of ecstatic Bhakti. A more surprising note of dissent to Keshab's experiments with Bhakti appears in the writings of his cousin and most trusted lieutenant, Protap Chandra Mozoomdar (1840–1905). Mozoomdar bitterly complains of how Vaishnava Bhakti emotionalism had emasculated a good many 'unripe minds' in Keshab's church with *kirtan* parties degenerating into 'mobbish assemblies'.

It is something of an irony that while the Brahmo Rammohun appears as the first major critic of Chaitanya and Vaishnavism in modern India, the Brahmo Samaj after him provided the Chaitanya movement with the earliest and many illustrious recruits. Among those who, notwithstanding their Brahmo past, took to a piously Vaishnava life were Aswini Kumar Dutta, Sisir Kumar Ghosh, Manoranjan Guhathakurta, Tarakishore Raychaudhuri, and Bipinchandra Pal. Most of these figures took initiation under Bejoykrishna Goswami who was instrumental in introducing Bhakti to the Brahmo way of life and cast a significant influence on Keshab himself. Brahmo theologian Hemchandra Sarkar wrote an influential work titled *Gaudiya Vaishnavharma O Chaitanyadev* (Gaudiya Vaishnavism and Chaitanya, 1932) in which he showed Chaitanya to have carried out important changes in the everyday religious and cultural life of the Hindu Bengali.

It might also be justly argued that the Bhakti experiments of Keshab or the neo-Puranism of Bankimchandra and Bipinchandra Pal were, on one level, correctives to the position once adopted by Rammohun himself. There were, however, unrelenting critics too. Writing in the popular Bengali journal *Sahitya* (1896–7), Brahmo Umeshchandra Batabyal (1852–1892) viewed Chaitanya as a paranoid figure who had developed signs of madness after his first marriage. Batabyal was also among those who took Vaishnavism to be a residual aberration from degenerating Buddhism and even portrayed Radha herself as a promiscuous Buddhist nun.

A relatively unexplored aspect to the study of Chaitanya and Vaishnavism in colonial Bengal is the response from Ramakrishna and the movement that grew around him. In part, the explanation may lie in perceiving Ramakrishna as a Sakta-Tantrik figure and Vivekananda as primarily an *advaitin*, not expected to take much interest in the rival tradition of Vaishnavism. Such perceptions are easily contested by turning to sources, of which *Sri Sri Ramakrishnakathamrita* (The Gospel of Ramakrishna) by Mahendranath Gupta is easily the most valuable. For one, there is the issue of Ramakrishna's Vaishnava ancestry. His father was a devotee of Raghuvir, a synonym for Rama, and Ramakrishna's siblings were given names beginning with the prefix 'Ram', such as Ramkumar or Ramsila. Second, by one estimate, in the *Kathamrita* itself, there are over a dozen instances of Ramakrishna referring euphorically to the '*mahabhava*' of Chaitanya, to his extreme renunciation, and his conquest of worldliness. Closer to our time, there have been at least two serious attempts at comparing the religious views of Chaitanya and Ramakrishna: first by A.K. Majumdar in *Chaitanya: His Life and Doctrine* (1969), followed by Rabindra Kumar Dasgupta in the work *Sri Ramakrishner Chaitanya O Ramprosad* (Chaitanya and Ramprosad in the Eyes of Ramakrishna) (2015). Dasgupta has gone to the extent of claiming that Chaitanya and Ramakrishna were but the two faces of the same person.

Ramakrishna recalled with delight Chaitanya revealing the ecstatic moods of Radha, even chiding the novelist Bankimchandra for expressing some reservations on this score. The *Kathamrita* also records how, on his visit to Vrindavan, Ramakrishna himself was taken to be a manifestation of Radha by local followers. Not surprisingly, some of his *bhadralok* devotees viewed the saint as 'Chaitanya of the 19th century', a perception occasionally affirmed by Ramakrishna himself. Two popular plays launched on the contemporary Bengali stage, both dealing with the life of Chaitanya—*Chaitanya Lila* (The Divine Sports of Chaitanya, 1884) and *Nimai Sanyas* (The Ascetic Life of Chaitanya, 1885)—were authored and directed by the well-known playwright and Ramakrishna devotee Girishchandra Ghosh (1844–1912). Interestingly though, *bhadralok* validation of the lives and work of these two figures also reveal subtle differences in approach and strategy. When speaking of Chaitanya, Sisir Kumar Ghosh pointedly refers to Chaitanya's birth in a highly educated community; Mahendranath Gupta, on the contrary, is crestfallen upon gathering that 'Thakur' (Ramakrishna) has no use for books. In the first instance, arguably, the intention was to situate the 'reformist' Chaitanya in the tradition of 'high' learning; in the second, it was to pronounce the vacuity of formal learning, especially that produced in a culturally alienating environment and colonial educational institutions. The *Kathamrita* takes some pride in reporting how the Western-educated community of Calcutta felt itself humbled in the presence of a semi-literate Brahmin priest.

His great attachment to goddess Kali or fleeting experiments with esoteric Tantric *sadhana* did not come in the way of Ramakrishna warmly socializing with his Vaishnava visitors, some of whom such as Radhikamohan Goswami of Santipur, belonged to distinguished Vaishnava spiritual lineages. There were recurring *kirtan* recitals at Dakshineswar as also at other places in Calcutta which Ramakrishna visited, and such performative aspects of devotion were, without a doubt, an important part of his religious life. Ramakrishna was a regular visitor at the annual Panihati Vaishnava festival associated with Nityananda and Raghunath Das Goswami. Between 1882 and 1884, he is known to have visited at least four important Vaishnava icons and institutions within the close vicinity of Dakshineswar: Kansaripara Haribhaktipradayini Sabha, Gadadhar Patbari at Ariadaha, *Shadabhuja Gauranga* (the six-armed image of Chaitanya) at Garanhata, and *Jorasanko Harisabha*. On the other hand, he had two strong points of criticism directed against the Gaudiya Vaishnavas. First, he disliked the exaggerated humility and self-denial in the Vaishnava, always seeking God's forgiveness and redemption for his frailties and sins. His position in the matter, also often articulated before the Brahmos, was that the devotee ought really to stand by the belief that having taken the Divine Name, no sin could possibly touch him. Second, somewhat surprisingly, there is at least one instance of his favourably comparing the intellectual Bhakti of the *Gita* to that of the emotionally charged Bhakti in the *Bhagavat Purana*—surprising, that is, for a man who otherwise took 'Radhabhava' to be an exalted state of love for the Divine. He compared the Bhakti of the *Bhagavat*, which privileged the clandestine but selfless love of the *gopis*, to the enticingly coquettish foreplay of the public woman. By comparison, devotion found in the *Gita* was pure and chaste, exhibited as it was by the faithful and chaste wife. Indeed, some of Ramakrishna's devotees were heard complaining against singing Radha–Krishna love songs at home since, reportedly, its effects on wives and children was far from salutary.

In most ways, Swami Vivekananda, Ramakrishna's most eminent pupil, carried forward his master's views on Chaitanya and on

Vaishnavism. For Vivekananda, Chaitanya was best understood as the founder of a movement that placed the greatest emphasis on undiscriminating human love and bonding:

> His love knew no bounds. The saint or the sinner, the Hindu or the Mohammedan, the pure and the impure, the prostitute the street-walker—all had a share in his love, all had a share in his mercy ... his sect is the refuge of the poor, of the downtrodden, the outcast, of the weak, of those who have been rejected by all society. (Complete Works of Swami Vivekananda)

Speaking at Madras immediately upon his return to India in 1897, Vivekananda found Chaitanya's influence to be truly pan-Indian in scope and character, penetrating all areas that had come under the influence of Bhakti Marga. In 1899, responding to questions put to him publicly, the Swami was to also observe that the Gaudiya movement had made way for a wide range of Hindu converts to re-enter the Hindu fold. It was Chaitanya and his movement which had saved Hinduism from extinction, Vivekananda concluded.

In Vivekananda's perception, the error with Chaitanya's methods, as also those of his spiritual successors, lay in following the tactically disastrous strategy of universalizing the path of love (*madhurbhava*). In the hands of the common man and woman, the Swami alleged, this was likely to be seriously misapprehended and abused. Evidently, the implication here was that discrimination was a function of class; the lowly and the uneducated could not possibly tell lust from love. On the whole, the Swami did validate the path of Bhakti or else he would not have chosen to write on *Bhakti Yoga* as devotedly as he wrote on *Jnan Yoga* and on *Karma Yoga*. And yet, he found Bhakti to be marred by the lack of discrimination. Somewhat echoing his master, Vivekananda sincerely recommended that Bhakti be suitably tempered by Jnan.

Appendix A

Chronology of Events in Chaitanya's Life

18 February 1486 (according to Julian calendar), 27 February 1486 (according to Gregorian calendar)	Born to Jagannath Misra (also known as Purandar Misra) and Sachi Devi on the day of a lunar eclipse
1500–1	Admitted to Gangadas Pandit's *tol*
1501–2	Marries Lakshmi, daughter of Vallabha
1505	Opens own *tol* for instructing local students
1506	Tours east Bengal, possibly covering Sylhet; Lakshmi dies of snakebite while Chaitanya is on tour
1507	Second marriage to Vishnupriya, daughter of Sanatan Misra

October 1508	Visits Gaya
January 1509	Returns from Gaya; devotees gather at Sribas's place for *kirtan*
1509	Resumes teaching at *tol* and continues teaching until April
31(?) January 1510	Leaves home; reaches Katwa on the following day; initiated into *sanyas* on 3 February 1510; wanders about in ecstasy for the next three days aimlessly
March 1510	Leaves for Puri
March–April 1510	Stays at Puri for 18 days
1510	Leaves for tour of south India
1510–12	Tours southern India—Rajamundry, Venkatagiri, Kanjivaram, Vishnukanchi, Pakshitirtham, Vridhhachalam, Chidambaram, Vedavanna, Kumbhokonam, Srirangam (spends four months on account of rains), Rishva Parvata (Madura); meets Paramananda Puri; visits Rameswaram, Dhanuskodi, Sri Vaikuntha, Cape Comorin; travels along banks of Truvattaur river in Travancore; visits temple of Keshava at Trivandrum (acquires copy of *Brahma Samhita*), Sringeri Matha, Udipi, Pandharpur; passes through the territory between rivers Krishna and Venva (Bhima) to the west of Sholapur; obtains copy of *Krishnakarnamrita* by Lilasuka; crosses Tapti and Narmada; takes to south-easterly course passing through Dhanustirtha, Nasik, Kusavarta (source of Godavari); travels along Godavari to Rajamundry; meets Ramananda; also visits Somnath, Dwarka, and Prabhasa according to *Govidadaser Kadcha*; may have met Ramananda Ray twice, for the first time in the summer of 1510 and subsequently on his way back to Puri in May 1512

1513	Meets Panchasakha at Puri (Ananta, Achyuta, Yashovanta, Balaram, Jagannath); meets Odiya King Prataprudra; meets Bengali devotees (including Nityananda and Advaita) on their annual pilgrimage; launches *nagar sankirtan* on the occasion of Ratha Yatra; keen to visit Mathura–Vrindvan; sets out for Gaur; sends emissaries Goswamis Bhugarbha and Lokenath to Vrindavan; tours Panihati, Kumarhatta (meets Srinivas Acharya), Kanchrapara (meets Sivananda Sen and Basudev Dutta), Ramkeli (meets Rup and Sanatan); directs Rup and Sanatan to go to Prayag and Kashi; journey to Vrindavan postponed on account of potential trouble on route
Autumn, 1515	Leaves for Vrindavan with two companions, including Balabhadra Bhattacharya; travels through Jharkhand; converts Pathan Bijuli Khan en route to Prayag; reaches Kashi, halts for 10 days; meets Raghunath Bhatta, Tapan Misra, and Chandrashekhar; travels through Allahabad to reach Mathura and Vrindavan; visits Vishramghat; discovers Radhakunda
January 1516	Camps at Prayag; meets Vallabha (may be Vallabhacharya of Pushtimarga); meets Rup, teaches him Bhakti Shastra; directs him to go to Vrindavan; meets Sanatan at Kashi, directs him to leave for Vrindavan; debate with Prakashananda a/o *Vedanta Siddhanta Muktavali* (A Treatise on Vedanta), mentioned only in *Chaitanya Charitamrita*
May 1516	Returns to Puri to the garden house of Tapan Misra; spends the rest of his life at Puri
27 April 1533 (according to Julian calendar), 29 June 1533 (according to Gregorian calendar)	Dies at Puri

Appendix B

Printing History of Major Sanskrit and Bengali Hagiographies of Chaitanya (c.19th–20th Century): Select Editions

(Chronologically Arranged)

Bengali

Chaitanya Bhagavata by Vrindavan Das

1. 1838: Published by Tarapada Tarkabagish at Padmalay Press, Sovabazar.
2. 1843: Published by Radhanadhav Sil, Ramgovinda Sil, and Madhusudan Sil at Jnanratnakar Press, Ahiritola.
3. 1854: Published by Keshavchandra Ray at Gyanpurnodaya Press, Srirampur.

4. 1877: Published by Mahendralal Shila at Chaitanya Chandrodaya Press, Calcutta.
5. 1908: Edited by Kaliprasanna Vidyaratna. Published by Purnachandra Mukhopadhyay at Electric Machine Press, Calcutta.
6. 1910: Edited by Ambikacharan Brahmachari. Published by Gopendubhushan Vidyavinod at Kalna.

Chaitanya Charitamrita by Krishnadas Kaviraj[1]

1. 1844:'Antya Lila', edited by Gyanchandra Siddhantabagish. Published at Gyananjana Press in Calcutta; Adi and Madhya Lila, 1845.
2. 1851: Edited by Radhamadhav Vidyabagish. Published by Benimadhav De. Co. in Calcutta.
3. 1858: With commentary (tika) Anandachandrika of Utsavananda. Published by Benimadhav De at Vidyaratna Press, Calcutta.
4. 1868: Published by Ramkanai Das at Sudhasindhu Press, Calcutta.
5. 1878: Published by Akshaykumar Ray & Co. at Harihara Press, Calcutta.
6. 1878: Published by Vinodbihari Shila in Calcutta.
7. 1884: With commentary Anandachandrika of Utsavananda. Published by Vaneswar Ghosh; 'Adi Lila' (1884), 'Madhya Lila', and 'Antya Lila' (n.d).
8. 1886, reprinted in 1889: Edited with tika and vyakhya by Jagadiswara Gupta. Published by Debiprasanna Raychaudhuri in Calcutta.

Chaitanya Mangal by Jayananda Misra

1. 1905: Edited by Nagendranath Basu and Kalidas Nath. Published by Bangiya Sahitya Parishat, Calcutta.

---

[1] According to one source, the earliest printed copy of this work came out in 1827. See Ghoshel 1986, pp. 265–70. However, Tony K. Stewart cites Ramakanta Chakravarti claiming that Chaitanya Charitamrita was advertised in the Samachar Darpan as early as 1818. According to Stewart, the earliest Vaishnava texts to be printed were Narottam Vilas and Jagadishacharitravijay in 1815. No further details are available. See Chaitanyachandrodayanatakam by Krishnadas Kaviraj. Translation and commentary by Edward C. Dimock. Edited by Tony K. Stewart. Department of Sanskrit and Indian Studies, Harvard University, Cambridge (Massachusetts), 1999.

2. 1971: Edited by Bimanbihari Majumdar and Sukhomoy Mukhopadhyay, with English and Bengali introductions. Published by Asiatic Society, Calcutta.

Chaitanya Mangal by Lochandas

1. 1856: Edited by Radhamadhav Vidyabagish. Published by Benimadhav De at Bhagavatratna Press, Calcutta.
2. 1903: Edited by Atulkrishna Goswami. Published by Arunodaya Ray in Calcutta.
3. 1903: Published at Gaurvishnupriya Press, Calcutta.

Gauranga Vijaya by Chudamani Das

1. 1957: Edited by Sukumar Sen. Published by Asiatic Society, Calcutta.

Govindadaser Kadcha

1. 1926: Edited by Dineshchandra Sen and Banwarilal Goswami, 2nd edition. Published at Calcutta University Press, Calcutta.
2. 1997: Edited by Madhusudan Karmakar, with summary of Bengali proses and appendices. Published at Dey's Publishing, Calcutta.

Sanskrit

Chaitanyachandrodayanatakam by Kavi Karnapur

1. 1853: Sanskrit text with Bengali translation by Premdas. Published at Kamalasan Press, Calcutta.
2. 1854: Edited by Rajendralal Mitra, with the commentary of Viswanath Sastri explaining the Prakrit passages. In *Bibliotheca Indica*, nos. 40, 48, and 80. Published by Asiatic Society, Calcutta.
3. 1885: Edited with a commentary by Jivananda Vidyasagara. Published at Saraswati Press, Calcutta.
4. 1906: Edited by Pandit Kedarnath. In *Kavyamala* 87. Published by Tukaram Jayaji in Bombay.

Chaitanyacharitamrita Mahakavya by Kavi Karnapur

1. 1925: Edited with a Bengali translation by Ramnarayan Vidyaratna. 2nd edition. Published at Radharaman Press, Behrampore.
2. 1970?: Edited with a Bengali translation by Prankishore Goswami. Published by the editor of journal *Gauranga Mandira*, Calcutta.

Krishnachaitanyacharitamritam by Murari Gupta

1. 1975: Edited by Mrinalkanti Ghosh, with a Bengali translation by Haridas Das, 4th edition. Published by The Editor, Calcutta.
2. 1975: Translated into Bengali as *Srisrikrishnachaitanyacharitamritam ba Murari Gupter Kadcha* by Madanmohan Goswami. Published by Pushparani Mandal in Calcutta.

Chaitanyachandramritam by Probodhananda Saraswati

1. 1912: Edited with a Bengali translation by Ramnarayan Vidyaratna, with the commentary *Rasikavadini* by Anandi, 3rd edition. Published at Radharaman Press, Murshidabad.
2. 1926: Edited with a Bengali translation by Bhaktisiddhanta Saraswati. Published by Gaudiya Matha, Calcutta.
3. 1970: Edited with a Bengali translation by Manindranath Guha, with the commentary *Rasikavadini*. Published by Savitri Buha in 24 Paraganas.

Sources:
Basudev Ghoshel. 'Chaitanya Samparkita Granthabali'. In *Chaitanya Parikrama*, edited by Barun Kumar Chakravarti. Calcutta Harisabha, 1986 [1827].
J.F. Blumhardt. *Catalogue of Bengali Printed Books in the Library of the British Museum.* London: British Museum, 1886.
———. *Catalogue of the Library of the India Office*, vol. II, part IV. Bengali, Oriya and Assamese Books London: Eyre & Spottishwoode, 1905.
Tony K. Stewart. *The Final Word: The Grammar of a Religious Tradition.* Oxford and New York: Oxford University Press, 2010.
Vrindavan Das. *Chaitanya Bhagavata*, edited by Sukumar Sen, reprint. New Delhi: Sahitya Akademi, 1991.
Winand M. Callewaert and Rupert Snell, eds. *According to Tradition: Hagiographical Writing in India.* Wiesbaden: Harrasowitz, Verlag. 1994.

Appendix C

Major Biographical Works on Prominent Devotees and Followers of Chaitanya, in Print (c.19th–20th Century): Select Editions*

Abhirama Dasa

Abhirama Lilarahasya. Compiled by Kishoridasa Babaji. Sripat Krishnanangar: Prangopala Goswami, 1980.

Bhattacharya, Bidhubhushan. *Abhirama Goswami*. Howrah: Karmayogi Press. 1920.

Dasa, Tilak Ram. *Abhiram Lilamrita*, edited by Kishori Dasa Babaji. Sripata, 24 Paraganas: The Editor, 1981.

Ramdasa. *Abhiram Lilamrita*, edited by Natabar Tarkabagish. Calcutta, 1895; Calcutta. Reprinted at Basu Press, 1922.

* Complete publishing details could not be determined in every case.

Advaita Acharya

Das, Haricharana. *Advaita Mangal*, edited by Rabindranath Maiti. Burdwan: Burdwan University, 1966.

Krishnadas, Lauriya. *Balyalilasutra*, edited with a Bengali translation by Achyutacharan Chaudhuri Tattwanidhi, Charitmalika Series. No. 2. Karimganj: Sridhar Library, 1915.

Nagara, Ishan. *Advaita Prakash*, edited by Mrinal Kanti Ghosh, 3rd edition. Calcutta: Amrit Bazar Patrika Office, 1932.

Pramanik, Bireswar. *Advaita Vilas*, Part 1. Calcutta, 1899.

Haridas Thakur

Dasgupta, Surendramohan. *Thakur Haridas*. Bogra: Serendramohan Dasgupta, 1922.

Mitra, Satishchandra. *Haridas Thakur*. Calcutta: Ashutosh Library, 1925.

Sen, Revatimohan. *Thakur Haridas*. Calcutta: Bhattacharya & Sons, 1920.

Upadhyaya, Viswabandhaba. *Thakur Haridas*. Dacca: Brojomohan Dey, 1923.

Jahnava Devi

Das, Nityananda. *Premvilas*. (See works listed under Narottam Das).

Goswami, Rajvallabha. *Murali Vilas*, edited by Nilkantha and Binodbihari Goswamis. Baghnapara: Surendranath Bandopadhyay, 1895.

Also see *Narottam Vilas* listed under Narottam Das.

Narahari Sarkar

Thakur, Gaurgunananda. *Srikhander Prachin Vaishnava*, 3rd edition. Burdwan: Srikhanda Madhumati Samiti, n.d.

Narottam Das

Narahari Chakravarti: *Bhaktiratnakara*, edited by Ramnarayan Vidyaratna, 3rd edition. Haribhaktipradayini Sabha, Radharamana Press, 1915.

Narahari Chakravarti: *Bhaktiratnakara*, edited by Nandalal Vidyasagar. Calcutta: Gaudiya Mission, 1960.[†]

[†] According to one source, the *Bhaktiratnakara* was the first Vaishnava text to be printed in 1815. See Ghoshel, Basudev. 'Chaitanyadev Samparkita

Chakravarti, Narahari. *Narottam Vilas*. Calcutta: Barabazar Vaishnav Office, 1889.

Chakravarti, Narahari. *Narottam Vilas*, edited by Ramnarayan Vidyaratna. Murshidabad: Radharaman Press, 1893. [2nd edition, 1921]

Chakravarti, Narahari. *Narottam Vilas*, edited by Rakhaldas Kaviratna. Calcutta: Tara Library, 1924. 5th edition, Calcutta: Tarachandra Das & Sons, 1973.

Ghosh, Sisir Kumar. *Narottam Charita*. Calcutta, 1903.

Goswami, Brajendralal. *Narottam Lila*. Batila, Dacca: Brajendralal Goswami, 1923.

Das, Nityananda. *Prema Vilas*, edited by Ramnarayan Vidyaratna. Murshidabad, Haribhakti Pradayini, Radharaman Press (Behrampore). 1891.

Das, Nityananda. *Prema Vilas*, edited by Rashbihari Sankhyatirtha, 2nd edition. Murshidabad: Radharaman Press, 1911.

Das, Nityananda. *Prema Vilas*, edited by Yashodalal Talukdar. Calcutta: The Editor, 1913.

Nityananda

Anonymous. *Nityananda Charitamrita* (in verse). Haricharan Mallik, 1902.

Bhattacharya, Jagyeshwar. *Nityananda Charita*. Calcutta: Student's Library, 1929.

Das, Vrindavan. *Nityananda Charitamrita*, edited by Kishoridas Babaji. Sri Sri Gaudiya Vaishnava Sastra No. 8. Sripat Kumarhatta, 1980. [first published in 1914 but publisher unknown]

Das, Vrindavan. *Nityananda Vamsa Vistar*, edited by Nabinchandra Adya. Calcutta, 1874

Das, Vrindavan. *Nityananda Vamsa Vistar*, edited by Kishoridas Babaji. Sri Sri Gaudiya Vaishnava Sastra No. 9. Sripata Kumarhatta: The Editor, 1978.

Goswami, Khirodbihari. *Nityanander Vamsabali Gangadevir Vamsavali O Vaishnavadiger Sadhana*, 2 parts. Calcutta: 1914.

Pal, Janakinath. *Dayal Nitai*. Calcutta, 1905.

Granthabali'. In *Chaitanya Parikrama*, edited by Barun Kumar Chakravarti. Calcutta Harisabha, 1986. Several late texts such as *Narottam Vilas*, *Anurragavalli*, *Karnananda*, *Murali Vilas*, and so on carry biographical information on multiple figures.

Pal, Janakinath. *Nityananda Charit,* edited by Maheshchandra Bhattacharya. Calcutta, 1910.

Prabodhananda Saraswati

Das, Balaram. *Prabodhananda Saraswatir Jeebon Charit.* Calcutta, 1889.
Ghosh, Sisir Kumar. *Prabodhananda O Gopal Bhatta,* 2nd edition. Calcutta: Piyush Kanti Ghosh, 1923.

Prataprudra

Das, Vaishnavcharan. *Sri Prataprudra Charit.* Hooghly: 1914.

Raghunath Das Goswami

Chakravarti, Rasikmohan. *Srimat Das Goswami.* Calcutta, 1906.
Chattopadhyay, Aghorenath. *Raghunath Das Goswamir Jeebon Charit.* Calcutta, 1893.
Chaudhuri, Achyutacharan. *Raghunath Das Goswamir Jeebon Charit.* Mayna (Sylhet), 1893.
Chaudhuri, Priyanath. *Bairagi Raghunath Das Goswami.* Calcutta, 1925.
Datta, Prankrishna. *Bairagi Raghunath Das.* Calcutta(?). 1903.
Goswami, Padmalochan. *Raghunath Lilamrita.* Calcutta(?). 1905.
Goswami Raghunath Das. Calcutta: R. Datta, 1908.

Ramananda Ray

Vidyabhushan, Rasikmohan. *Ray Ramananda.* Calcutta: Goverdhan Press, 1900.

Rasik Murari

Das, Gopijanaballabha. *Rasik Mangal,* edited by Gopalagovindanandana Dev Goswami. Gopijanavallabhapur: The Editor1941.
Das, Gopijanaballabha. *Rasik Mangal,* edited by Kishoridas Babaji. Gaudiya Vaishnava Sastra No. 40. Halishahar: Sri Nitai Gauranga Gurudhama, 1997
Das, Gopijanaballabha. *Rasik Mangal,* edited by Sarada Prasad Mitra. Tamluk: The Editor, n.d.

Goswamis Rup and Sanatan

Gupta, Rajeswar. *Rup Sanatan*. Calcutta, 1877.

Gupta, Aghorenath. *Bhakta Charitamala*. Calcutta: Gurudas Chattopadhya, 1894.

Adhikari, Dhankrishna. *Sanatan Goswami O Rupa Goswamir Jeebon Charit*. Calcutta, 1891.

Pal, Janakinath. *Rup Sanatan*. Calcutta, 1904.

Chattopadhyay, Sachischandra. *Sri Sanatan Goswami*. Calcutta: Gurudas Chattopadhyay & Sons, 1924.

Mukhopadhyay, Durgamohan. *Rup Sanatan*. Calcutta, 1931.

Mitra, Satischandra. *Sapta Gowami*. Calcutta: Ashutosh Library, 1927.[§]

Sita Devi

Das, Lokenath. *Sita Charita*, edited by Achyutacharan Chaudhuri Tattwanidhi. Calcutta: 1926.

Sribas

Das, Vaishnavcharan, *Sribas Charit*, edited by Rashbihari Sankhyatirtha. Murshidabad: Ramdev Misra, 1909.

Srinivas Acharya

Chakravarti, Narahari. *Bhaktiratnakara*. (See works listed under Narottam Das.)

Das, Jadunandana. *Karnananda*, edited by Ramnarain Vidyaratna. Behrampore: Radharaman Press, 1892.

Das, Manohar. *Anuragvalli*. Calcutta: Tarit Kanti Biswas, 1909; edited by Mrinalkanti Ghosh. Calcutta: Amrita Bazar Patrika Office, 1931.

Das, Nityananda. *Prem Vilas*. (See works listed under Narottam Das.)

Shyamananda

Das Adhikari, Madhusudan. *Shyamananda Charita*. Elati: Vaishnava Sangini Office, 1911.

[§] The seventh Goswami in this case is Lokenath Goswami.

Das, Krishnacharan. *Shyamananda Prakash*, edited by Amulyacharan Raybhatta. Calcutta, 1928.

Das, Gopijanavallabha. *Rasik Mangal*. (See works listed under Rasik Murari.)

Vamsivadan Thakur

Misra, Premdas. *Vamshishiksha*, edited by Bhagavatkumara Deva Goswami. Calcutta: Saratchandra Das, n.d.

———. *Vamshishiksha*, edited by Nimai Chand Goswami. Nabadwip: The Editor, n.d.

Vishnupriya Devi

Dasi, Niradasundari. *Vishnupriya*. Brahmanberia: Nabadwip Chandra Roy, 1918.

De, Vaikunthanath. *Vishnupriya Charitamrita*, Part 1. Calcutta: Yogindramohan Chaudhuri, 1917.

Goswami, Haridas. *Gambhiray Vishnupriya*. Calcutta, 1923.

Sarkar, Vidhubhushan. *Vishnupriya*, 2 parts. Calcutta: Vidhubhushan Sarkar, 1915–26.

Sri Sri Vishnupriya Charita, 2nd edition. Calcutta: Ramnivas Dhandariya, 1962.

Vidyabhushan, Rasikmohan. *Gour Vishnupriya*. Calcutta, 1893.

Sources:

Basudev Ghoshel. 'Chaitanyadev Samparkita Grantahbali'. In *Chaitanya Parikrama*, edited by Barun Kumar Chakravarti. Calcutta: Harisabha, 1986.

National Library Catalogue of Bengali Printed Books. Calcutta. Multiple volumes.

Ramakanta Chakravarti. *Vaishnavism in Bengal*. Calcutta: Sanskrit Pustak Bhandar, 1985.

Appendix D

(i) List of Prominent Temples Dedicated to Chaitanya and Nityananda: Bengal (c.16th–19th Century)

Icon(s)	Location	Constructed in	Constructed by
Gour-Nitai	Kalna (Burdwan)	early 16th century	Gauridas Pandit[1]
Mahaprabhu	Mahaprabhu Para (Nabadwip)	early 16th century	Vishnupriya Devi[2]

(Cont'd)

---

[1] Intimate follower of Chaitanya.

[2] Wife of Chaitanya. Legend has it that she had the wooden image of Chaitanya constructed by a craftsman called Nabindnanda Acharya at the request of Vamshibadan Thakur, a close companion of Chaitanya.

Icon(s)	Location	Constructed in	Constructed by
Mahaprabhu	Tamluk (Midnapore)	early 16th century	Basudev Ghosh[3]
Nitai-Gour	Antisara (South 24 Paraganas)	early 16th century	Ananta Pandit[4]
Nitai Gour	Barahanagar (North 24 Parganas)	early 16th century	Raghunath Bhattacharya[5]
Gour-Nitai	Saptagram (Hooghly)	early 16th century	Uddharan Datta[6]
Gour-Nitai	Chakandi (Burdwan)	mid-16th century	Bhattacharya Family
Gauranga	Katwa (Burdwan)		Gadadhar Das[7]
Gauranga	Srikhanda (Burdwan)	mid-16th century	Narahari Sarkar[8]
Gauranga	Bhasakola, Bagura (Bangladesh)	mid-16th century	?
Gauranga	Chatra-Srirmpur (Hooghly)	late 16th century	?
Gauranga	Guptipara (Hooghly)	late 16th century	?
Nitai-Gaur	Kankutia (Birbhum)	end of 16th century	?
Gauranga	Moynadal (Birbhum)	early 17th century	Mitra family
Gaur-Nitai	Bodogatchi (Nadia)	1704	Khemababa[9]

[3] Follower of Chaitanya.
[4] Follower of Chaitanya.
[5] Follower of Chaitanya.
[6] Follower of Nityananda.
[7] Follower of Chaitanya.
[8] Poet and intimate follower of Chaitanya.
[9] Vaishnav mendicant.

Icon(s)	Location	Constructed in	Constructed by
Gaur-Nitai	Sundalpur (Nadia)	1790	Das Sarkar family
Mahaprabhu	Manipur (Nadia)	1798	Manipur Royalty
Gauranga	Joflai (Birbhum)	late 18th century	Thakur family[10]
Mahaprabhu	Patnabazar, Midnapore city		Goswami family[11]
Gaur-Nitai	Kadilpur (Midnapore)	late 18th century	?
Gaur-Nitai	Gadbalia (Howrah)	late 18th century	?
Gaur-Nitai	Kulia Paat (Nadia)	19th century	Dhar family[12]
Shadabhuja	Panchrol (Midnapore)	19th century	Mahapatra family[13]
Mahaprabhu	Sonamui (Midnapore)	1824	Adhikari family[14]
Mahaprabhu	Vrindavanpur (Midnapore)	1827	?
Mahaprabhu	Vasudevpur (Midnapore)	1833	Dasthakur family[15]
Mahaprabhu	Gaura (Midnapore)	mid-19th century	Adhikari[16]
Sonar Gauranga	Nadia	mid-19th century	Goswami family[17]
Mahaprabhu	Ilambazar (Birbhum)	mid-19th century	?

(Cont'd)

[10] Baidya by *jati*.
[11] Brahman by *jati*.
[12] Subarnabanik by *jati*.
[13] Local landowners.
[14] Jat Vaishnavs.
[15] Jat Vaishnavs.
[16] Brahmans by *jati*.
[17] Brahmans by *jati*.

Icon(s)	Location	Constructed in	Constructed by
Mahaprabhu	Maruibazar, Vishnupur (Bankura)	late 19th century	Goswami family

Note: There are 36 other temples of this category which could be identified, but for which there is no information on the date of construction or the name of the patron(s). Of these, as many as 19 are located at various places in Midnapore district and eight in Nadia.

The Mallabhum Rajas of Mallabhum (Bankura-Vishnupur region) built 82 temples in all between c.1600–1758. Of these temples, dates are not known for seven. Only one temple (no dates available) is dedicated to Chaitanya.

Source:
Abanti Kumar Sanyal and Ashok Bhattacharya (eds). *Chaitanyadeb: Itihas O Abadan.* Kolkata: Saraswat Library, 2002.
Pradyot Goswami. *Nabadwiper Samaj O Sanskriti.* Kolkata: Pustak Bipani, 2006.

(ii)   Extant Terracotta Figures of Shadabhuja (Six-Armed) Chaitanya: Bengal c.17th–19th Century

District	Location	Constructed in
Bankura	Shyam Ray Temple, Vishnupur	1643
	Keshto Ray Temple	1655
	Madanmohan Temple	1694
	Radhadamodar Temple	c.19th century
Burdwan	Shilla Village, P.S. Galsi	c.18th century
Birbhum	Ilambazar#	c.19th century
	Uchkaran, P.S. Nannur#	1768
	Angora village, P.S. Nannur	unknown
Murshidabad	Bhattabati, P.S. Nabagram#	c.18th century
Hooghly	Harirampur, P.S Jangipara#	1738

	Balidiwanganj, P.S Goghat	1822
	Kamarpukur, P.S. Goghat	c.19th century[18]
Midnapore	Alui village, P.S. Ghatal	1860
	Kotalpur village, P.S.Daspur	1713
	Ramkrishnapur, P.S. Daspur	1792
	Khirpai village, P.S. Ghatal	unknown[19]
	Panchkhuri village, P.S Midnapore	1821
	Anandapur village, P.S. Keshpur	1893
	Garkrishnapur village, P.S. Narayangrh	1892
	Aguria village, P.S. Daspur	1871
	Samat village, P.S. Daspur	1828
	Maqsoodpur, P.S. Kharagpur	1821
	Kaliyara, P.S. Kharagpur	1862
	Purvagopalpur, P.S Panshkura	1774
	Mirpur village, P.S. Pingla	1763
	Baranga village, P.S. Ramnagar	c.19th century
	Panchrol, P.S. Egra	unknown
	24 Parganas(N) Kharda, P.S. Kharda	unknown
Nadia	Santipur, P.S. Santipur	unknown
Bankura	Tejpal, P.S. Vishnupur	unknown
Hooghly Shandeswartala	P.S. Chinsura	unknown
	Kolkata 69/3, Nimtala Street	unknown

Note: # Shaiva temples
Source:
Abanti Kumar Sanyal and Ashok Bhattacharya (eds). *Chaitanyadeb: Itihas O Abadan.* Kolkata: Saraswat Library, 2002.
Pradyot Goswami. *Nabadwiper Samaj O Sanskriti.* Kolkata: Pustak Bipani, 2006.

---

[18] Private shrine belonging to the Laha family, possibly built by Dharmadas Laha, which Ramakrishna Paramahamsa refers to in his reminiscences.
[19] Private shrine belonging to the Chaudhuri family.

(iii) Images of Chaitanya and Nityananda on Terracotta Panels: Bengal c.19th–20th Century

District	Location	Date of Installation
Burdwan	Kalna	1849
Birbhum	Ghurisar, P.S. Ilambazar	c.19th century
	Mehgram, P.S. Nalhati*	c.19th century
	Sherandi, P.S. Bolpur*	1867
Midnapore	Astigram, P.S. Pingla	1909
	Iswarpur, P.S. Ghatal	1863
	Krishnapur–Udayganj, P.S. Ghatal	1877
	Khirpai, P.S. Chandrakona	unknown

Note: * Shaiva temples
Source:
Abanti Kumar Sanyal and Ashok Bhattacharya (eds). *Chaitanyadeb: Itihas O Abadan*. Kolkata: Saraswat Library, 2002.
Pradyot Goswami. *Nabadwiper Samaj O Sanskriti*. Kolkata: Pustak Bipani, 2006.

(iv) Sankirtana Processions Depicted on Terracotta Panels: Bengal c.18th–19th Century

District	Location	Date of Installation
Hooghly	Bali-Diwanganj, P.S. Goghat	1822
Howrah	Jaipur village, P.S. Amta	1784
Burdwan	Bonpash village, P.S. Bhatar	1882*
	Kalna, Pratapeswar temple	1749*
Bankura	Hridaynarayanpur, P.S. Patrasayar	c.19th century
	Shyam Ray temple, Vishnupur	1643
	Maynapur, P.S. Jaipur	1845
	Sridhar Jiu, Vishnupur	c.19th century
Birbhum	Ilambazar, P.S. Ilambazar	1846
	Ghurisar, P.S. Ilambazar	c.19th century
	Supur, P.S. Bolpur	c.19th century*

District	Location	Date of Installation
Midnapore	Alui village, P.S. Ghatal	1860
	Ajuria village, P.S. Daspur	1871
	Aurangabad village, P.S. Keshiari	1894
	Khirpai village, P.S. Chandrakona	1817
	Gopalpur village, P.S. Patashpur	1814
	Jamna, P.S. Pingla	c.19th century
	Palashi village, P.S. Debra	1824
	Belitara village, P.S. Daspur	1852
	Mahakalpota village, P.S. Daspur	1819
	Mirpur village, P.S. Pingla	1793
	Mirzapur village, P.S Patashpur	c.19th century
	Raghunathpur village, P.S. Daspur	1822
	Lalgarh village, P.S. Binpur	c.18th century
	Srirampur village, P.S. Daspur	1836

Note: * Shaiva temples
Source: Tarapada Santra. 'Bangalir Shilpa Sadhanay Chaitanyalila' (Chaitanya's Place in the Artistic Achievements of the Bengalis). In *Chaitanya Parikrama*, edited by Barunkumar Chakravarti. Calcutta: Khidirpur Harisabha, 1986.

(v) Prominent Chaitanya Temples in Odisha

(i) Solitary Images of Chaitanya

Location	Remarks
Banki, District Cuttack	Installed by Raja of Banki
Pratappur, District Mayurbhanj	Believed to have been installed by Prataprudra
Gaurangapur, District Balasore	Installed by Bansimadhav Mahapatra, zemindar-turned-monk; image made of Neem wood
Kuans, District Balasore	
Jagannath Puri, District Puri	Seated image of Chaitanya as a monk, only one of its kind in Orissa

(ii) Chaitanya Maths and Temples

Math/Temple	Location
Ganjam District	
Chaitanya Temple	Village and P.O. Rambha
Chaitanya Math	Village and P.O Berguda
Chaitanya Swami Temple	Village and P.O Sergoda
Chaitanya Temple	Village and P.O. Athagarahipatna
Chaitanya–Nityananda Temple	Village and P.O. Ganjam
Chaitanya Temple	Burligad, P.O. Humma
Chaitanya Temple	Belkhandi, near Behrampore
Chaitanya–Nityananda Temple	Village and P.O. Bodokhemdi
Chaitanya–Nityananda Temple	Village Nimakhandipenth, P.O. Nimakhendi
Chaitanya Temple	Bhimapore, near Behrampore
Chaitanya Temple	Bhavanipur, near Behrampore
Chaitanya–Nityananda Temple	Village and P.O. Dighphandi

Math/Temple	Location
Chaitanya Temple	Village and P.O. Surangi
Chaitanya Mahaprabhu Temple	Village and P.O. Palasera
Chaitanya–Nityananda Temple	Chingudiadas near Kodla
Chaitanya Temple	Village and P.O. Baragada
Chaitanya Temple	Parlakamedi
Chaitanya Temple	Dhanija, P.O. Aska
Mayurbhanj District	
Chaitanya–Nityananda Temple	Kantakanathi
Chaitanya–Nityananda Temple	Hatashi
Chaitanya Temple	Kanpur
Balasore	
Chaitanya–Nityananda Temple	Mangalpur, P.O. Sopo
Chaitanya Temple	Nuagna, P.O Bankipara
Chitanya–Nityananda Temple	Dayi Singh, P.O. Kanpur
Chaitanya Jiu Temple	Totapara, P.O Ghanteswar
Chaitanya Mahaprabhu Temple	Village and P.O. Basudebpur
Nitai Gaur Temple	Bhadrak
Chaitanya Mahaprabhu Temple	Mahapada
Chaitanya–Nityananda Temple	Damodarpur, near Balasore
Cuttack	
Chaitanya Temple	Gurudaspur, P.O. Mathashahi
Chaitanya Mahaprabhu Math	Muhammadiya Bazar[20]
Gauranga–Nityananda Temple	Bangali Shahi
Chaitanya–Nityananda Temple	Purushottampur, P.O. Kabirpur
Chaitanya Mahaprabhu Temple	Nilkantha, P.O. Patamundai
Chaitanya Mahaprabhu Temple	Village and P.O Kapila

(Cont'd)

[20] According to the records at the Board of Revenue office at Cuttack, dated 28 May 1858, this shrine had been receiving an annual donation of Rs. 55 and eight annas from the Maratha government. This was renewed by the East India Company.

Math/Temple	Location
Chaitanya Mahaprabhu Temple	Barada, P.S. Binjharpur
Chaitanya Mahaprabhu Temple	Rampa, P.O. Bari, P.S. Binjharpur
Chaitanya Temple	Dubakana, P.O. Mangalpur. P.S. Jajpur
Gauranga–Nityananda Temple	Kapileswar, P.O. Jajpur
Puri	
Chaitanya Deva Temple	Vishnupur, P.O. Nimapada
Chaitanya–Nityananda Temple	Patapur
Chaitanya Temple	Chatak hill, Puri
Chaitanya Deva Temple	Barabati, P.O Begunia
Chaitanya Temple	Channagiri?, P.O. Olsingh
Chaitanya Deva Temple	Manasibag, P.O. Balanga
Chaitanya Deva Temple	Banamalipur, P.O Khandapara
Chaitanya Math	Teltumb, P.O Pichukuli
Chaitanya Thakura Temple	Ghantagharpatna, P.O. Satapatna
Chaitanya Mahaprabhu Temple	Sanagudam, P.O. Kaipada
Chaitanya Deva Temple	Robena, P.O. Brahmagiri
Chaitanya Mahaprabhu Temple	Salatara, P.O. Gadiapalli
Sonar Gauranga Temple	on the sea coast of Puri
Chaitanya Deva Temple	Balakathi
Chaitanya–Nityananda Temple	Pirjipur, P.O. Brahmagiri
Koraput	
Urdha Bahu Chaitanya Temple	Jeypore
Chaitanya–Nityananda Temple	Jeypore

(iii) Recently Constructed Images (end of the 19th and early 20th century)

Shadabhuja (six-armed images of Chaitanya)[21]

Temple	Location
Jagannatha Temple	Puri
Old Bhuvaneswar	Bhuvaneswar
Sohela	P.S. Sargarh, district Sambalpur
Balisahi	near Ali, district Cuttack
Baladeva Temple	Kendrapara, district Cuttack
Kesonda Math	Tendakuda, Cuttack
Barabati	near Balasore

(iv) Vishnupriya Gauranga Temples[22]

Name of Math (monastery)	Location
Vishnupriya Gaur Math	Sambalpur
Gaura Govinda Math	Anandapara, Keonjhar
Gaura Govinda Math	Ghodabara, Cuttack
Jhankarpal	Sambalpur

Note: Images of Chaitanya, Nityananda, and Advaita were also installed at a shrine attached to the tomb of Haridas at Puri by Bhramaravara Jagadev, zemindar of Kendrapara. Chaitanya, Nityananda, and Advaita are also worshipped at the Auliya Math at Puri and at the private shrine owned by the De family at Motiganj, Balasore.
Source: Prabhat Mukherjee. *History of the Chaitanya Faith in Orissa.* Delhi: Manohar Publishers, 1979.

[21] In 1885, Shadabhuja images of Chaitanya, Nityananda, and Advaita were installed within the precincts of the Jagannath temple by Pachata Ananta Mahapatra, a priest. In the 1940s, a similar image was installed by one S. Mukherjee.

[22] In all these temples, Lakshmipriya, the first wife of Chaitanya, is also worshipped.

Appendix E

Major Anthologies of Vaishnava Verse in Print (c. 19th–20th Century)*

n.d.: *Vaishnava Mahajan Padabali*, edited by Satishchandra Mukhopadhyay, vol. 1 (Chandidas), vol. 2 (Vidyapati); vol. 3 (Govindadas), vol. 4 (Gyandas). Calcutta.

n.d.: *Padakalpataru*. Compiled by Vaishnav Das. Published by Kishorilal Roy under the supervision of Sisir Kumar Ghosh. Calcutta.

n.d.: *Rayshekharer Padabali*, edited by Nityaswarup Brahmachari. Calcutta.

n.d.: *Lochan Daser Dhamali*, edited by Nanigopal Sheel. Calcutta.

1849: *Padakalpalatika*. Compiled by Gourmohan Das. Calcutta.

---

* Arranged chronologically by date of publication and not the date of compilation of the work.

1871: *Govindadas (Kavya Sangraha)*. Calcutta: Gupta Press.

1872: *Vidyapati O Chandidaser Padabali* (only Vidyapati's verses printed) edited by Jagatbandhu Bhadra. Calcutta.

1878: *Padamritasamudra*. Compiled by Radhamohan Thakur, edited by Ramnarayan Vidyaratna. Behrampore.

1878: *Govindadas Krita Padabali*, edited by Akhaychandra Sarkar. Chinsura.

1878: *Padamritasamudra*. Compiled by Radhamohan Thakur, edited by Ramnarayan Vidyaratna. Behrampore.

1876: *Prachin Kavya Sangraha (Vidyapati)*. Compiled by Akshaychandra Sarkar. Chinsura.

1885: *Padaratnavali*. Compiled by Rabindranath Tagore and Srisha-chandra Majumdar. Calcutta.

1886: *Padakalpataru*. Compiled by Vaishnav Das, edited by Banseswar Ghosh. Calcutta.

1890: *Mahajan Padabali*, edited by Brajadas Vairagi. Calcutta.

1890: *Geeta Ratnavali*. Compiled Bankubihari Das. Calcutta.

1893: *Chandidas*. Compiled by Ramanimohan Mallik. Calcutta.

1894: *Vidyapati*, edited by Panchanan Tarkaratna. Calcutta.

1895: *Gyandas*, edited by Ramanimohan Mallik. Calcutta.

1897: *Prachin Kabir Granthabali*. Calcutta: Basumati Press (Upendranath Mukhopadhyay).

1898: *Padakalpataru*. Compiled by Vaishnav Das, edited by Viswambhar Laha. Calcutta.

1899: *Balaram Das*, edited by Ramanimohan Mallik. Calcutta.

1899: *Jagadananda Padabali*, edited by Kalidas Nath. Calcutta.

1900: *Mahajan Padabali (Chandidas O Vidyapati)*, edited by Akshay Kumar De, 2nd edition.

1901: *Sashishekhar*, edited by Ramanimohan Mallik. Calcutta. Bangiya Sahitya Parishat.

1902: *Govindadas Padabali*, edited by Kalidas Nath. Calcutta.

1902: *Gaurapadatarangini*. Compiled by Jagatbandhu Bhadra. Calcutta.

1902: *Basu Ghosher Padabali*, edited by Jagatbandhu Bhadra. Calcutta.

1902: *Narottam Das*, edited by Ramanimohan Mallik. Calcutta.

1903: *Rayshekhar Padabali*, edited by Kalidas Nath. Calcutta.

1904: *Musalman Vaishnav Kabi*, edited by Brajasundar Sanyal. Rajshahi.

1905: *Vaishnav Padabali (Basudev Ghosh Birachita)*. Edited by Mrinalkanti Ghosh. Calcutta. Bangiya Sahitya Parishat.

1909: *Khanada Geeta Chintamani.* Compiled by Viswanath Chakravarti, 3rd edition. Nityalal Sheel.

1909: *Vidyapati Thakurer Padabali,* edited by Nagendranath Gupta. Calcutta: Bangiya Sahitya Parishat.

1914: *Narottam Das,* edited by Surendramohan Bhattacharya. Calcutta.

1915–27: *Padakalpataru.* Compiled by Vaishnav Das, edited by Satishchandra Ray, 5 Vols. Calcutta: Bangiya Sahitya Parishat.

1920: *Aprakashita Padabali,* edited by Satishchandra Ray. Calcutta.

1921: *Balaram Das Thakurer Jeeboni O Padavali,* edited by Haridas Goswami. Calcutta.

1924: *Vidyapati,* edited by Kaliprasanna Kavyavisharad. Calcutta.

1924: *Khanda Geeta Chintamani,* edited by Radhanath Kabasi. Calcutta.

1924: *Padakalpataru.* Compiled by Vaishnav Das, edited by Radhanath Kabasi. Calcutta.

1931: *Lochandaser Dhamali,* edited by Mrinalkanti Ghosh, 2nd edition. Calcutta.

1934: *Gaurcharitra Chintamani,* edited by Mrinalkanti Ghosh. 2nd edition. Calcutta.

1934: *Chandidas Padabali,* edited by Harekrishna Mukhopadhyay and Sunitikumar Chattopadhyay. Calcutta: Bangiya Sahitya Parishat.

1935, 1938: *Deena Chandidaser Padabali,* 2 Vols, edited by Manindramohan Basu. Calcutta.

1947: *Gaurcharitra Chintamani.* Compiled by Narahari Chakravarti. Haridas Das.

1949: *Banglar Vaishnava Bhavapanna Musalman Kabi,* edited by Jatindramohan Bhattacharya. Calcutta.

1952: *Vidyapatir Padabali,* edited by Khagendranath Mitra and Bimanbihari Majundar. Calcutta.

1956: *Gyandas O Tahar Padabali,* edited by Harekrishna Mukhopadhyay and Srikumar Bandopadhyay. Calcutta: Calcutta University.

1960: *Chandidas Padabali,* edited by Nilratan Mukhopadhyay. Calcutta: Bangiya Sahitya Parishat.

1961: *Chandidaser Padabali,* edited by Bimanbihari Majumdar. Calcutta: Bangiya Sahitya Parishat.

1961: *Vaishnav Padabali,* edited by Harekrishna Mukhopadhyay. Calcutta.

1962: *Khanda Geeta Chintamani,* edited by Bimanbihari Majumdar. Calcutta.

1965: *Gyandas O Tahar Padabali*, edited by Bimanbihari Majumdar. Calcutta.

Source:

Bimanbihari Majumdar and Nareshchanda Jana. *Vaisnava Padabalir Anukramanika*. Calcutta: Calcutta University, 1975. Majumdar and Jana list a total of about 102 such works, some of which were not yet published at the time. Complete publication details could not be ascertained in each case.

Appendix F

Bengali Translations of the Bhagavat Purana (in part or whole) in Print (c. 19th Century)

1820: *Raspanchadhyay: Sri Sukadev Pranita, Sanskrit Mul O Bhashay Artha* (Sanskrit Text of Canto X, chapters 28–33 and Bengali prose translation). Calcutta.

1854: *Rasbilasgrantha* (Canto X, Chapters 28–33), metrical translation by Narayan Chattaraj Gunandhi. Serampore. Jnanarunoday Press.

1855: *Bhagavat*, prose translation by Purnachandra Sampadak. Calcutta.

1858: *Srimadbhagavat-Ekadas Skandha*, text and translation by Sanatan Chakravarti, 2nd edition. Calcutta.

1859: *Raspanchadhyay* (Canto X, chapters 28–33), metrical paraphrase by Narayan Chattaraj Gunandhi. Calcutta.

1861: *Srimadbhagavat-Dasam Skandha*, text and translation by Birbhadra Goswami. Calcutta.

1870–5: Prose translation by Durgacharan Bandopadhyay, 2 vols. Calcutta: Kavyaprakash Press.

1871: *Srimadbhagavat*, Part I, translated by Kaliprasanna Sarkar. Calcutta: Bharat Press.

1876: Abridged metrical translation by Rameswar Tarkaratna. Calcutta.

1877: Translated by Rohininandan Sarkar, 2nd edition. Calcutta.

1877(?): Translated by Brahmavrata Bhattacharya (Cantos 1–3 only). Calcutta.

1878: *Srimadbhagavata*. Prose translation by Brahmavrata Bhattacharya. Calcutta: Kavyaprakash Press.

1881: *Bhagavattattwakaumudi*. Verse translation by Ishanchandra Basu. Burdwan.

1884: Translated and edited by Satyacharan Gupta. Calcutta: Durgacharan Gupta.

1884: Translated by Pratapchandra Ray (Cantos 1–8 only). Calcutta.

1885–7: Translated by Pratapchandra Ray. Calcutta.

1886: Translated by Durgacharan Gupta (Cantos 1–7 only). Calcutta.

1889: Verse translation by Tinkari Biswas (Cantos 1–7 only). Calcutta: Biharilal Sarkar.

1893–5: Text with commentary (Sridhari?) and Bengali translation by Ramnarayan Vidyaratna. Murshidabad.

1896: Translation and notes by Radhikanath Goswami. Calcutta: Basak & Sons.

1896: Verse translation by Ramnarayan Vidyaratna and Batakrishna Chattopadhyay. Calcutta: Garanhata Public Library.

1899: Translation by Aswini Kumar Haldar. Calcutta.

Notes: From the brief descriptions given in catalogues and other sources, it is not clear in every case if the translation was in verse or prose. Complete publication details could not be ascertained in every case.

There is reference to an unpublished prose translation by Henry Sergeant which was once part of the Fort William collection. According to Ramakanta Chakravarti, one Upendranath Mitra translated the *Bhagavat* as early as 1816. Reportedly, a translated five-volume edition of the *Bhagavat* along with select commentaries, financed by Birchandra Manikya Burman of Tripura and published between 1872 and 1877, was available for private circulation only. Perhaps the most popular edition was the prose translation by Pandit Panchanan Tarkaratna published by the Bangabasi Press in 1903, which underwent its fourth and, apparently, the last edition in 1925.

Source: National Library. Author Catalogue of Printed Books in the Bengali Language. Multiple Volumes. Calcutta. Various Dates; West Bengal State Central Library (Digital). Available at http://www.wbpublibnet. gov.in/.

Annotated Bibliography

For a general understanding of devotional cultures in pre-modern South Asia, especially in their relation to Bengal Vaishnavism, the following works will prove extremely useful:

Bhattacharya, N.N., ed. *Medieval Bhakti Movements in India: Sri Caitanya Quincentenary Commemorative Volume*. Delhi: Munshiram Manoharlal, 1999.

Chakravarti, Kunal. *Religious Process: The Puranans and the Making of a Regional Tradition*. Delhi: Oxford University Press, 2001.

Curley, David L. *Poetry and History: Bengali Mangal- kābya and Social Change in pre-colonial Bengal*. New Delhi: Chronicle Books, 2008.

Hardy, Friedhelm. 'Madhavendra Puri: A Link between Bengal Vaishnavism and South Indian Bhakti'. *Journal of the Royal Asiatic Society of Great Britain and Ireland* 1, 1974, pp. 23–41.

———. *Viraha Bhakti: The Early History of Krishna Devotion in South India*. Delhi: Oxford University Press, 1983.

Hawley, J.S. *A Storm of Songs: India and the Idea of the Bhakti Movement*. Cambridge (Massachusetts) and London: Harvard University Press, 2015.

Majumdar, A. K. *Bhakti Renaissance*. Bombay: Bharatiya Vidya Bhavan, 1965.

Novetzke, Christian Lee. 'Bhakti and Its Public'. *International Journal of Hindu Studies* 11(3), December 2007, pp. 257–72.

Sharma, Krishna. *Bhakti and the Bhakti Movement: A New Perspective, A Study in the History of Ideas*. Delhi: Munshiram Manoharlal, 1987.

Of these works, those by Sharma, Novetzke, and Hawley significantly engage with the theoretical aspects of bhakti.

An interesting and useful introduction to medieval bhakti literature can be found in

b">
Schelling, Andrew, ed. *The Oxford Anthology of Bhakti Literature*. Delhi: Oxford University Press, 2011.

J.S. Hawley's older anthology, though quite excellent, carries no reference to Chaitanya Vaishnavism. See

b">
Hawley, J.S. *Three Bhakti Voices*. Delhi: Oxford University Press, 2005.

For the evolution of Radha as a literary and religious symbol in medieval Indian literature, see

b">
Dasgupta, Sashibhushan. *Shri Radhar Kromobikash: Darshane O Sahitye* (The Evolution of Radha in Philsophy and Literature). Calcutta: A. Mukherjee & Co., 1952.

A highly feminist reading of Radha occurs in

b">
Bandopadhyay, Atin. *Jodi Radha Na Hoto* (What If There Was No Radha). Calcutta: New Bengal Press, 1961.

The following works are recommended for an introduction to the portrayal of Krishna in pre-modern Indian literature, history and legend:

b">
Beck, Guy L., ed. *Alternative Krishnas: Regional and Vernacular Variations on a Hindu Deity*. New York: SUNY, 2005.

Bryant, Edwin. *Krishna: A Sourcebook*. New York: Oxford University Press, 2007.

Dimock, Edward C., and Denise Levertov, eds and trans. *In Praise of Krishna*. New York: Doubleday, 1967.

Giri, Satyabati. *Bangla Sahitye Krishnakothar Kromobikash* (The Evolution of the Krishna Tradition in Bengali Literature). Kolkata: Dey's Publishing, 2006.

Holdrege, Barbara A. *Bhakti and Embodiment: Fashioning Divine Bodies and Devotional Bodies in Krishna Bhakti.* London and New York: Routedge, 2015.

Majumdar, B.B. *Krishna in History and Legend.* Calcutta: University of Calcutta. 1969.

Pal, Bipinchandra. *Shree Krishna: Letters Written to a Christian Friend.* Calcutta: Yugayatri Prakashan, 1964.

For a modern Bengali retelling of the Krishna tradition, see

Chattopadhyay, Bankimchandra: *Krishna Charitra* (The Life of Krishna). 1892. Included in J.C. Bagal, ed. *Bankim Rachanavali* (The Collected Works of Bankimchandra Chattopadhyay), vol. II, 15th reprint, pp. 353–524. Kolkata: Sahitya Samsad, 2005.

Given the importance attached to the *Bhagavat Purana* as a sourcebook for Vaishnava Bhakti in Bengal, I recommend that the interested reader especially consult the works listed below:

Chattopadhayay, Geeta. *Bhagavat O Bangla Sahitya* (The Bhagavat and Bengali Literature). Calcutta: Kabi O Kabita, 1962.

Hopkins, Thomas. 'Bhakti in the Bhagavat Purana'. *Journal of Vaishnava Studies* 2(3), Summer, 1994, pp. 7–43.

Rukmani, T.S. *A Critical Study of the Bhagavat Purana (with special reference to bhakti).* Varanasi: Chowkambha Sanskrit Series, 1970.

Vaudeville, Charlotte. 'Love Symbolism in the Bhagavata'. *Journal of the American Oriental Society*, 82, 1962, pp. 31–40.

For a more recent and comprehensive study in this field, see

Gupta, Ravi M., and Kenneth Valpey. *The Bhagavat Purana: Sacred Text and Living Tradition.* New York: Columbia University Press, 2013.

The vexed issue of the interrelationship between philosophical non-dualism and dualist Vaishnava bhakti is adequately treated in the following:

Chaudhuri, Bhavesh Chandra. 'Some Vaishnava Legends in Vedantic Test Tube'. *Journal of the Ganganath Jha Research Institute* XVIII (1–4), November 1961–August 1962, pp. 53–72.

Gupta, Sanjukta. *Advaita Vedanta and Vaishnavism: The Philosophy of Madhusudan Saraswati*. London and New York: Routledge, 2006.

Venkatkrishnan Anand. 'Love in the Time of Scholarship: An Advaita Vedantin Reads the Bhakti Sutra'. *Journal of Hindu Studies* 8, 2015, pp. 139–53.

There are several works that provide an analytical survey of the history, religion, and culture of pre-modern Bengal. Of these, I have found the following to be particularly important for the study of pre-modern Bengali literature:

Ghosh, J.C. *Bengali Literature*. London: Curzon Press, 1948.

Nyayratna, Ramgati. *Bangla Bhasha O Sahitya Bishayak Prostab* (A Proposition Regarding the Bengali Language and Literature), 2nd edition. Chinsurah: Ram Press, 1887.

Sen, Dineshchandra. *Vanga Sahitya Parichay or Selections from the Bengali literature from the earliest time to the middle of the nineteenth century*, 2 vols. Calcutta: University of Calcutta, 1914.

———. *History of Bengali Language and Literature: A Series of Lectures Delivered as Reader to the Calcutta University*. Delhi: Gian Publishing House, reprint, 1986.

Sen, Sukumar. *Bangla Sahityer Itihas* (A History of Bengali Literature), vol. 1, 6th edition Calcutta: Ananda Publishers, 1971.

Pre-modern and early modern religious culture in Bengal receives excellent treatment in the following:

Banerji, Suresh Chandra. *Sanskrit Culture of Bengal*, reprint. Delhi: Sharda Publishing House, 2004.

Dasgupta, S.B. *Aspects of Indian Religious Thought*. Calcutta: A. Mukherjee & Co., 1957.

———. *Obscure Religious Cults*, 2nd edition. Calcutta: Firma K.L. Mukhopadhyay Pvt. Ltd., 1962.

McDermott, Rachel Fell. 'The Vaishnavized Uma of Bengali Devotionalism'. *Journal of Vaishnava Studies* 4(1), Winter, 1995–6, pp. 105–24.

———, ed. *Singing to the Goddess: Songs to Kali and Uma*. Oxford: Oxford University Press, 2001.

McDaniel, June. *The Madness of Saints: Ecstatic Religion in Bengal*. Chicago: University of Chicago Press, 1989.

———. 'Folk Vaishnavism and the Thakur Panchayat: Life and Status among Village Statues'. In *Alternative Krishnas: Regional and Vernacular Variations on a Hindu Deity*, edited by Guy L. Beck. Albany: SUNY, 2000.

———. 'The Tantric Radha: Some Controversies about the Nature of Radha in Bengali Vaishnavism and the Radha Tantra'. *Journal of Vaishnava Studies* 8(2), Spring, 2000, pp. 131–46.

Mukhopadhyay, Harekrishna. *Banglar Kirtan O Kirtaniya* (Kirtanas and Kirtana Singers of Bengal). Calcutta: Sahitya Samsad, 1971.

Sarkar, Tanika. 'Caste, Sect and Hagiography: The Balakdashis of Early Modern Bengal'. In *Rebels, Wives, Saints: Designing Selves and Nations in Colonial Times*, pp. 69-120. Delhi: Permanent Black, 2009.

Sen, Amiya P. 'Bhakti Paradigms, Syncretism and Social Restructuring in Kaliyuga: A Reappraisal of Some Aspects of Bengali Religious Culture'. *Studies in History* 14(1) (NS), 1998, pp. 89–126.

Sen, Kshitimohan. *Bharaitya Madhyayuge Sadhanar Dhara* (Religious Praxis in the Indian Middle Ages). Calcutta: University of Calcutta, 1930.

Sen, Sukumar. *Vaishnaviya Nibandha* (Essays on Vaishnavism). Calcutta: Rupa, 1970.

Sinha, Samita. 'The Nadia School of Sanskrit Learning'. *Bengal Past and Present* CVIII (1–2), January–December, 1989, pp. 89–102.

The social and political history of medieval Bengal is well narrated in the following volumes:

Banerji, Rakhaldas. *Banglar Itihas* (History of Bengal), vol. 2, reprint. Calcutta: Nababharat Publications, 1971.

Gupta, Tamonash Chandra Das. 'Aspects of Bengali Society: From Old Bengali Literature'. *Journal of the Department of Letters* XIV. Calcutta: University of Calcutta, 1927, pp. 1–134.

Mallik, Kumud Nath. *Nadiya Kahini* (The Saga of (district) Nadia), 3rd edition. Calcutta: Pustak Bipani.

Nizami, K.A. *Some Aspects of Religion and Politics in India during the 13th Century*. Delhi, 1961.

Ray, Aniruddha. 'State and Composite Culture in Sultanate Bengal, ca. 1200–1600'. In *Historical Diversities: Societies, Politics and Culture. Essays for Prof. V.N.Dutta*, edited by K.L.Tuteja and Smriti Pathania, pp. 97–124. Delhi: Manohar Publishers, 2008.

Ray, Niharranjan. *History of the Bengali People (Ancient Period)*, translated with an introduction by John W. Wood. Calcutta: Orient Longman, 1994.

Raychaudhuri, Tapan Kumar. *Bengal under Akbar and Jehangir. An Introductory Study in Social History*. Calcutta: A Mukherjee & Co., 1953.

Sarkar, Jadunath. *The History of Bengal: Muslim Period 1200-1757*. Patna: Academic Asiatic, 1957.

Sen, Dineshchandra. *Brihat Banga*, 2 vols, reprint. Kolkata: Dey's Publishing, 2006.

Sen, Kshitimohan. *Chinmoy Bongo*. Calcutta: Ashutosh Kumar Sarkar, 1958.

As sources on Chaitanya's life and teachings, medieval hagiographies written in Sanskrit or Bengali and produced between the 16th and 17th centuries are indispensable. These constitute our primary sources of information. Some later works whose authenticity is in some doubt have been left out of this list:

Chaitanya Charitamritam by Krishnadas Kaviraj: A Translation and Commentary by Edward C. Dimock and Tony K. Stewart. Edited by Tony K. Stewart. Cambridge (Massachusetts): Harvard University Press, 1999.

Das, Chudamani. *Gauranga Vijaya*, edited by Sukumar Sen. Calcutta: The Asiatic Society, 1957.

Das, Vrindavan. *Chaitanya Bhagavata*, edited by Sukumar Sen, 2nd reprint. New Delhi: Sahitya Akademi, 1991.

Gupta, Murari. *Sri Chaitanya Charita Mahakavyam*, translated into English by Bhaktivedanta Bhagavat Mahraj, edited by Purnaprajna Das. Vrindavan: Rashbihari Lal & Sons, 2006.

Jayananda. *Chaitanya Mangal*, edited by Bimanbihari Majumdar and Sukhomoy Mukhopadhyay, reprint. Kolkata: Asiatic Society, 2006.

Karmakar, Govindadas. *Govindadaser Kadcha*. Kolkata: Dey's Publishing, 1997.

Karnapur, Kavi. *Chaitanyacharitamritam Mahakavya*, edited with an introduction by Prankishore Goswami. Calcutta: Prankishore Goswami, n.d.

———. *Chaitanyacandrodaya Natakam*. Mumbai: Nirnaya Sagar Press, 1917.

Kaviraj, Krishnadas. *Sri Sri Chaitanya Charitamrita*, edited by Sukumar Sen and Tarapada Mukhopadhyay, 5th edition. Calcutta: Ananda Publishers, 1991.

Lochandas. *Chaitanya Mangal*, reprint. Kolkata: Benimadhav Shil's Library, 2014.

Saraswati, Prabodhananda. *Sri Sri Chaitanya Chandramritam*, with a commentary by Anandi called *Rasikavadini Tika*, translated into English by Sri Sarvabhavana Das Adhikari, edited by Kunjabihari Das. Vrindavan: Rashbihari Lal & Sons, 2010.

The work *Govindadaser Kadcha* created an intense controversy in 19th-century Calcutta. It was attributed to one Govindadas of the Karmakar caste and was acclaimed by some to be the earliest hagiographical work related to Chaitanya. The work was reviewed in contemporary journals. These reviews now make interesting reading.

The first of these by an anonymous reviewer appeared in the *Calcutta Review* of October 1895. Three other reviews by Haraprasad Shastri also successively appeared in the *Calcutta Review* in the January, April, and July 1898 issues. Dineshchandra Sen followed this up with a review in the same journal in 1925.

The following full length critiques of the work were also authored:

Dasgupta, B.V. *Govindas's Kadcha: A Black Forgery*, with a Foreword by Jadunath Sarkar. Dacca: S.N. Dasgupta, n.d.
Ghosh, Mrinal Kanti. *Govindadaser Kadcha Rahasya*. Calcutta: ABP Office, 1936.

Three important supplementary studies specifically on the *Chaitanya Charitamrita* are as follows:

Dimock, Edward C. 'Religious Biographies in India: The Nectar of the Acts of Caitanya'. In *The Biographical Process: Studies in the History of Psychology of Religions*, edited by Frank E. Reynolds and Donald Capp, pp. 68–80. The Hague, Paris: Mouton, 1976.
Stewart, Tony K. *The Final Word: The Caitanya Caritamrita and the Grammar of Religious Tradition*. New York: Oxford University Press, 2010.
———. 'One Text for Many: Caitanya Caritamrita as a "Classic" and "Commentary"'. In *According to Tradition: Hagiographic Writings in India*, edited by Winand Callewaert and H. Rupert Snell, pp. 229–56. Wiesbaden: Harrossowitz Verlag, 1994.

A general survey of the subject can be found in

O'Connell, Joseph T. 'Historicity in the Biographies of Chaitanya'. *Journal of Vaishnava Studies* 1(2), Winter, 1993. pp. 102–32.

In reconstructing the life of Chaitanya, pre-modern hagiographic sources have to be carefully supplemented by modern works that began to be published from about the late 19th century. There is a wealth of biographical literature on Chaitanya in English and Bengali, particularly in the latter, not all of which can be listed here. A select list of important sources is as follows:

Bandhu, Bhagirath. *Chaitanya Sangita* (A Biography in Verse). Calcutta: Chaitanya Chandrodaya Press, 1857?

Bhaduri, Nrisingha Prasad. *Chaitanyadev*. Kolkata: Patralekha, 2013.

Brezenski, Jan. 'Sri Chaitanya's Shikshastakam: Comparing the original with two translations'. *Journal of Vaishnava Studies* 12(1), Spring, 2003, pp. 87–111.

Chakravarti, Janardan. *Bengal Vaishnavism and Chaitanya*, Dr. Bimanbihari Majumdar Memorial Lecture, 1973. Calcutta: The Asiatic Society, 1975.

Chatterjee, A.N. *Sri Krishna Chaitanya: A Historical Study on Gaudiya Vaishnavism*. New Delhi: Associated Publishing, 1983.

Chatterjee, Amar Nath: *Madhyajuge Sri Chaitanya, Vaishnav Dharma, Sanskriti O Samaj*. (Chaitanya, Vaishnavism, Religion, Culture and Society in the Middle Ages). New Delhi: Associated Publishing, 2002.

Das, H.C., ed. *Sri Chaitanya in the Religious Life of India*. Calcutta: Punthi Pustak, 1989.

Dasgupta, Rabindra Kumar. *Sri Ramakrishner Chaitanya O Ramprosad* (Chaitanya and Ramprosad in the Eyes of Ramakrishna). Kolkata: Sutradhar, 2015.

De, S.K. 'Chaitanya as an Author'. *Indian Historical Quarterly* X, 1934, pp. 301–17.

———. *Early History of the Vaishnava Faith and Movement in Bengal: From Sanskrit and Bengali Sources*. Calcutta: Firma K.L. Mukhopadhyay, 1961.

Dey, Lal Behari. 'Chaitanya and the Vaishnavas of Bengal'. *Calcutta Review* 15(29), January–June 1857, pp. 169–201.

Deuskar, Sakharam Ganesh. 'Sri Gauranga O Tukaram' (Gauranga and Tukaram). *Dasi Patrika* 4(11), November, 1895, pp. 609–25.

Dutta, Bhavatosh. 'Rabindranath and Chaitanyadev: A Humanist Perspective'. *The Viswabharati Quarterly* 13(1–2), October 2003, pp. 9–16.

Dutta, Kedarnath. *Sri Gauranga Smaranamangal or Chaitanya: His Life and Precepts*. Calcutta: The Author, 1896.

———. *Srimanmahaprabhur Shiksha*. Mayapur: Sri Chaitanya Math, 1958.

Ghosh, Sisir Kumar. *Amiya Nimai Charit*, 6 vols, 16th edition. Calcutta: Tushar Kanti Ghosh, 1975.

Gupta, Jagadish, compiled. *Chaitanyalilamrita-Purvabhag* (The Divine Play of Chaitanya). Calcutta. Deviprasanna Raychaudhuri. 1890;

Jana, Yudhistir (Malibudo). *Sri Chaitanyer Antardhan Rahasya* (The Mystery Surrounding the Disappearance of Chaitanya). Kolkata: Bakprotima, 2012.

Kapoor, O.B.L. *The Philosophy and Religion of Sri Chaitanya*. Delhi: Munshiram Manoharlal, 1977.

———. *Lord Chaitanya*. Vrindavan: Srimad Badrinarayan Bhagavat Bhushan Prabhu, 1997.

Kennedy, Melville T. *The Chaitanya Movement: A Study of Vaishnavism in Bengal*, reprint. Delhi: Munshiram Manoharlal, 1973.

Kopf, David. 'Keshab and Chaitanya: Brahmo Evangelism and the Indigenous Modernization of Vaishnavism in Bengal'. In *Aspects of India: Essays in Honour of Edward Cameron Dimock Jr.*, edited by Margaret Case and N. Gerald Barrier. Delhi: Manohar Publishers and the American Institute of Indian Studies, 1986, pp. 68–80.

Majumdar, A. K. *Chaitanya: His Life and Doctrines*. Bombay: Bharatiya Vidya Bhavan, 1969.

Majumdar, Bimanbihari. *Chaitanya Chariter Upadan* (Materials for Constructing the Life of Chaitanya). Calcutta: University of Calcutta, 1959.

Mitra, Rajendralal. 'On the Psychological Tenets of the Vaishnavas'. *Journal of the Asiatic Society of Bengal* LII (1.1), 1884, pp. 103–18.

Mukhopadhyay, Tuhin. *Lokayat Sri Chaitanya*. Kolkata: Gangchil, 2014.

Raychaudhuri, Girijasankar. *Bangla Charit Granthe Sri Chaitanya* (Chaitanya in Bengali Biographical Literature). Calcutta: University of Calcutta, 1949.

Rosen, Steven J. *Sri Chaitanya's Life and Teachings, The Golden Avatara of the Divine*. London: Lexington Books, 2017.

Sarkar, Hemchandra. *Gaudiya Vaishnavadharma O Chaitanyadev* (Gaudiya Vaishnavism and Chaitanya), vol. 2. Calcutta: Brahmo Mission Press, 1932.

Sen, Amulyacharan. *Itihaser Sri Chaitanya* (The Chaitanya of History). Calcutta: Saraswat Library, 1965.

Sen, Dineshchandra. *Chaitanya and His Age*, Ramtanu Lahiri Fellowship Lecture for 1920–21, reprint. Delhi: Aruna Prakashan, 2011.

Sen, Prabir. *Bangalir Chatanyalabh* (The Bengali Rediscovers Chaitanya). Kolkata: Patabahar, 2014.

Sheth, Noel. 'Hindu Avatars and Christian Incarnation: A Comparison'. *Philosophy East and West* 52(1), January 2002, pp. 98–125.

An interesting narrative in the fictional mould of Chaitanya is

Maharaj, Shanku. *Jodi Gour na Hoito* (What if There Was No Chaitanya?). Calcutta: Dey's Publishing, 1985.

A comparable work but with more radical leaps in historical imagination is

Mitra, Shaibal, *Gora*. Calcutta: Dey's Publishing, 2013.

Useful biographical information on the close companions and followers of Chaitanya is available in the following volumes:

Das, Haridas. *Sri Sri Gaudiya Vaishnava Jeebon*, vol. 2. Nabadwip: Haribol Kutir, 1951.

Dey, Satish Chandra. *Gaurangadev O Kanchanpalli* (Chaitanya and Kanchanpalli). Calcutta: The Author, 1923.

Maiti, Rabindranath. *Chaitanya Parikar* (Those Who Served Chaitanya). Calcutta: Janakinath Bose, 1962.

Raychaudhuri, Girijasankar. *Sri Chaitanya O Tahar Parshadgan* (Chaitanya and His Followers). Calcutta: University of Calcutta, 1957.

A one of a kind study is

Brezenski, Jan. 'Women Saints in Gaudiya Vaishnavism'. *Journal of Vaishnava Studies* 3(4), Fall, 1995, pp. 57–85.

There are several useful, though at times apocryphal, accounts of post-Chaitanya Vaishnavism in ethnic Bengal and outside. The authors of some of these works were important Vaishnava figures themselves. Some of these accounts are as follows:

Chakravarti, Narahari. *Sri Sri Bhaktiratnakar*. Calcutta: The Gaudiya Mission, 1960.

Das, Manohar. *Anurag Balli*, 2nd edition. Calcutta: Patrika Office, Tarit Kanti Biswas, 1910.

Das, Narahari. *Narottam Vilas*, revised by Rakhaldas Kaviraj, 2nd edition. Calcutta: Tara Library, 1924.

Das, Nityananda. *Premvilas*. Calcutta: Yashodalal Talukdar, 1913.

Das, Yadunandan. *Karnananda*. Behrampore: Ramnarayan Vidyaratna, 1891.

Goswami, Rajballabha. *Sri Sri Murali Vilas*, edited with notes by Nilkanta Goswami and Vinodbihari Goswami. Mathura: Sri Krishna Janmasthan Seva Sansthan, 1987.

Thakur, Gaurgunananda. *Srikhander Prachin Vaishnava*, 3rd edition. Burdwan: Madhumati Smriti, n.d.

Two classic works on the history of Vaishnavism in ethnic Bengal produced more recently are as follows:

Chakravarti, Ramakanta. *Vaishnavism in Bengal 1486–1900*. Calcutta: Sanskrit Pustak Bhandar, 1985.

De, Sushil Kumar. *Early History of the Vaishnava Faith and Movement in Bengal: From Sanskrit and Bengali Sources*, 2nd edition. Calcutta: Firma K.L. Mukhopadhyay, 1961.

Chakravarti's 1985 work is adequately supported and supplemented in his two Bengali language studies:

Bangalir Dharma Samaj O Sanskriti (The Religion, Society and Culture of the Bengali People). Calcutta: Suvarnarekha, 2002.
Bonge Vaishnav Dharma (The Vaishnava Religion in Bengal), 6th reprint. Calcutta: Ananda Publisher, 2015.

A useful collection of essays on Bengal Vaishnavism is

Das, Rahul Peter. *Essays on Vaishnavism in Bengal*. Calcutta: Firma K.L. Mukhopadhyay, 1997.

For the spread of Gaudiya Vaishnava movement in the neighbouring states of Odisha and Manipur, see

Goswami, Dwijendra Narayan. *Origin and Development of Vaishnavism in Manipur*. Agartala: Akshar Prakashan, 2010.
Lahiri, Aloka. *Chaitanya Movement in Eastern India*. Calcutta: Punthi Pustak, 1993.
Mukherjee, Prabhat. *History of Medieval Vaishnavism in Orissa*. Calcutta: R.Chatterjee, 1940.
———. *History of the Chaitanya Faith in Orissa*. Delhi: Manohar Publishers, 1979.
Mukherjee, Prasenjit. 'Sri Chaitanya in Oriya Literature'. *Indian Literature* 22(1), January–February, 1879, pp. 113–21.
Parratt, Saroj Nalini. *The Religion of Manipur: Beliefs, Ritual and Historical Development*. Calcutta: Firma K.L. Mukhopadhyay, 1980.

A new trend in sub-regional studies of Gaudiya Vaishnavism is set by

Mandal, Rabindranath. *Vaishnavism and Vaishnavite Culture in Bengal: With Special Reference to Undivided Midnapore*. Kolkata: Punthi Pustak, 2014.

There are excellent biographies of modern Vaishnava figures who contributed much to the revival of Gaudiya Vaishnavism in colonial Bengal. There are accounts of Krishnakanta Singha, also known as Lala Babu in the north-western provinces, who was influential in setting up temples, hospices, and other institutions of Vaishnava charity in Vrindavan. See

Banerjee, Brajendranath. 'Lala Babu'. *Bengal Past and Present* XXXV (1), January–March 1928, pp. 56–9.

The standard biography of Sisir Kumar Ghosh is

Basu, Anath Nath. *Mahatma Sisir Kumar Ghosh*. Calcutta: Union Boro, 1920.

For an excellent biographical account of the influential Vaishnava theologian of colonial Bengal Kedarnath Dutta, see

Das, Shukavak N. *Hindu Encounter with Modernity: Kedarnath Datta Bhaktivinod, Vaishnava Theologian*. Los Angeles: SRI, 1999.

A recent and influential work which gives us a wealth of information and analysis on both Sisir Kumar and Kedarnath Dutta is

Bhatia, Varuni. *Unforgetting Chaitanya: Vaishnavism and the Cultures of Devotion in Colonial Bengal*, South Asia edition. Delhi: Oxford University Press, 2017.

Also useful is Jagadish Bhattacharya's biography of Maharaja Manindrachandra Nandi of the Kasimbazar Raj, a patron of several Vaishnava activities and institutions in Calcutta. See

Bhattacharya, Jagadish. *Maharaja Manindra Chandra*. Dacca: The Author, 1930.

A fuller history of the Kasimbazar Raj is available in

Nandy, Somendra Chandra. *History of the Cossimbazar Raj*, 2 vols. Calcutta: Dev-All, 1957.

It is instructive to go through the lives and work of two eminent researchers on Vaishnavism in modern India, Bimanbihari Majumdar and Sushil Kumar Dey. See

Dutta, Bhavatosh. *Sushil Kumar Dey*. Calcutta: Paschimbanga Bangla Academy, 1990.
Singha, Shukdev. *Bimanbihari Majumdar*. Calcutta: Paschimbanga Bangal Akademy, 1999.

Extremely passionate and a productive scholar of Vaishnavism, Dineshchandra Sen has an extremely interesting autobiography. See

Sen, Dineshchandra. *Ghorer Katha O Yuga Sahitya* (Memoirs on the Self and Contemporary Literature). Calcutta: Jignasa, 1922.

Modern writings on Gaudiya Vaishnava literature, theology, philosophy, and aesthetics are too numerous to be listed here. Given below are works that are especially useful and important:

Bandopadhyay, Sukhomoy. *Temples of Birbhum*. Delhi: B.R. Publishing Corporation, 1984.

Banerjee, Amiya Kumar. 'Temples in Calcutta and Its Neighbourhood'. *Bengal Past and Present*, January–June 1968, pp. 99–105.

Banerjee, Sumanta. *The Parlour and the Streets: Elite and Popular Culture in Nineteenth Century Calcutta*. Calcutta: Seagull Books, 1998.

———. *Logic in a Popular Form: Essays on Popular Religion in Bengal*. Calcutta: Seagull Books, 2002.

Basu, Hena. *Vaishnava Periodicals in Bengal: 1856–1983*. Calcutta: Basu Research and Documentation Service, 2009.

Bhattacharya, Bishnupada. *Gaudiya Vaishnava Sampradaya: Bhaktirasa and Alankarshastra* (Bhakti Theology and Rhetoric in the Gaudiya Vaishnava Sect), 2nd reprint. Kolkata: Ananda Publishers, 2015.

Bhattacharya, Sarabindu. *Sylheter Baul Sangite Shah Jelal O Chaitanyer Probhav* (The Influence of Saha Jelal and Chaitanya on the Baul songs of Sylhet District). Dhaka: Suchipatra, 2008.

Chakravarti, Sudhindra Chandra. *Philosophical Foundations of Bengal Vaishnavism*, 2nd reprint. Delhi: Munshiram Manoharlal, 2004.

Dey, Santanu. *Resuscitating or Restructuring Tradition? Issues and trends among Gaudiya Vaishnavas in the late nineteenth and early twentieth century Bengal*. Unpublished Ph.D dissertation. Jawaharlal Nehru University, 2014.

Dutta, K.K., and K.M. Purakayastha. *The Bengal Vaishnavism and Modern Life*. Calcutta: Sribhumi Publications, 1963.

Farquhar, J.N. *An Outline of Religious Literature of India*, reprint. Delhi: Motilal Banarasidass, 1967.

Ghosh, Pika. *Temple to Love: Architecture and Devotion in Seventeenth Century Bengal*. Bloomington: Indiana University Press, 2005.

Ghosh, Sisir Kumar. *Kalachand Gita*, with an introduction and commentary by Motilal Ghosh. Calcutta: Patrika Office, 1895.

Gupta, Ravi M. *The Chaitanya Vaishnava Vedanta of Jiva Gosvami: When knowledge meets devotion.* London and New York: Routledge, 2007.

Haque, M. Enamul. 'Impact of Islam on the Gaudiya Form of Vaishnavism'. *Journal of the Asiatic Society of Pakistan* XIII (2), August 1968, pp. 125–36.

Mitra, Khagendranath. *Vaishnava Rasa Sahitya.* Calcutta: Kamala Book Depot, 1946. Pal, Bipinchandra. *Memories of My Life and Times.* Calcutta: Modern Book Agency, 1932.

———. *Sahitya O Sadhana* (Literature and Praxis), 2 parts combined. Calcutta: Yugayatri Prakashan, 1959.

Majumdar, Bimanbihari, ed. *Panchshoto Botsorer Padabali: 1410-1910* (An Anthology of Vaishnava Verses: 1410-1910), 2nd edition. Calcutta: Jigyasa, 1985.

Majumdar, Bimanbihari, and Nareshchandra Jana, eds. *Vaishnava Padabalir Anukramanika* (An Annotated List of Vaishnava Verses). Calcutta: University of Calcutta, 1975.

Matilal, Bimal Krishna. *Neeti, Jukti O Dharma: Kahini Sahitye Ram O Krishna* (Morality, Logic and Religion: The Portrayal of Rama and Krishna in Indian Fiction), 5th reprint. Calcutta: Ananda, 2009.

O'Connell, Joseph T. 'Ethics and Practice: Chaitanya Vaishnava Ethics in Relation to the Devotional Community'. In *Chaitanya Vaishnavism: Philosophy, Tradition, Reason and Devotion,* edited by Ravi M. Gupta. Farnham: Ashgate, 2014, pp. 135–62.

Rosen, Steven J., ed. *Vaishnavism: Contemporary Scholars Discuss the Gaudiya Traditon.* New York: Folk Books, 1992.

Sanyal, Hiteshranjan. *Bangla Kirtaner Itihas.* Calcutta: Centre for the Study of Social Sciences and K.P. Bagchi, 1989.

Sen, Amiya P. 'Bankimchandra Chattopadhyay and the Vaishnava Revival in Colonial Bengal', edited by Arun Bandopadhyay and Sanjukta Das Gupta. In *In Quest of the Historian's Craft: Essays in Honour of Professor B.B. Chaudhuri.* Delhi: Manohar Publishers, 2018.

———, ed. *Bankim's Hinduism: An Anthology of Writings by Bankimchandra Chattopadhyay.* Delhi: Permanent Black, 2011.

Sen, Dineshchandra. *The Vaishnava Literature of Medieval Bengal: Being Lectures Delivered as Reader to the University of Calcutta in 1913,* with a preface by J.D. Anderson. Calcutta: University of Calcutta, 1917.

———. *Padabali Madhurya,* reprint. Calcutta: Patabahar, 2001.

Sen, Sukumar. *A History of Brajabuli literature: Being a Study of the Vaishnava Lyric Poetry and Poets of Bengal.* Calcutta: University of Calcutta, 1935.

Tarkabhushan, Pramathanath. *Banglay Vaishnava Dharma* (Vaishnavism in Bengal). Calcutta: University of Calcutta, 1939.

Other than the enumerative ethnology available through the colonial census, there is very important source material available on Bengal Vaishnavism in ethnographic insights and observations produced throughout the 19th and the early 20th century.

One of the earliest in this class of works is

Ward, William. *A view of the history, literature, and mythology of the Hindoos: Including a minute description of their manners and customs and translation from their principal works in two volumes.* London: Black, Parbury and Allen, 1817.

Another such work is

O'Connell, Joseph T. 'Jati Vaishnavas of Bengal: Sub Caste (Jati) without Caste (Varna)'. *Journal of Asian and African Studies*, VIII (3–4), 1982, pp.189–207.

A volume that is rich in information on contemporary Vaishnavas, albeit in a somewhat pejorative vein is

Dey, Lal Behari. *Bengal Peasant Life: Folk Tales of Bengal and Recollections of My School Days*, edited by Mahadev Prasad Sinha. Calcutta: Editions Indian, 1969.

The following volume is partly based on field work in some chosen districts of Bengal:

Dutta, Bhupendranath. *Vaishnava Sahitye Samajtattwa* (Sociology in Vaishnava Literature), reprint. Kolkata: Chirayat, 2011.

The multivolume *A Statistical Account of Bengal* by W.W. Hunter is immensely rich in ethnographic descriptions of various Vaishnava communities and sub-communities. See in particular volumes 1 to 5, 8, 9 and 19. Delhi: D. K Publishers reprint, various dates.

Also important are

Bhattacharya, Jogendra Nath. *Hindu Castes and Sects*, reprint. Calcutta: Editions Indian, 1968.
Risley, H.H. *Tribes and Castes of Bengal: Ethnographic Glossary.* Calcutta: Bengal Secretariat Press, 1892.

For regional studies of select Bengal districts, see

Allen, B.C. *Eastern Bengal District Gazetteer: Dacca.* Allahabad: The Pioneer Press, 1912.

Bhattacharya, Kalikrishna. *Shantipur Parichay* (A Descriptive Account of Santipur), vol. 1. Calcutta: The Author, 1939.

Chattopadhyay, Ekkari. *Bardhaman Jelar Itihas o Sanskriti* (The History and Folk Culture of Burdwan District), vol. 2. Calcutta: Radical, 2000.

Majumdar, Durgadas. *West Bengal District Gazetteers: Nadia.* Calcutta: Government of West Bengal, 1978.

For modern studies on Bengal Vaishnavism, especially related to the complex social structure it produced, see

O'Connell, Joseph T. 'Jati Vaishnavas of Bengal: Subcaste (Jati) without Caste (Varna)'. *Journal of Asian and African Studies* XVII (3–4), 1982, pp. 189–207.

————. *Religious Movements and Social Structure: The Case of Chaitanya Vaishnavas in Bengal.* Occasional Paper No. 4. Shimla: Indian Institute of Advanced Study, 1993.

————. 'Do Bhakti Movements Change Hindu Social Structure: The Case of Chaitanya Vaishnavas in Bengal'. In *Boeings and Bullock Carts: Studies in Change and Continuity in Indian Civilization: Religious Movements and Social Identity*, edited by Bardwell L. Smith. Calcutta: National Book Agency, 2004, pp. 539–53.

Index

About the Author

Amiya P. Sen was a professor of modern Indian history at Jamia Millia Islamia, New Delhi. His main area of interest is the intellectual and cultural history of colonial Bengal, especially of the 19th century. Sen was Visiting Fellow to St Antony's College and the Oxford Centre for Hindu Studies, both in Oxford, UK, Indian Institute of Advanced Study, Shimla, Nehru Memorial Museum and Library, New Delhi, and the South Asia Institute, Heidelberg, Germany. Next, he plans to research Gandhi and Tagore as religious figures. Till date, he has authored and edited 13 books.